13th Conference of the European Chapter of the Association for Computational Linguistics 2012 (EACL 2012)

Demonstrations

AA005479

Avignon, France
23 – 27 April 2012

ISBN: 978-1-62276-500-3

Printed from e-media with permission by:

Curran Associates, Inc.
57 Morehouse Lane
Red Hook, NY 12571

Some format issues inherent in the e-media version may also appear in this print version.

Copyright© (2012) by the Association for Computational Linguistics
All rights reserved.

Printed by Curran Associates, Inc. (2012)

For permission requests, please contact the Association for Computational Linguistics
at the address below.

Association for Computational Linguistics
209 N. Eighth Street
Stroudsburg, Pennsylvania 18360

Phone: 1-570-476-8006
Fax: 1-570-476-0860

acl@aclweb.org

Additional copies of this publication are available from:

Curran Associates, Inc.
57 Morehouse Lane
Red Hook, NY 12571 USA
Phone: 845-758-0400
Fax: 845-758-2634
Email: curran@proceedings.com
Web: www.proceedings.com

Organizers:

Frédérique Segond, XEROX

Table of Contents

Conference Program

Wednesday, April, 25, 2012

Session 1: (16:10 -16:40)

Language Resources Factory: case study on the acquisition of Translation Memories
Marc Poch, Antonio Toral and Núria Bel

Harnessing NLP Techniques in the Processes of Multilingual Content Management
Anelia Belogay, Diman Karagyozov, Svetla Koeva, Cristina Vertan, Adam Przepiórkowski, Dan Cristea and Plovios Raxis

Collaborative Machine Translation Service for Scientific texts
Patrik Lambert, Jean Senellart, Laurent Romary, Holger Schwenk, Florian Zipser, Patrice Lopez and Frédéric Blain

Session 2: (16:50 - 17.20)

TransAhead: A Writing Assistant for CAT and CALL
Chung-chi Huang, Ping-che Yang, Mei-hua Chen, Hung-ting Hsieh, Ting-hui Kao and Jason S. Chang

SWAN - Scientific Writing AssistaNt. A Tool for Helping Scholars to Write Reader-Friendly Manuscripts
Tomi Kinnunen, Henri Leisma, Monika Machunik, Tuomo Kakkonen and Jean-Luc LeBrun

ONTS: "Optima" News Translation System
Marco Turchi, Martin Atkinson, Alastair Wilcox, Brett Crawley, Stefano Bucci, Ralf Steinberger and Erik Van der Goot

Just Title It! (by an Online Application)
Cédric Lopez, Violaine Prince and Mathieu Roche

Thursday, April, 26, 2012 (continued)

Session 5: (16:50 - 17.20)

Automatic Analysis of Patient History Episodes in Bulgarian Hospital Discharge Letters
Svetla Boytcheva, Galia Angelova and Ivelina Nikolova

ElectionWatch: Detecting Patterns in News Coverage of US Elections
Saatviga Sudhahar, Thomas Lansdall-Welfare, Ilias Flaounas and Nello Cristianini

Query log analysis with LangLog
Marco Trevisan, Eduard Barbu, Igor Barsanti, Luca Dini, Nikolaos Lagos, Frédérique Segond, Mathieu Rhulmann and Ed Vald

Session 6: (17:30 - 18:00)

A platform for collaborative semantic annotation
Valerio Basile, Johan Bos, Kilian Evang and Noortje Venhuizen

HadoopPerceptron: a Toolkit for Distributed Perceptron Training and Prediction with MapReduce
Andrea Gesmundo and Nadi Tomeh

brat: a Web-based Tool for NLP-Assisted Text Annotation
Pontus Stenetorp, Sampo Pyysalo, Goran Topić, Tomoko Ohta, Sophia Ananiadou and Jun'ichi Tsujii

Language Resources Factory: case study on the acquisition of Translation Memories*

Marc Poch
UPF Barcelona, Spain
marc.pochriera@upf.edu

Antonio Toral
DCU Dublin, Ireland
atoral@computing.dcu.ie

Núria Bel
UPF Barcelona, Spain
nuria.bel@upf.edu

Abstract

This paper demonstrates a novel distributed architecture to facilitate the acquisition of Language Resources. We build a *factory* that automates the stages involved in the acquisition, production, updating and maintenance of these resources. The factory is designed as a platform where functionalities are deployed as web services, which can be combined in complex acquisition chains using workflows. We show a case study, which acquires a Translation Memory for a given pair of languages and a domain using web services for crawling, sentence alignment and conversion to TMX.

1 Introduction

A fundamental issue for many tasks in the field of Computational Linguistics and Language Technologies in general is the lack of Language Resources (LRs) to tackle them successfully, especially for some languages and domains. It is the so-called LRs bottleneck.

Our objective is to build a factory of LRs that automates the stages involved in the acquisition, production, updating and maintenance of LRs required by Machine Translation (MT), and by other applications based on Language Technologies. This automation will significantly cut down the required cost, time and human effort. These reductions are the only way to guarantee the continuous supply of LRs that Language Technologies demand in a multilingual world.

* We would like to thank the developers of Soaplab, Taverna, myExperiment and Biocatalogue for solving our questions and attending our requests. This research has been partially funded by the EU project PANACEA (7FP-ICT-248064).

2 Web Services and Workflows

The factory is designed as a platform of web services (WSs) where the users can create and use these services directly or combine them in more complex chains. These chains are called workflows and can represent different combinations of tasks, e.g. "extract the text from a PDF document and obtain the Part of Speech (PoS) tagging" or "crawl this bilingual website and align its sentence pairs". Each task is carried out using NLP tools deployed as WSs in the factory.

Web Service Providers (WSPs) are institutions (universities, companies, etc.) who are willing to offer services for some tasks. WSs are services made available from a web server to remote users or to other connected programs. WSs are built upon protocols, server and programming languages. Their massive adoption has contributed to make this technology rather interoperable and open. In fact, WSs allow computer programs distributed in different locations to interact with each other.

WSs introduce a completely new paradigm in the way we use software tools. Before, every researcher or laboratory had to install and maintain all the different tools that they needed for their work, which has a considerable cost in both human and computing resources. In addition, it makes it more difficult to carry out experiments that involve other tools because the researcher might hesitate to spend time resources on installing new tools when there are other alternatives already installed.

The paradigm changes considerably with WSs, as in this case only the WSP needs to have a deep knowledge of the installation and maintenance of the tool, thus allowing all the other users to benefit from this work. Consequently, researchers think about tools from a high level and solely regarding their functionalities, thus they can focus on their work and be more productive as the time resources that would have been spent to install software are freed. The only tool that the users need to install in order to design and run experiments is a WS client or a Workflow editor.

3 Choosing the tools for the platform

During the design phase several technologies were analyzed to study their features, ease of use, installation, maintenance needs as well as the estimated learning curve required to use them. Interoperability between components and with other technologies was also taken into account since one of our goals is to reach as many providers and users as possible. After some deliberation, a set of technologies that have proved to be successful in the Bioinformatics field were adopted to build the platform. These tools are developed by the myGrid[1] team. This group aims to develop a suite of tools for researchers that work with e-Science. These tools have been used in numerous projects as well as in different research fields as diverse as astronomy, biology and social science.

3.1 Web Services: Soaplab

Soaplab (Senger et al., 2003)[2] allows a WSP to deploy a command line tool as a WS just by writing a metadata file that describes the parameters of the tool. Soaplab takes care of the typical issues regarding WSs automatically, including temporary files, protocols, the WSDL file and its parameters, etc. Moreover, it creates a Web interface (called Spinet) where WSs can be tested and used with input forms. All these features make Soaplab a suitable tool for our project. Moreover, its numerous successful stories make it a safe choise; e.g., it has been used by the European Bioinformatics Institute[3] to deploy their tools as WSs.

3.2 Registry: Biocatalogue

Once the WSs are deployed by WSPs, some means to find them becomes necessary. Biocatalogue (Belhajjame et al., 2008)[4] is a registry where WSs can be shared, searched for, annotated with tags, etc. It is used as the main registration point for WSPs to share and annotate their WSs and for users to find the tools they need. Biocatalogue is a user-friendly portal that monitors the status of the WSs deployed and offers multiple metadata fields to annotate WSs.

3.3 Workflows: Taverna

Now that users can find WSs and use them, the next step is to combine them to create complex chains. Taverna (Missier et al., 2010)[5] is an open source application that allows the user to create high-level workflows that integrate different resources (mainly WSs in our case) into a single experiment. Such experiments can be seen as simulations which can be reproduced, tuned and shared with other researchers.

An advantage of using workflows is that the researcher does not need to have background knowledge of the technical aspects involved in the experiment. The researcher creates the workflow based on functionalities (each WS provides a function) instead of dealing with technical aspects of the software that provides the functionality.

3.4 Sharing workflows: myExperiment

MyExperiment (De Roure et al., 2008)[6] is a social network used by workflow designers to share workflows. Users can create groups and share their workflows within the group or make them publically available. Workflows can be annotated with several types of information such as description, attribution, license, etc. Users can easily find examples that will help them during the design phase, being able to reuse workflows (or parts of them) and thus avoiding *reinveinting the wheel.*

4 Using the tools to work with NLP

All the aforementioned tools were installed, used and adapted to work with NLP. In addition, several tutorials and videos have been prepared[7] to help partners and other users to deploy and use WSs and to create workflows.

Soaplab has been modified (a patch has been developed and distributed)[8] to limit the amount of data being transfered inside the SOAP message in

[1] `http://www.mygrid.org.uk`

[2] `http://soaplab.sourceforge.net/soaplab2/`

[3] `http://www.ebi.ac.uk`

[4] `http://www.biocatalogue.org/`

[5] `http://www.taverna.org.uk/`

[6] `http://www.myexperiment.org/`

[7] `http://panacea-lr.eu/en/tutorials/`

[8] `http://myexperiment.elda.org/files/5`

order to optimize the network usage. Guidelines that describe how to limit the amount of concurrent users of WSs as well as to limit the maximum size of the input data have been prepared.[9]

Regarding Taverna, guidelines and workflow examples have been shared among partners showing the best way to create workflows for the project. The examples show how to benefit from useful features provided by this tool, such as "retries" (to execute up to a certain number of times a WS when it fails) and "parallelisation" (to run WSs in parallel, thus increasing trhoughput). Users can view intermediate results and parameters using the provenance capture option, a useful feature while designing a workflow. In case of any WS error in one of the inputs, Taverna will report the error message produced by the WS or processor component that causes it. However, Taverna will be able to continue processing the rest of the input data if the workflow is robust (i.e. makes use of retry and parallelisation) and the error is confined to a WS (i.e. it does not affect the rest of the workflow).

An instance of Biocatalogue and one of myExperiment have been deployed to be the Registry and the portal to share workflows and other experiment-related data. Both have been adapted by modifying relevant aspects of the interface (layout, colours, names, logos, etc.). The categories that make up the classification system used in the Registry have been adapted to the NLP field. At the time of writing there are more than 100 WSs and 30 workflows registered.

5 Interoperability

Interoperability plays a crucial role in a platform of distributed WSs. Soaplab deploys SOAP[10] WSs and handles automatically most of the issues involved in this process, while Taverna can combine SOAP and REST[11] WSs. Hence, we can say that communication protocols are being handled by the tools. However, parameters and data interoperability need to be addressed.

5.1 Common Interface

To facilitate interoperability between WSs and to easily exchange WSs, a Common Interface (CI) has been designed for each type of tool (e.g. PoS-taggers, aligners, etc.). The CI establishes that all WSs that perform a given task must have the same mandatory parameters. That said, each tool can have different optional parameters. This system eases the design of workflows as well as the exchange of tools that perform the same task inside a workflow. The CI has been developed using an XML schema.[12]

5.2 Travelling Object

A goal of the project is to facilitate the deployment of as many tools as possible in the form of WSs. In many cases, tools performing the same task use in-house formats. We have designed a container, called "Travelling Object" (TO), as the data object that is being transfered between WSs. Any tool that is deployed needs to be adapted to the TO, this way we can interconnect the different tools in the platform regardless of their original input/output formats.

We have adopted for TO the XML Corpus Encoding Standard (XCES) format (Ide et al., 2000) because it was the already existing format that required the minimum transduction effort from the in-house formats. The XCES format has been used successfully to build workflows for PoS tagging and alignment.

Some WSs, e.g. dependency parsers, require a more complex representation that cannot be handled by the TO. Therefore, a more expressive format has been adopted for these. The Graph Annotation Format (GrAF) (Ide and Suderman, 2007) is a XML representation of a graph that allows different levels of annotation using a "feature–value" paradigm. This system allows different in-house formats to be easily encapsulated in this container-based format. On the other hand, GrAF can be used as a pivot format between other formats (Ide and Bunt, 2010), e.g. there is software to convert GrAF to UIMA and GATE formats (Ide and Suderman, 2009) and it can be used to merge data represented in a graph.

Both TO and GrAF address syntactic interoperability while semantic interoperability is still an open topic.

[9] http://myexperiment.elda.org/files/4

[10] http://www.w3.org/TR/soap/

[11] http://www.ics.uci.edu/~fielding/pubs/dissertation/rest_arch_style.htm

[12] http://panacea-lr.eu/en/info-for-professionals/documents/

6 Evaluation

The evaluation of the factory is based on its features and usability requirements. A binary scheme (yes/no) is used to check whether each requirement is fulfilled or not. The quality of the tools is not altered as they are deployed as WSs without any modification. According to the evaluation of the current version of the platform, most requirements are fulfilled (Aleksić et al., 2012).

Another aspect of the factory that is being evaluated is its performance and scalabilty. They do not depend on the factory itself but on the design of the workflows and WSs. WSPs with robust WSs and powerful servers will provide a better and faster service to users (considering that the service is based on the same tool). This is analogous to the user installing tools on a computer; if the user develops a fragile script to chain the tools the execution may fail, while if the computer does not provide the required computational resources the performance will be poor.

Following the example of the Bioinformatics field where users can benefit of powerful WSPs, the factory is used as a proof of concept that these technologies can grow and scale to benefit many users.

7 Case study

We introduce a case study in order to demonstrate the capabilities of the platform. It regards the acquisition of a Translation Memory (TM) for a language pair and a specific domain. This is deemed to be very useful for translators when they start translating documents for a new domain. As at that early stage they still do not have any content in their TM, having the automatically acquired TM can be helpful in order to get familiar with the characteristic bilingual terminology and other aspects of the domain. Another obvious potential use of this data would be to use it to train a Statistical MT system.

Three functionalities are needed to carry out this process: acquisition of the data, its alignment and its conversion into the desired format. These are provided by WSs available in the registry.

First, we use a domain-focused bilingual crawler[13] in order to acquire the data. Given a pair of languages, a set of web domains and a set of seed terms that define the target domain for these languages, this tool will crawl the webpages in the domains and gather pairs of web documents in the target languages that belong to the target domain. Second, we apply a sentence aligner.[14] It takes as input the pairs of documents obtained by the crawler and outputs pairs of equivalent sentences.Finally, convert the aligned data into a TM format. We have picked TMX[15] as it is the most common format for TMs. The export is done by a service that receives as input sentence-aligned text and converts it to TMX.[16]

The "Bilingual Process, Sentence Alignment of bilingual crawled data with Hunalign and export into TMX"[17] is a workflow built using Taverna that combines the three WSs in order to provide the functionality needed. The crawling part is ommitted because data only needs to be crawled once; crawled data can be processed with different workflows but it would be very inefficient to crawl the same data each time. A set of screenshots showing the WSs and the workflow, together with sample input and output data is available.[18]

8 Demo and Requirements

The demo aims to show the web portals and tools used during the development of the case study. First, the Registry[19] to find WSs, the Spinet Web client to easily test them and Taverna to finally build a workflow combining the different WSs. For the live demo, the workflows will be already designed because of the time constraints. However, there are videos on the web that illustrate the whole process. It will be also interesting to show the myExperiment portal,[20] where all public workflows can be found. Videos of workflow executions will also be available.

Regarding the requirements, a decent internet connection is critical for an acceptable performance of the whole platform, specially for remote WSs and workflows. We will use a laptop with Taverna installed to run the workflow presented in Section 7.

[13] `http://registry.elda.org/services/127`

[14] `http://registry.elda.org/services/92`

[15] `http://www.gala-global.org/oscarStandards/tmx/tmx14b.html`

[16] `http://registry.elda.org/services/219`

[17] `http://myexperiment.elda.org/workflows/37`

[18] `http://www.computing.dcu.ie/~atoral/panacea/eacl12_demo/`

[19] `http://registry.elda.org`

[20] `http://myexperiment.elda.org`

References

Vera Aleksić, Olivier Hamon, Vassilis Papavassiliou, Pavel Pecina, Marc Poch, Prokopis Prokopidis, Valeria Quochi, Christoph Schwarz, and Gregor Thurmair. 2012. Second evaluation report. Evaluation of PANACEA v2 and produced resources (PANACEA project Deliverable 7.3). Technical report.

Khalid Belhajjame, Carole Goble, Franck Tanoh, Jiten Bhagat, Katherine Wolstencroft, Robert Stevens, Eric Nzuobontane, Hamish McWilliam, Thomas Laurent, and Rodrigo Lopez. 2008. Biocatalogue: A curated web service registry for the life science community. In *Microsoft eScience conference*.

David De Roure, Carole Goble, and Robert Stevens. 2008. The design and realisation of the myexperiment virtual research environment for social sharing of workflows. *Future Generation Computer Systems*, 25:561–567, May.

Nancy Ide and Harry Bunt. 2010. Anatomy of annotation schemes: mapping to graf. In *Proceedings of the Fourth Linguistic Annotation Workshop*, LAW IV '10, pages 247–255, Stroudsburg, PA, USA. Association for Computational Linguistics.

Nancy Ide and Keith Suderman. 2007. GrAF: A Graph-based Format for Linguistic Annotations. In *Proceedings of the Linguistic Annotation Workshop*, pages 1–8, Prague, Czech Republic, June. Association for Computational Linguistics.

Nancy Ide and Keith Suderman. 2009. Bridging the Gaps: Interoperability for GrAF, GATE, and UIMA. In *Proceedings of the Third Linguistic Annotation Workshop*, pages 27–34, Suntec, Singapore, August. Association for Computational Linguistics.

Nancy Ide, Patrice Bonhomme, and Laurent Romary. 2000. XCES: An XML-based encoding standard for linguistic corpora. In *Proceedings of the Second International Language Resources and Evaluation Conference. Paris: European Language Resources Association.*

Paolo Missier, Stian Soiland-Reyes, Stuart Owen, Wei Tan, Aleksandra Nenadic, Ian Dunlop, Alan Williams, Thomas Oinn, and Carole Goble. 2010. Taverna, reloaded. In M. Gertz, T. Hey, and B. Ludaescher, editors, *SSDBM 2010*, Heidelberg, Germany, June.

Martin Senger, Peter Rice, and Thomas Oinn. 2003. Soaplab - a unified sesame door to analysis tools. In *All Hands Meeting*, September.

Harnessing NLP Techniques in the Processes of Multilingual Content Management

Anelia Belogay
Tetracom IS Ltd.
anelia@tetracom.com

Diman Karagyozov
Tetracom IS Ltd.
diman@tetracom.com

Svetla Koeva
Institute for Bulgarian Language
svetla@dcl.bass.bg

Cristina Vertan
Universitaet Hamburg
cristina.vertan@uni-hamburg.de

Adam Przepiórkowski
Instytut Podstaw Informatyki Polskiej Akademii Nauk
adamp@ipipan.waw.pl

Polivios Raxis
Atlantis Consulting SA
raxis@atlantisresearch.gr

Dan Cristea
Universitatea Alexandru Ioan Cuza
dcristea@info.uaic.ro

Abstract

The emergence of the WWW as the main source of distributing content opened the floodgates of information. The sheer volume and diversity of this content necessitate an approach that will reinvent the way it is analysed. The quantitative route to processing information which relies on content management tools provides structural analysis. The challenge we address is to evolve from the process of streamlining data to a level of understanding that assigns value to content.

We present an open-source multilingual platform ATALS that incorporates human language technologies in the process of multilingual web content management. It complements a content management software-as-a-service component i-Publisher, used for creating, running and managing dynamic content-driven websites with a linguistic platform. The platform enriches the content of these websites with revealing details and reduces the manual work of classification editors by automatically categorising content. The platform ASSET supports six European languages.

We expect ASSET to serve as a basis for future development of deep analysis tools capable of generating abstractive summaries and training models for decision making systems.

Introduction

The advent of the Web revolutionized the way in which content is manipulated and delivered. As a result, digital content in various languages has become widely available on the Internet and its sheer volume and language diversity have presented an opportunity for embracing new methods and tools for content creation and distribution. Although significant improvements have been made in the field of web content management lately, there is still a growing demand for online content services that incorporate language-based technology.

Existing software solutions and services such as Google Docs, Slingshot and Amazon implement some of the linguistic mechanisms addressed in the platform. The most used open-source multilingual web content management systems (Joomla, Joom!Fish, TYPO3, Drupal)[1] offer low level of multilingual content management, providing abilities for building multilingual sites. However, the available services are narrowly focused on meeting the needs of very specific target groups, thus leaving unmet the rising demand for a comprehensive solution for multilingual content management addressing the issues posed by the growing family of languages spoken within the EU.

We are going to demonstrate the open-source content management platform ATLAS and as proof of concept, a multilingual library i-librarian, driven by the platform. The demonstration aims to prove that people reading websites powered by ATLAS can easily find documents, kept in order via the automatic classification, find context-sensitive content, find similar documents in a massive multilingual data collection, and get short summaries in different languages that help the users to discern essential information with unparalleled clarity.

The "Technologies behind the system" chapter describes the implementation and the integration approach of the core linguistic processing framework and its key sub-components – the categorisation, summarisation and machine-translation engines. The chapter "i-Librarian – a case study" outlines the functionalities of an intelligent web application built with our system and the benefits of using it. The chapter "Evaluation" briefly discusses the user evaluation of the new system. The last chapter "Conclusion and Future Work" summarises the main achievements of the system and suggests improvements and extensions.

Technologies behind the system

The linguistic framework ASSET employs diverse natural language processing (NLP) tools technologically and linguistically in a platform, based on UIMA [2]. The UIMA pluggable component architecture and software framework are designed to analyse content and to structure it. The ATLAS core annotation schema, as a uniform representation model, normalizes and harmonizes the heterogeneous nature of the NLP tools[3].

The processing of text in the system is split into three sequentially executed tasks.

Firstly, the text is extracted from the input source (text or binary documents) in the "pre-processing" phase.

Secondly, the text is annotated by several NLP tools, chained in a sequence in the "processing" phase. The language processing tools are integrated in a language processing chain (LPC), so that the output of a given NLP tool is used as an input for the next tool in the chain. The baseline LPC for each of the supported languages includes a sentence and paragraph splitter, tokenizer, part of speech tagger, lemmatizer, word sense disambiguation, noun phrase chunker and named entity extractor (Cristea and Pistiol, 2008). The annotations produced by each LPC along with additional statistical methods are subsequently used for detection of keywords and concepts, generation of summary of text, multi-label text categorisation and machine translation.

Finally, the annotations are stored in a fusion data store, comprising of relational database and high-performance Lucene[4] indexes.

The architecture of the language processing framework is depicted in Figure 1.

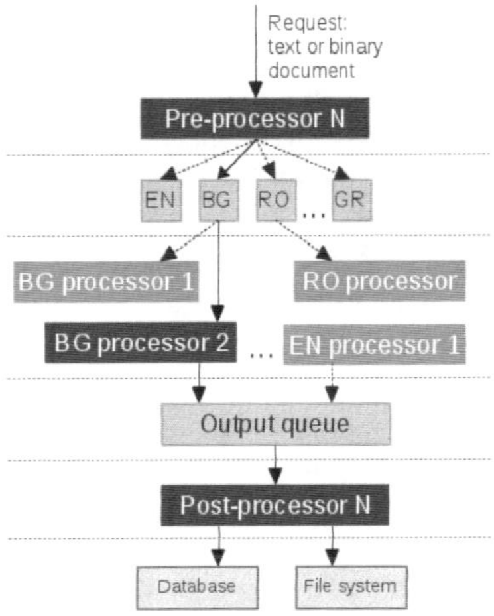

Figure 1. Architecture and communication channels in our language processing framework.

The system architecture, shown in Figure 2, is based on asynchronous message processing

[1] http://www.joomla.org/, http://www.joomfish.net/, http://typo3.org/, http://drupal.org/

[2] http://uima.apache.org/

[3] The system exploits heterogeneous NLP tools, for the supported natural languages, implemented in Java, C++ and Perl. Examples are: OpenNLP (http://incubator.apache.org/opennlp/), RASP (http://ilexir.co.uk/applications/rasp/), Morfeusz (http://sgjp.pl/morfeusz/), Panterra (http://code.google.com/p/pantera-tagger/), ParsEst (http://dcl.bas.bg/), TnT Tagger (http://www.coli.uni-saarland.de/~thorsten/tnt/).

[4] http://lucene.apache.org/

patterns (Hohpe and Woolf, 2004) and thus allows the processing framework to be easily scaled horizontally.

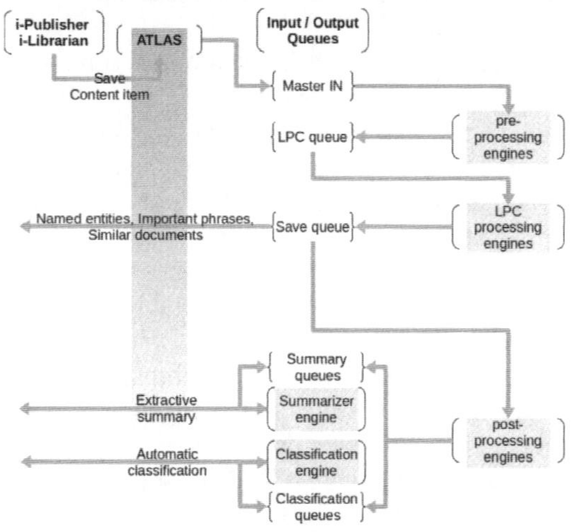

Figure 2. Top-level architecture of our CMS and its major components.

Text Categorisation

We implemented a language independent text categorisation tool, which works for user-defined and controlled classification hierarchies. The NLP framework converts the texts to a series of natural numbers, prior sending the texts to the categorisation engine. This conversion allows high level compression of the feature space. The categorisation engine employs different algorithms, such as Naïve Bayesian, relative entropy, Class-Feature Centroid (CFC) (Guan et. al., 2009), and SVM. New algorithms can be easily integrated because of the chosen OSGi-based architecture (OSGi Alliance, 2009). A tailored voting system for multi-label multi-class tasks consolidates the results of each of the categorisation algorithms.

Summarisation (prototype phase)

The chosen implementation approach for coherent text summarisation combines the well-known LexRank algorithm (Erkan and Radev, 2004) and semantic graphs and word-sense disambiguation techniques (Plaza and Diaz, 2011). Furthermore, we have automatically built thesauri for the top-level domains in order to produce domain-focused extractive summaries. Finally, we apply clause-boundaries splitting in order to truncate the irrelevant or subordinating clauses in the sentences in the summary.

Machine Translation (prototype phase)

The machine translation (MT) sub-component implements the hybrid MT paradigm, combining an example-based (EBMT) component and a Moses-based statistical approach (SMT). Firstly, the input is processed by the example-based MT engine and if the whole or important chunks of it are found in the translation database, then the translation equivalents are used and if necessary combined (Gavrila, 2011). In all other cases the input is processed by the categorisation sub-component in order to select the top-level domain and respectively, the most appropriate SMT domain- and POS-translation model (Niehues and Waibel, 2010).

The translation engine in the system, based on MT Server Land (Federmann and Eisele, 2010), is able to accommodate and use different third party translation engines, such as the Google, Bing, Lusy or Yahoo translators.

Case Study: Multilingual Library

i-Librarian[5] is a free online library that assists authors, students, young researchers, scholars, librarians and executives to easily create, organise and publish various types of documents in English, Bulgarian, German, Greek, Polish and Romanian. Currently, a sample of the publicly available library contains over 20 000 books in English.

On uploading a new document to i-Librarian, the system automatically provides the user with an extraction of the most relevant information (concepts and named entities, keywords). Later on, the retrieved information is used to generate suggestions for classification in the library catalogue, containing 86 categories, as well as a list of similar documents. Finally, the system compiles a summary and translates it in all supported languages. Among the supported formats are Microsoft Office documents, PDF, OpenOffice documents, books in various electronic formats, HTML pages and XML documents. Users have exclusive rights to manage content in the library at their discretion.

The current version of the system supports English and Bulgarian. In early 2012 the Polish, Greek, German and Romanian languages will be in use.

[5] i-Librarian web site is available at http://www.i-librarian.eu/. One can access the i-Librarian demo content using "**demo@i-librarian.eu**" for username and "**sandbox**" for password.

Evaluation

The technical quality and performance of the system is being evaluated as well as its appraisal by prospective users. The technical evaluation uses indicators that assess the following key technical elements:

- overall quality and performance attributes (MTBF6, uptime, response time);
- performance of specific functional elements (content management, machine translation, cross-lingual content retrieval, summarisation, text categorisation).

The user evaluation assesses the level of satisfaction with the system. We measure non functional elements such as:

- User friendliness and satisfaction, clarity in responses and ease of use;
- Adequacy and completeness of the provided data and functionality;
- Impact on certain user activities and the degree of fulfilment of common tasks.

We have planned for three rounds of user evaluation; all users are encouraged to try online the system, freely, or by following the provided base-line scenarios and accompanying exercises. The main instrument for collecting user feedback is an online interactive electronic questionnaire[7].

The second round of user evaluation is scheduled for Feb-March 2012, while the first round took place in Q1 2011, with the participation of 33 users. The overall user impression was positive and the Mean value of each indicator (in a 5-point Likert scale) was measured on AVERAGE or ABOVE AVERAGE.

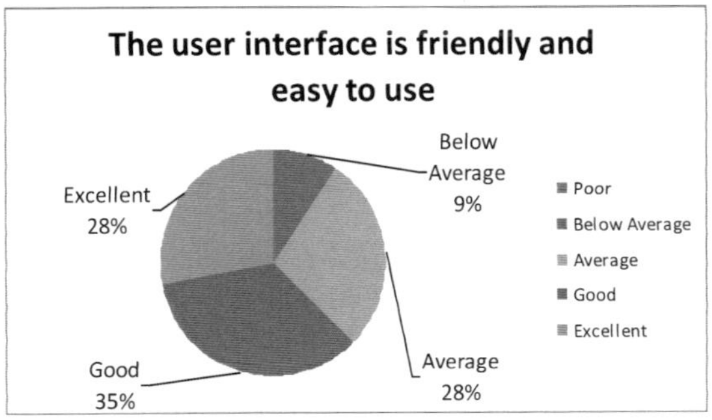

Figure 3. User evaluation – UI friendliness and ease of use.

[6] Mean Time Between Failures

[7] The electronic questionnaire is available at http://ue.atlasproject.eu

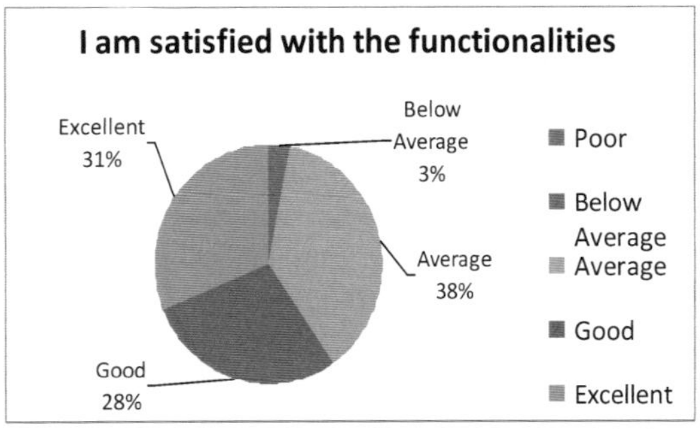

Figure 4. User evaluation – user satisfaction with the available functionalities in the system.

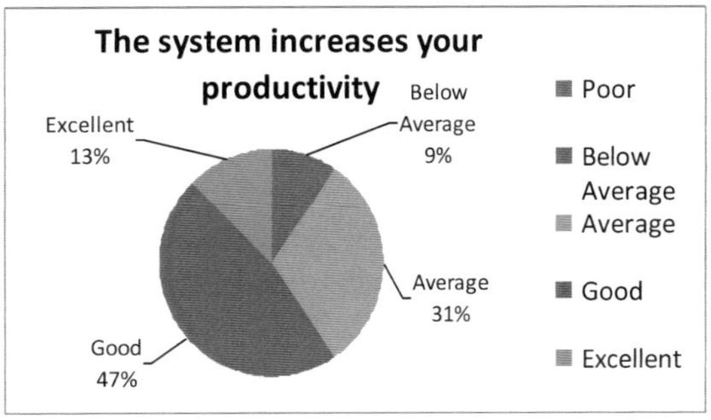

Figure 5. User evaluation – users productivity incensement.

Acknowledgments

ATLAS (Applied Technology for Language-Aided CMS) is a European project funded under the CIP ICT Policy Support Programme, Grant Agreement 250467.

Conclusion and Future Work

The abundance of knowledge allows us to widen the application of NLP tools, developed in a research environment. The tailor made voting system maximizes the use of the different categorisation algorithms. The novel summary approach adopts state of the art techniques and the automatic translation is provided by a cutting edge hybrid machine translation system.

The content management platform and the linguistic framework will be released as open-source software. The language processing chains for Greek, Romanian, Polish and German will be fully implemented by the end of 2011. The summarisation engine and machine translation tools will be fully integrated in mid 2012.

We expect this platform to serve as a basis for future development of tools that directly support decision making and situation awareness. We will use categorical and statistical analysis in order to recognise events and patterns, to detect opinions and predictions while processing extremely large volumes of disparate data resources.

Demonstration websites

The multilingual content management platform is available for testing at http://i-publisher.atlasproject.eu/atlas/i-publisher/demo . One can access the CMS demo content using "demo" for username and "sandbox2" for password.

The multilingual library web site is available at http://www.i-librarian.eu/. One can access the i-Librarian demo content using "demo@i-librarian.eu" for username and "sandbox" for password.

References

Dan Cristea and Ionut C. Pistol, 2008. Managing Language Resources and Tools using a Hierarchy of Annotation Schemas. In the proceedings of workshop 'Sustainability of Language Resources and Tools for Natural Language Processing', LREC, 2008

Gregor Hohpe and Bobby Woolf. 2004. Enterprise Integration Patterns: Designing, Building, and Deploying Messaging Solutions. Addison-Wesley Professional.

Hu Guan, Jingyu Zhou and Minyi Guo. A Class-Feature-Centroid Classifier for Text Categorization. 2009. WWW 2009 Madrid, Track: Data Mining / Session: Learning, p201-210.

OSGi Alliance. 2009. OSGi Service Platform, Core Specification, Release 4, Version 4.2.

Gunes Erkan and Dragomir R. Radev. 2004. LexRank: Graph-based Centrality as Salience in Text Summarization. Journal of Artificial Intelligence Research 22 (2004), p457–479.

Laura Plaza and Alberto Diaz. 2011. Using Semantic Graphs and Word Sense Disambiguation Techniques to Improve Text Summarization. Procesamiento del Lenguaje Natural, Revista nº 47 septiembre de 2011 (SEPLN 2011), pp 97-105.

Monica Gavrila. 2011. Constrained Recombination in an Example-based Machine Translation System, In the Proceedings of the EAMT-2011: the 15th Annual Conference of the European Association for Machine Translation, 30-31 May 2011, Leuven, Belgium, p. 193-200

Jan Niehues and Alex Waibel. 2010. Domain adaptation in statistical machine translation using factored translation models. EAMT 2010: Proceedings of the 14th Annual conference of the European Association for Machine Translation, 27-28 May 2010, Saint-Raphaël, France.

Christian Federmann and Andreas Eisele. 2010. MT Server Land: An Open-Source MT Architecture. The Prague Bulletin of Mathematical Linguistics. NUMBER 94, 2010, p57–66

Collaborative Machine Translation Service for Scientific texts

Patrik Lambert
University of Le Mans
patrik.lambert@lium.univ-lemans.fr

Jean Senellart
Systran SA
senellart@systran.fr

Laurent Romary
Humboldt Universität Berlin /
INRIA Saclay - Ile de France
laurent.romary@inria.fr

Holger Schwenk
University of Le Mans
holger.schwenk@lium.univ-lemans.fr

Florian Zipser
Humboldt Universität Berlin
f.zipser@gmx.de

Patrice Lopez
Humboldt Universität Berlin /
INRIA Saclay - Ile de France
patrice.lopez@inria.fr

Frédéric Blain
Systran SA /
University of Le Mans
frederic.blain@lium.univ-lemans.fr

Abstract

French researchers are required to frequently translate into French the description of their work published in English. At the same time, the need for French people to access articles in English, or to international researchers to access theses or papers in French, is incorrectly resolved via the use of generic translation tools. We propose the demonstration of an end-to-end tool integrated in the HAL open archive for enabling efficient translation for scientific texts. This tool can give translation suggestions adapted to the scientific domain, improving by more than 10 points the BLEU score of a generic system. It also provides a post-edition service which captures user post-editing data that can be used to incrementally improve the translations engines. Thus it is helpful for users which need to translate or to access scientific texts.

1 Introduction

Due to the globalisation of research, the English language is today the universal language of scientific communication. In France, regulations require the use of the French language in progress reports, academic dissertations, manuscripts, and French is the official educational language of the country. This situation forces researchers to frequently translate their own articles, lectures, presentations, reports, and abstracts between English and French. In addition, students and the general public are also challenged by language, when it comes to find published articles in English or to understand these articles. Finally, international scientists not even consider to look for French publications (for instance PhD theses) because they are not available in their native languages. This problem, incorrectly resolved through the use of generic translation tools, actually reveals an interesting generic problem where a community of specialists are regularly performing translations tasks on a very limited domain. At the same time, other communities of users seek translations for the same type of documents. Without appropriate tools, the expertise and time spent for translation activity by the first community is lost and do not benefit to translation requests of the other communities.

We propose the demonstration of an end-to-end tool for enabling efficient translation for scientific texts. This system, developed for the COSMAT ANR project,[1] is closely integrated into the HAL open archive,[2] a multidisciplinary open-access archive which was created in 2006 to archive publications from all the French scientific community. The tool deals with handling of source document format, generally a pdf file, specialised translation of the content, and user-friendly user-interface allowing to post-edit the output. Behind

[1] http://www.cosmat.fr/
[2] http://hal.archives-ouvertes.fr/?langue=en

the scene, the post-editing tool captures user post-editing data which are used to incrementally improve the translations engines. The only equipment required by this demonstration is a computer with an Internet browser installed and an Internet connection.

In this paper, we first describe the complete work-flow from data acquisition to final post-editing. Then we focus on the text extraction procedure. In Section 4, we give details about the translation system. Then in section 5, we present the translation and post-editing interface. We finally give some concluding remarks.

The system will be demonstrated at EACL in his tight integration with the HAL paper deposit system. If the organizers agree, we would like to offer the use of our system during the EACL conference. It would automatically translate all the abstracts of the accepted papers and also offers the possibility to correct the outputs. This resulting data would be made freely available.

2 Complete Processing Work-flow

The entry point for the system are "ready to publish" scientific papers. The goal of our system was to extract content keeping as many meta-information as possible from the document, to translate the content, to allow the user to perform post-editing, and to render the result in a format as close as possible to the source format. To train our system, we collected from the HAL archive more than 40 000 documents in physics and computer science, including articles, PhD theses or research reports (see Section 4). This material was used to train the translation engines and to extract domain bilingual terminology.

The user scenario is the following:

- A user uploads an article in PDF format[3] on the system.
- The document is processed by the open-source Grobid tool (see section 3) to extract the content. The extracted paper is structured in the TEI format where title, authors, references, footnotes, figure captions are identified with a very high accuracy.
- An entity recognition process is performed for markup of domain entities such as: chemical compounds for chemical papers, mathematical formulas, pseudo-code and object references in computer science papers, but also miscellaneous acronyms commonly used in scientific communication.
- Specialised terminology is then recognised using the Termsciences[4] reference terminology database, completed with terminology automatically extracted from the training corpus. The actual translation of the paper is performed using adapted translation as described in Section 4.
- The translation process generates a bilingual TEI format preserving the source structure and integrating the entity annotation, multiple terminology choices when available, and the token alignment between source and target sentences.
- The translation is proposed to the user for post-editing through a rich interactive interface described in Section 5.
- The final version of the document is then archived in TEI format and available for display in HTML using dedicated XSLT style sheets.

3 The Grobid System

Based on state-of-the-art machine learning techniques, Grobid (Lopez, 2009) performs reliable bibliographic data extraction from scholar articles combined with multi-level term extraction. These two types of extraction present synergies and correspond to complementary descriptions of an article.

This tool parses and converts scientific articles in PDF format into a structured TEI document[5] compliant with the good practices developed within the European PEER project (Bretel et al., 2010). Grobid is trained on a set of annotated

[3]The commonly used publishing format is PDF files while authoring format is principally a mix of Microsoft Word file and LaTeX documents using a variety of styles. The originality of our approach is to work on the PDF file and not on these source formats. The rationale being that 1/ the source format is almost never available, 2/ even if we had access to the source format, we would need to implement a filter specific to each individual template required by such or such conference for a good quality content extraction

[4]http://www.termsciences.fr

[5]http://www.tei-c.org

scientific article and can be re-trained to fit templates used for a specific conference or to extract additional fields.

4 Translation of Scientific Texts

The translation system used is a Hybrid Machine Translation (HMT) system from French to English and from English to French, adapted to translate scientific texts in several domains (so far physics and computer science). This system is composed of a statistical engine, coupled with rule-based modules to translate special parts of the text such as mathematical formulas, chemical compounds, pseudo-code, and enriched with domain bilingual terminology (see Section 2). Large amounts of monolingual and parallel data are available to train a SMT system between French and English, but not in the scientific domain. In order to improve the performance of our translation system in this task, we extracted in-domain monolingual and parallel data from the HAL archive. All the PDF files deposited in HAL in computer science and physics were made available to us. These files were then converted to plain text using the Grobid tool, as described in the previous section. We extracted text from all the documents from HAL that were made available to us to train our language model. We built a small parallel corpus from the abstracts of the PhD theses from French universities, which must include both an abstract in French and in English. Table 1 presents statistics of these in-domain data.

The data extracted from HAL were used to adapt a generic system to the scientific literature domain. The generic system was mostly trained on data provided for the shared task of Sixth Workshop on Statistical Machine Translation[6] (WMT 2011), described in Table 2.

Table 3 presents results showing, in the English–French direction, the impact on the statistical engine of introducing the resources extracted from HAL, as well as the impact of domain adaptation techniques. The baseline statistical engine is a standard PBSMT system based on Moses (Koehn et al., 2007) and the SRILM tookit (Stolcke, 2002). Is was trained and tuned only on WMT11 data (out-of-domain). Incorporating the HAL data into the language model and tuning the system on the HAL development set,

[6]http://www.statmt.org/wmt11/translation-task.html

Set	Domain	Lg	Sent.	Words	Vocab.
Parallel data					
Train	cs+phys	En	55.9 k	1.41 M	43.3 k
		Fr	55.9 k	1.63 M	47.9 k
Dev	cs	En	1100	25.8 k	4.6 k
		Fr	1100	28.7 k	5.1 k
	phys	En	1000	26.1 k	5.1 k
		Fr	1000	29.1 k	5.6 k
Test	cs	En	1100	26.1 k	4.6 k
		Fr	1100	29.2 k	5.2 k
	phys	En	1000	25.9 k	5.1 k
		Fr	1000	28.8 k	5.5 k
Monolingual data					
Train	cs	En	2.5 M	54 M	457 k
		Fr	761 k	19 M	274 k
	phys	En	2.1 M	50 M	646 k
		Fr	662 k	17 M	292 k

Table 1: Statistics for the parallel training, development, and test data sets extracted from thesis abstracts contained in HAL, as well as monolingual data extracted from all documents in HAL, in computer science (cs) and physics (phys). The following statistics are given for the English (En) and French (Fr) sides (Lg) of the corpus: the number of sentences, the number of running words (after tokenisation) and the number of words in the vocabulary (M and k stand for millions and thousands, respectively).

yielded a gain of more than 7 BLEU points, in both domains (computer science and physics). Including the theses abstracts in the parallel training corpus, a further gain of 2.3 BLEU points is observed for computer science, and 3.1 points for physics. The last experiment performed aims at increasing the amount of in-domain parallel texts by translating automatically in-domain monolingual data, as suggested by Schwenk (2008). The synthesised bitext does not bring new words into the system, but increases the probability of in-domain bilingual phrases. By adding a synthetic bitext of 12 million words to the parallel training data, we observed a gain of 0.5 BLEU point for computer science, and 0.7 points for physics.

Although not shown here, similar results were obtained in the French–English direction. The French–English system is actually slightly better than the English–French one as it is an easier translation direction.

Translation Model	Language Model	Tuning Domain	CS		PHYS	
			words (M)	Bleu	words (M)	Bleu
wmt11	wmt11	wmt11	371	27.3	371	27.1
wmt11	wmt11+hal	hal	371	36.0	371	36.2
wmt11+hal	wmt11+hal	hal	287	38.3	287	39.3
wmt11+hal+adapted	wmt11+hal	hal	299	38.8	307	40.0

Table 3: Results (BLEU score) for the English–French systems. The type of parallel data used to train the translation model or language model are indicated, as well as the set (in-domain or out-of-domain) used to tune the models. Finally, the number of words in the parallel corpus and the BLEU score on the in-domain test set are indicated for each domain: computer science and physics.

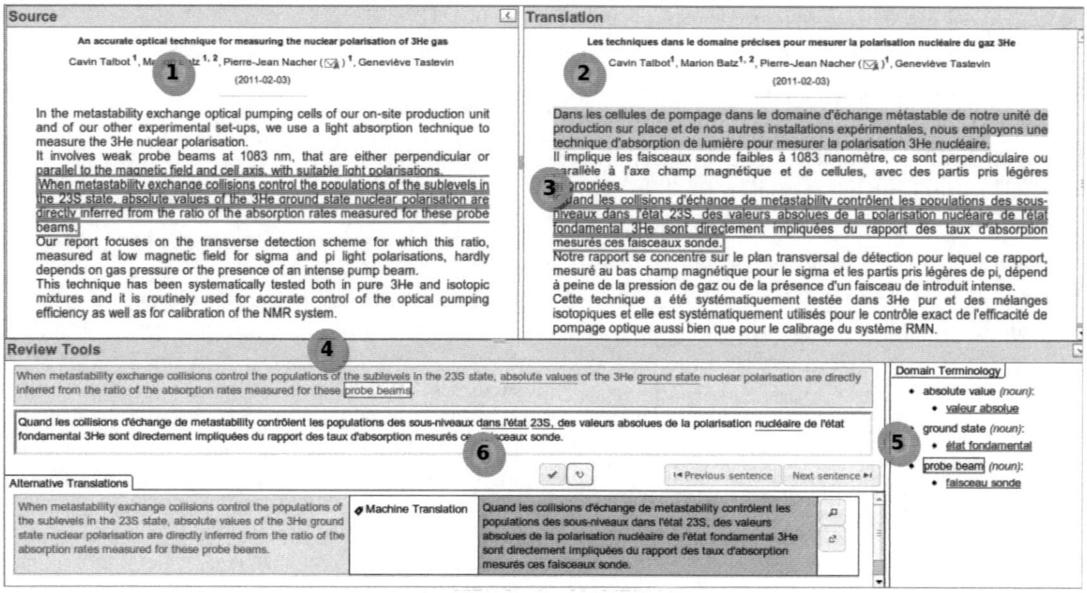

Figure 1: Translation and post-editing interface.

Corpus	English	French
Bitexts:		
Europarl	50.5M	54.4M
News Commentary	2.9M	3.3M
Crawled (10^9 bitexts)	667M	794M
Development data:		
newstest2009	65k	73k
newstest2010	62k	71k
Monolingual data:		
LDC Gigaword	4.1G	920M
Crawled news	2.6G	612M

Table 2: Out-of-domain development and training data used (number of words after tokenisation).

5 Post-editing Interface

The collaborative aspect of the demonstrated machine translation service is based on a post-editing tool, whose interface is shown in Figure 1. This tool provides the following features:

- WYSIWYG display of the source and target texts (Zones 1+2)
- Alignment at the sentence level (Zone 3)
- Zone to review the translation with alignment of source and target terms (Zone 4) and terminology reference (Zone 5)
- Alternative translations (Zone 6)

The tool allows the user to perform sentence level post-editing and records details of post-editing activity, such as keystrokes, terminology selection, actual edits and time log for the complete action.

6 Conclusions and Perspectives

We proposed the demonstration of an end-to-end tool integrated into the HAL archive and enabling efficient translation for scientific texts. This tool consists of a high-accuracy PDF extractor, a hybrid machine translation engine adapted to the scientific domain and a post-edition tool. Thanks to in-domain data collected from HAL, the statistical engine was improved by more than 10 BLEU points with respect to a generic system trained on WMT11 data.

Our system was deployed for a physic conference organised in Paris in Sept 2011. All accepted abstracts were translated into author's native languages (around 70% of them) and proposed for post-editing. The experience was promoted by the organisation committee and 50 scientists volunteered (34 finally performed their post-editing). The same experience will be proposed for authors of the LREC conference. We would like to offer a complete demonstration of the system at EACL. The goal of these experiences is to collect and distribute detailed "post-editing" data for enabling research on this activity.

Acknowledgements

This work has been partially funded by the French Government under the project COSMAT (ANR ANR-09-CORD-004).

References

Foudil Bretel, Patrice Lopez, Maud Medves, Alain Monteil, and Laurent Romary. 2010. Back to meaning – information structuring in the PEER project. In *TEI Conference*, Zadar, Croatie.

Philipp Koehn, Hieu Hoang, Alexandra Birch, Chris Callison-Burch, Marcello Federico, Nicola Bertoldi, Brooke Cowan, Wade Shen, Christine Moran, Richard Zens, Chris Dyer, Ondrej Bojar, Alexandra Constantin, and Evan Herbst. 2007. Moses: Open source toolkit for statistical machine translation. In *Proc. of the 45th Annual Meeting of the Association for Computational Linguistics (Demo and Poster Sessions)*, pages 177–180, Prague, Czech Republic, June. Association for Computational Linguistics.

Patrice Lopez. 2009. GROBID: Combining automatic bibliographic data recognition and term extraction for scholarship publications. In *Proceedings of ECDL 2009, 13th European Conference on Digital Library*, Corfu, Greece.

Holger Schwenk. 2008. Investigations on large-scale lightly-supervised training for statistical machine translation. In *IWSLT*, pages 182–189.

A. Stolcke. 2002. SRILM: an extensible language modeling toolkit. In *Proc. of the Int. Conf. on Spoken Language Processing*, pages 901–904, Denver, CO.

TransAhead: A Writing Assistant for CAT and CALL

[*]Chung-chi Huang [++]Ping-che Yang [*]Mei-hua Chen [*]Hung-ting Hsieh [+]Ting-hui Kao [+]Jason S. Chang

[*]ISA, NTHU, HsinChu, Taiwan, R.O.C.
[++]III, Taipei, Taiwan, R.O.C.
[+]CS, NTHU, HsinChu, Taiwan, R.O.C.

{u901571,maciaclark,chen.meihua,vincent732,maxis1718,jason.jschang}gmail.com

Abstract

We introduce a method for learning to predict the following grammar and text of the ongoing translation given a source text. In our approach, predictions are offered aimed at reducing users' burden on lexical and grammar choices, and improving productivity. The method involves learning syntactic phraseology and translation equivalents. At run-time, the source and its translation prefix are sliced into ngrams to generate subsequent grammar and translation predictions. We present a prototype writing assistant, TransAhead[1], that applies the method to where computer-assisted translation and language learning meet. The preliminary results show that the method has great potentials in CAT and CALL (significant boost in translation quality is observed).

1. Introduction

More and more language learners use the MT systems on the Web for language understanding or learning. However, web translation systems typically suggest a, usually far from perfect, one-best translation and hardly interact with the user.

Language learning/sentence translation could be achieved more interactively and appropriately if a system recognized translation as a collaborative sequence of the user's learning and choosing from the machine-generated predictions of the next-in-line grammar and text and the machine's adapting to the user's accepting /overriding the suggestions.

Consider the source sentence "我們在結束這個交易上扮演重要角色" (We play an important role in closing this deal). The best learning environment is probably not the one solely providing the automated translation. A good learning environment might comprise a writing assistant that gives the user direct control over the target text and offers text and grammar predictions following the ongoing translations.

We present a new system, TransAhead, that automatically learns to predict/suggest the grammatical constructs and lexical translations expected to immediately follow the current translation given a source text, and adapts to the user's choices. Example TransAhead responses to the source "我們在結束這個交易上扮演重要角色" and the ongoing translation "we" and "we play an important role" are shown in Figure 1[2](a) and (b) respectively. TransAhead has determined the probable subsequent grammatical constructions with constituents lexically translated, shown in pop-up menus (e.g., Figure 1(b) shows a prediction "IN[*in*] VBG[*close*, *end*, …]" due to the history "play role" where lexical items in square brackets are lemmas of potential translations). TransAhead learns these constructs and translations during training.

At run-time, TransAhead starts with a source sentence, and iteratively collaborates with the user: by making predictions on the successive grammar patterns and lexical translations, and by adapting to the user's translation choices to reduce source ambiguities (e.g., word segmentation and senses). In our prototype, TransAhead mediates between users and automatic modules to boost users' writing/ translation performance (e.g., productivity).

2. Related Work

CAT has been an area of active research. Our work addresses an aspect of CAT focusing on language learning. Specifically, our goal is to build a human-computer collaborative writing assistant: helping the language learner with in-text grammar and translation and at the same

[1]Available at http://140.114.214.80/theSite/TransAhead/ which, for the time being, only supports Chrome browsers.

[2] Note that grammatical constituents (in all-capitalized words) are represented using Penn parts-of-speech and the history based on the user input is shown in shades.

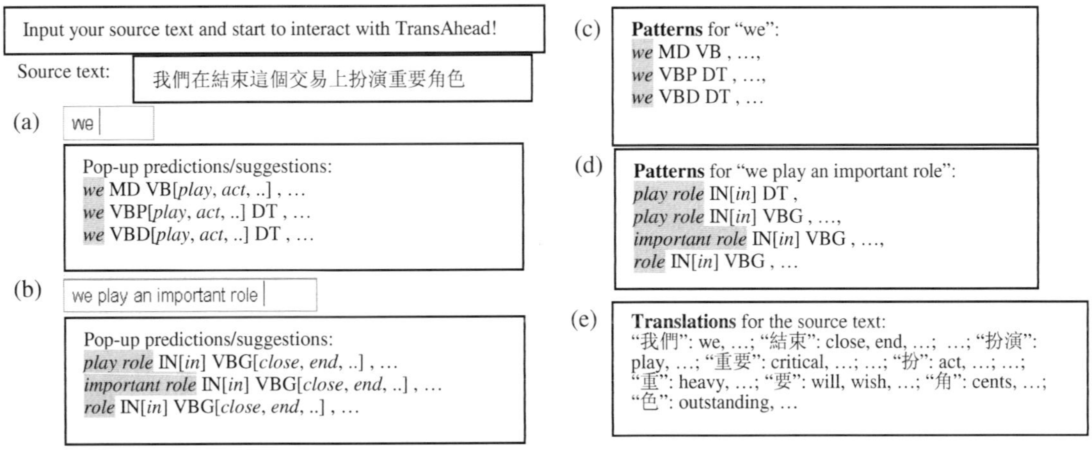

Figure 1. Example TransAhead responses to a source text under the translation (a) "we" and (b) "we play an important role". Note that the grammar/text predictions of (a) and (b) are not placed directly under the current input focus for space limit. (c) and (d) depict predominant grammar constructs which follow and (e) summarizes the translations for the source's character-based ngrams.

time updating the system's segmentation /translation options through the user's word choices. Our intended users are different from those of the previous research focusing on what professional translator can bring for MT systems (e.g., Brown and Nirenburg, 1990).

More recently, interactive MT (IMT) systems have begun to shift the user's role from analyses of the source text to the formation of the target translation. TransType project (Foster et al., 2002) describes such pioneering system that supports next word predictions. Koehn (2009) develops caitra which displays one phrase translation at a time and offers alternative translation options. Both systems are similar in spirit to our work. The main difference is that we do not expect the user to be a professional translator and we provide translation hints along with grammar predictions to avoid the generalization issue facing phrase-based system.

Recent work has been done on using fully-fledged statistical MT systems to produce target hypotheses completing user-validated translation prefix in IMT paradigm. Barrachina et al. (2008) investigate the applicability of different MT kernels within IMT framework. Nepveu et al. (2004) and Ortiz-Martinez et al. (2011) further exploit user feedbacks for better IMT systems and user experience. Instead of trigged by user correction, our method is triggered by word delimiter and assists in target language learning.

In contrast to the previous CAT research, we present a writing assistant that suggests subsequent grammar constructs with translations and interactively collaborates with learners, in view of reducing users' burden on grammar and word choice and enhancing their writing quality.

3. The TransAhead System

3.1 Problem Statement

For CAT and CALL, we focus on predicting a set of grammar patterns with lexical translations likely to follow the current target translation given a source text. The predictions will be examined by a human user directly. Not to overwhelm the user, our goal is to return a reasonable-sized set of predictions that contain suitable word choices and correct grammar to choose and learn from. Formally speaking,

Problem Statement: We are given a target-language reference corpus C_t, a parallel corpus C_{st}, a source-language text S, and its target translation prefix T_p. Our goal is to provide a set of predictions based on C_t and C_{st} likely to further translate S in terms of grammar and text. For this, we transform S and T_p into sets of ngrams such that the predominant grammar constructs with suitable translation options following T_p are likely to be acquired.

3.2 Learning to Find Pattern and Translation

We attempt to find syntax-based phraseology and translation equivalents beforehand (four-staged) so that a real-time system is achievable.

Firstly, we syntactically analyze the corpus C_t. In light of the phrases in grammar book (e.g., *one's* in "make up *one's* mind"), we resort to parts-of-speech for syntactic generalization. Secondly, we build up inverted files of the words in C_t for the next stage (i.e., pattern grammar generation). Apart from sentence and position information, a word's lemma and part-of-speech (POS) are also recorded.

We then leverage the procedure in Figure 2 to generate grammar patterns for any given sequence of words (e.g., contiguous or not).

```
procedure PatternFinding(query,N,C_t)
(1)  interInvList=findInvertedFile(w_1 of query)
     for each word w_i in query except for w_1
(2)     InvList=findInvertedFile(w_i)
(3a)    newInterInvList= φ ; i=1; j=1
(3b)    while i<=length(interInvList) and j<=lengh(InvList)
(3c)       if interInvList[i].SentNo==InvList[j].SentNo
(3d)          Insert(newInterInvList, interInvList[i],InvList[j])
           else
(3e)          Move i,j accordingly
(3f)    interInvList=newInterInvList
(4) Usage= φ
     for each element in interInvList
(5)     Usage+={PatternGrammarGeneration(element,C_t)}
(6) Sort patterns in Usage in descending order of frequency
(7) return the N patterns in Usage with highest frequency
```

Figure 2. Automatically generating pattern grammar.

The algorithm first identifies the sentences containing the given sequence of words, *query*. Iteratively, Step (3) performs an AND operation on the inverted file, *InvList*, of the current word w_i and *interInvList*, a previous intersected results.

Afterwards, we analyze *query*'s syntax-based phraseology (Step (5)). For each *element* of the form ([wordPosi(w_1),…,wordPosi(w_n)], *sentence number*) denoting the positions of *query*'s words in the *sentence*, we generate grammar pattern involving replacing words with POS tags and words in wordPosi(w_i) with lemmas, and extracting fixed-window[3] segments surrounding *query* from the transformed sentence. The result is a set of grammatical, contextual patterns.

The procedure finally returns top N predominant syntactic patterns associated with the query. Such patterns characterizing the query's word usages follow the notion of pattern grammar in (Hunston and Francis, 2000) and are collected across the target language.

In the fourth and final stage, we exploit C_{st} for bilingual phrase acquisition, rather than a manual dictionary, to achieve better translation coverage and variety. We obtain phrase pairs through leveraging IBM models to word-align the bitexts, "smoothing" the directional word alignments via grow-diagonal-final, and extracting translation equivalents using (Koehn et al., 2003).

3.3 Run-Time Grammar and Text Prediction

Once translation equivalents and phraseological tendencies are learned, TransAhead then predicts/suggests the following grammar and text of a translation prefix given the source text using the procedure in Figure 3.

We first slice the source text S and its translation prefix T_p into character-level and word-level ngrams respectively. Step (3) and (4) retrieve the translations and patterns learned from Section 3.2. Step (3) acquires the active target-language vocabulary that may be used to translate the source text. To alleviate the word boundary issue in MT raised by Ma et al. (2007), TransAhead non-deterministically segments the source text using character ngrams and proceeds with collaborations with the user to obtain the segmentation for MT and to complete the translation. Note that a user vocabulary of preference (due to users' domain of knowledge or errors of the system) may be exploited for better system performance. On the other hand, Step (4) extracts patterns preceding with the history ngrams of $\{t_j\}$.

```
procedure MakePrediction(S,T_p)
(1) Assign sliceNgram(S) to {s_i}
(2) Assign sliceNgram(T_p) to {t_j}
(3) TransOptions=findTranslation({s_i},T_p)
(4) GramOptions=findPattern({t_j})
(5) Evaluate translation options in TransOptions
         and incorporate them into GramOptions
(6) Return GramOptions
```

Figure 3. Predicting pattern grammar and translations.

In Step (5), we first evaluate and rank the translation candidates using linear combination:

$$\lambda_1 \times \left(P_1\left(t \mid s_i\right) + P_1\left(s_i \mid t\right)\right) + \lambda_2 \times P_2\left(t \mid T_p\right)$$

where λ_i is combination weight, P_1 and P_2 are translation and language model respectively, and t is one of the translation candidates under S and T_p. Subsequently, we incorporate the lemmatized translation candidates into grammar constituents in *GramOptions*. For example, we would include "close" in pattern "*play role* IN[*in*] VBG" as "*play role* IN[*in*] VBG[*close*]".

At last, the algorithm returns the representative grammar patterns with confident translations expected to follow the ongoing translation and further translate the source. This algorithm will be triggered by word delimiter to provide an interactive environment where CAT and CALL meet.

4. Preliminary Results

To train TransAhead, we used British National Corpus and Hong Kong Parallel Text and deployed GENIA tagger for POS analyses.

To evaluate TransAhead in CAT and CALL, we introduced it to a class of 34 (Chinese) first-year college students learning English as foreign language. Designed to be intuitive to the general public, esp. language learners, presentational tutorial lasted only for a minute. After the tutorial, the participants were asked to translate 15

[3] Inspired by (Gamon and Leacock, 2010).

Chinese texts from (Huang et al., 2011a) one by one (half with TransAhead assistance, and the other without). Encouragingly, the experimental group (i.e., with the help of our system) achieved *much* better translation quality than the control group in BLEU (Papineni et al., 2002) (i.e., 35.49 vs. 26.46) and *significantly* reduced the performance gap between language learners and automatic decoder of Google Translate (44.82). We noticed that, for the source "我們在結束這個交易上扮演重要角色", 90% of the participants in the experimental group finished with more grammatical and fluent translations (see Figure 4) than (less interactive) Google Translate ("We conclude this transaction plays an important role"). In comparison, 50% of the translations of *the* source from the control group were erroneous.

1. we play(ed) a critical role in closing/sealing this/the deal. 2. we play(ed) an important role in ending/closing this/the deal.

Figure 4. Example translations with TransAhead assistance.

Post-experiment surveys indicate that a) the participants found TransAhead intuitive enough to collaborate with in writing/translation; b) the participants found TransAhead suggestions satisfying, accepted, and learned from them; c) interactivity made translation and language learning more fun and the participants found TransAhead very recommendable and would like to use the system again in future translation tasks.

5. Future Work and Summary

Many avenues exist for future research and improvement. For example, in the linear combination, the patterns' frequencies could be considered and the feature weight could be better tuned. Furthermore, interesting directions to explore include leveraging user input such as (Nepveu et al., 2004) and (Ortiz-Martinez et al., 2010) and serially combining a grammar checker (Huang et al., 2011b). Yet another direction would be to investigate the possibility of using human-computer collaborated translation pairs to re-train word boundaries suitable for MT.

In summary, we have introduced a method for learning to offer grammar and text predictions expected to assist the user in translation and writing (or even language learning). We have implemented and evaluated the method. The preliminary results are encouragingly promising, prompting us to further qualitatively and quantitatively evaluate our system in the near future (i.e., learners' productivity, typing speed and keystroke ratios of "del" and "backspace" (possibly hesitating on the grammar and lexical choices), and human-computer interaction, among others).

Acknowledgement

This study is conducted under the "Project Digital Convergence Service Open Platform" of the Institute for Information Industry which is subsidized by the Ministry of Economy Affairs of the Republic of China.

References

S. Barrachina, O. Bender, F. Casacuberta, J. Civera, E. Cubel, S. Khadivi, A. Lagarda, H. Ney, J. Tomas, E. Vidal, and J.-M. Vilar. 2008. Statistical approaches to computer-assisted translation. *Computer Linguistics*, 35(1): 3-28.

R. D. Brown and S. Nirenburg. 1990. Human-computer interaction for semantic disambiguation. In *Proceedings of COLING*, pages 42-47.

G. Foster, P. Langlais, E. Macklovitch, and G. Lapalme. 2002. TransType: text prediction for translators. In *Proceedings of ACL Demonstrations*, pages 93-94.

M. Gamon and C. Leacock. 2010. Search right and thou shalt find ... using web queries for learner error detection. In *Proceedings of the NAACL Workshop on Innovative Use of NLP for Building Educational Applications*, pages 37-44.

C.-C. Huang, M.-H. Chen, S.-T. Huang, H.-C. Liou, and J. S. Chang. 2011a. GRASP: grammar- and syntax-based pattern-finder in CALL. In *Proceedings of ACL*.

C.-C. Huang, M.-H. Chen, S.-T. Huang, and J. S. Chang. 2011b. EdIt: a broad-coverage grammar checker using pattern grammar. In *Proceedings of ACL*.

S. Hunston and G. Francis. 2000. *Pattern Grammar: A Corpus-Driven Approach to the Lexical Grammar of English*. Amsterdam: John Benjamins.

P. Koehn, F. J. Och, and D. Marcu. 2003. Statistical phrase-based translation. In *Proceedings of NAACL*.

P. Koehn. 2009. A web-based interactive computer aided translation tool. In *Proceedings of ACL*.

Y. Ma, N. Stroppa, and A. Way. 2007. Bootstrapping word alignment via word packing. In *Proceedings of ACL*.

L. Nepveu, G. Lapalme, P. Langlais, and G. Foster. 2004. Adaptive language and translation models for interactive machine translation. In *Proceedings of EMNLP*.

Franz Josef Och and Hermann Ney. 2003. A systematic Comparison of Various Statistical Alignment Models. *Computational Linguistics*, 29(1):19-51.

D. Ortiz-Martinez, L. A. Leiva, V. Alabau, I. Garcia-Varea, and F. Casacuberta. 2011. An interactive machine translation system with online learning. In *Proceedings of ACL System Demonstrations*, pages 68-73.

K. Papineni, S. Roukos, T. Ward, W.-J. Zhu. 2002. Bleu: a method for automatic evaluation of machine translation. In *Proceedings of ACL*, pages 311-318.

SWAN – Scientific Writing AssistaNt
A Tool for Helping Scholars to Write Reader-Friendly Manuscripts

`http://cs.joensuu.fi/swan/`

Tomi Kinnunen* **Henri Leisma** **Monika Machunik** **Tuomo Kakkonen** **Jean-Luc Lebrun**

Abstract

Difficulty of reading scholarly papers is significantly reduced by *reader-friendly* writing principles. Writing reader-friendly text, however, is challenging due to difficulty in recognizing problems in one's own writing. To help scholars identify and correct potential writing problems, we introduce SWAN (Scientific Writing AssistaNt) tool. SWAN is a rule-based system that gives feedback based on various quality metrics based on years of experience from scientific writing classes including 960 scientists of various backgrounds: life sciences, engineering sciences and economics. According to our first experiences, users have perceived SWAN as helpful in identifying problematic sections in text and increasing overall clarity of manuscripts.

1 Introduction

A search on "tools to evaluate the quality of writing" often gets you to sites assessing only one of the qualities of writing: its *readability*. Measuring ease of reading is indeed useful to determine if your writing meets the reading level of your targeted reader, but with scientific writing, the statistical formulae and readability indices such as Flesch-Kincaid lose their usefulness.

In a way, readability is subjective and dependent on how familiar the reader is with the specific vocabulary and the written style. Scientific papers are targeting an audience at ease with a more specialized vocabulary, an audience expecting sentence-lengthening precision in writing. The readability index would require recalibration for such a specific audience. But the need for readability indices is not questioned here. "Science is often hard to read" (Gopen and Swan, 1990), even for scientists.

Science is also hard to *write*, and finding fault with one's own writing is even more challenging since we understand ourselves perfectly, at least most of the time. To gain objectivity scientists turn away from silent readability indices and find more direct help in checklists such as the peer review form proposed by Bates College[1], or scoring sheets to assess the quality of a scientific paper. These organise a systematic and critical walk through each part of a paper, from its title to its references in peer-review style. They integrate readability criteria that far exceed those covered by statistical lexical tools. For example, they examine how the text structure frames the contents under headings and subheadings that are consistent with the title and abstract of the paper. They test whether or not the writer fluidly meets the expectations of the reader. Written by expert reviewers (and readers), they represent them, their needs and concerns, and act as their proxy. Such manual tools effectively improve writing (Chuck and Young, 2004).

Computer-assisted tools that support manual assessment based on checklists require natural language understanding. Due to the complexity of language, today's natural language processing (NLP) techniques mostly enable computers to deliver shallow language understanding when the

* T. Kinnunen, H. Leisma, M. Machunik and T. Kakkonen are with the School of Computing, University of Eastern Finland (UEF), Joensuu, Finland, e-mail: `tkinnu@cs.joensuu.fi`. Jean-Luc Lebrun is an independent trainer of scientific writing and can be contacted at `jllebrun@me.com`.

[1] `http://abacus.bates.edu/~ganderso/biology/resources/peerreview.html`

vocabulary is large and highly specialized – as is the case for scientific papers. Nevertheless, they are mature enough to be embedded in tools assisted by human input to increase depth of understanding. SWAN (*ScientificWriting AssistaNt*) is such a tool (Fig. 1). It is based on metrics tested on 960 scientists working for the research Institutes of the Agency for Science, Technology and Research (A*STAR) in Singapore since 1997.

The evaluation metrics used in SWAN are described in detail in a book written by the designer of the tool (Lebrun, 2011). In general, SWAN focuses on the areas of a scientific paper that create the first impression on the reader. Readers, and in particular reviewers, will always read these particular sections of a paper: title, abstract, introduction, conclusion, and the headings and subheadings of the paper. SWAN does *not* assess the overall quality of a scientific paper. SWAN assesses its fluidity and cohesion, two of the attributes that contribute to the overall quality of the paper. It also helps identify other types of potential problems such as lack of text dynamism, overly long sentences and judgmental words.

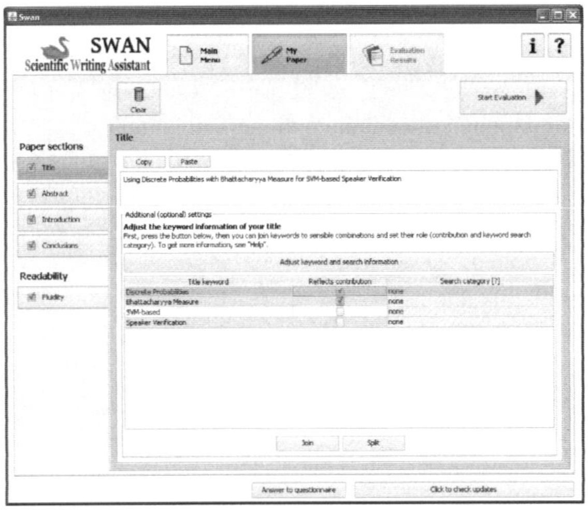

Figure 1: Main window of SWAN.

2 Related Work

Automatic assessment of student-authored texts is an active area of research. Hundreds of research publications related to this topic have been published since Page's (Page, 1966) pioneering work on automatic grading of student essays. The research on using NLP in support of writing scientific publications has, however, gained much less attention in the research community.

Amadeus (Aluisio et al., 2001) is perhaps the system that is the most similar to the work outlined in this system demonstration. However, the focus of the Amadeus system is mostly on non-native speakers on English who are learning to write scientific publications. SWAN is targeted for more general audience of users.

Helping our own (HOO) is an initiative that could in future spark a new interest in the research on using of NLP for supporting scientific writing (Dale and Kilgarriff, 2010). As the name suggests, the shared task (HOO, 2011) focuses on supporting non-native English speakers in writing articles related specifically to NLP and computational linguistics. The focus in this initiative is on what the authors themselves call "domain-and-register-specific error correction", i.e. correction of grammatical and spelling mistakes.

Some NLP research has been devoted to applying NLP techniques to scientific articles. Paquot and Bestgen (Paquot and Bestgen, 2009), for instance, extracted keywords from research articles.

3 Metrics Used in SWAN

We outline the evaluation metrics used in SWAN. Detailed description of the metrics is given in (Lebrun, 2011). Rather than focusing on English grammar or spell-checking included in most modern word processors, SWAN gives feedback on the core elements of any scientific paper: *title*, *abstract*, *introduction* and *conclusions*. In addition, SWAN gives feedback on *fluidity* of writing and paper structure.

SWAN includes two types of evaluation metrics, *automatic* and *manual* ones. Automatic metrics are solely implemented as text analysis of the original document using NLP tools. An example would be locating judgemental word patterns such as *suffers from* or locating sentences with passive voice. The manual metrics, in turn, require user's input for tasks that are difficult – if not impossible – to automate. An example would be highlighting title keywords that reflect the core contribution of the paper, or highlighting in the abstract the sentences that cover the relevant background.

Many of the evaluation metrics are strongly inter-connected with each other, such as

- Checking that abstract and title are consistent; for instance, frequently used abstract keywords should also be found in the title;

and the title should not include keywords absent in the abstract.

- Checking that all title keywords are also found in the paper structure (from headings or subheadings) so that the paper structure is self-explanatory.

An important part of paper quality metrics is assessing text *fluidity*. By fluidity we mean the ease with which the text can be read. This, in turn, depends on how much the reader needs to memorize about what they have read so far in order to understand new information. This memorizing need is greatly reduced if consecutive sentences do not contain rapid change in topic. The aim of the text fluidity module is to detect possible topic discontinuities within and across paragraphs, and to suggest ways of improving these parts, for example, by rearranging the sentences. The suggestions, while already useful, will improve in future versions of the tool with a better understanding of word meanings thanks to WordNet and lexical semantics techniques.

Fluidity evaluation is difficult to fully automate. Manual fluidity evaluation relies on the reader's understanding of the text. It is therefore superior to the automatic evaluation which relies on a set of heuristics that endeavor to identify text fluidity based on the concepts of *topic* and *stress* developed in (Gopen, 2004). These heuristics require the analysis of the sentence for which the Stanford parser is used. These heuristics are perfectible, but they already allow the identification of sentences disrupting text fluidity.More fluidity problems would be revealed through the manual fluidity evaluation.

Simply put, here *topic* refers to the main focus of the sentence (e.g. the subject of the main clause) while *stress* stands for the secondary sentence focus, which often becomes one of the following sentences' topic. SWAN compares the position of topic and stress across consecutive sentences, as well as their position inside the sentence (i.e. among its subclauses). SWAN assigns each sentence to one of four possible fluidity classes:

1. **Fluid**: the sentence is maintaining connection with the previous sentences.

2. **Inverted topic**: the sentence is connected to a previous sentence, but that connection only becomes apparent at the very end of the sentence ("The cropping should preserve all critical points. Images of the same size should also be kept by the cropping").

3. **Out-of-sync**: the sentence is connected to a previous one, but there are disconnected sentences in between the connected sentences ("The cropping should preserve all critical points. The face features should be normalized. The cropping should also preserve all critical points").

4. **Disconnected**: the sentence is not connected to any of the previous sentences or there are too many sentences in between.

The tool also alerts the writer when transition words such as *in addition*, *on the other hand*, or even the familiar *however* are used. Even though these expressions are effective when correctly used, they often betray the lack of a logical or semantic connection between consecutive sentences ("The cropping should preserve all critical points. However, the face features should be normalized"). SWAN displays all the sentences which could potentially break the fluidity (Fig. 2) and suggests ways of rewriting them.

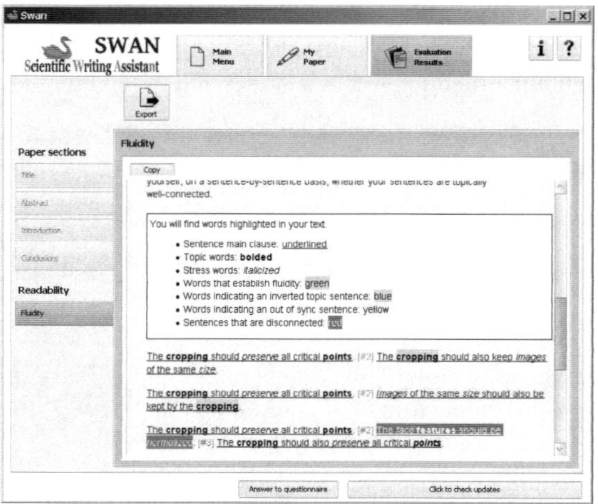

Figure 2: Fluidity evaluation result in SWAN.

4 The SWAN Tool

4.1 Inputs and outputs

SWAN operates on two possible evaluation modes: *simple* and *full*. In simple evaluation mode, the input to the tool are the title, abstract, introduction and conclusions of a manuscript. These sections can be copy-pasted as plain text to the input fields.

In full evaluation mode, which generally provides more feedback, the user provides a full paper as an input. This includes semi-automatic import of the manuscript from certain standard document formats such as TeX, MS Office and OpenOffice, as well as semi-automatic structure detection of the manuscript. For the well-known Adobe's portable document format (PDF) we use state-of-the-art freely available *PdfBox* extractor[2]. Unfortunately, PDF format is originally designed for layout and printing and not for structured text interchange. Most of the time, simple copy & paste from a source document to the simple evaluation fields is sufficient.

When the text sections have been input to the tool, clicking the *Evaluate* button will trigger the evaluation process. This has been observed to complete, at most, in a minute or two on a modern laptop. The evaluation metrics in the tool are straight-forward, most of the processing time is spent in the NLP tools. After the evaluation is complete, the results are shown to the user.

SWAN provides constructive feedback from the evaluated sections of your paper. The tool also highlights problematic words or sentences in the manuscript text and generates graphs of sentence features (see Fig. 2). The results can be saved and reloaded to the tool or exported to html format for sharing. The feedback includes tips on how to maintain authoritativeness and how to convince the scientist reader. Use of powerful and precise sentences is emphasized together with strategical and logical placement of key information.

In addition to these two main evaluation modes, the tool also includes a manual fluidity assessment exercise where the writer goes through a given text passage, sentence by sentence, to see whether the next sentence can be predicted from the previous sentences.

4.2 Implementation and External Libraries

The tool is a desktop application written in Java. It uses external libraries for natural language processing from Stanford, namely Stanford POS Tagger (Toutanova et al., 2003) and Stanford Parser (Klein and Manning, 2003). This is one of the most accurate and robust parsers available and implemented in Java, as is the rest of our system. Other external libraries include Apache Tika[3], which we use in extracting textual content from files. JFreeChart[4] is used in generating graphs and XStream[5] in saving and loading inputs and results.

5 Initial User Experiences of SWAN

Since its release in June 2011, the tool has been used in scientific writing classes in doctoral schools in France, Finland, and Singapore, as well as in 16 research institutes from A*STAR (Agency for Science Technology and Research). Participants to the classes routinely enter into SWAN either parts, or the whole paper they wish to immediately evaluate. SWAN is designed to work on multiple platforms and it relies completely on freely available tools. The feedback given by the participants after the course reveals the following benefits of using SWAN:

1. Identification and removal of the inconsistencies that make clear identification of the scientific contribution of the paper difficult.
2. Applicability of the tool across vast domains of research (life sciences, engineering sciences, and even economics).
3. Increased clarity of expression through the identification of the text fluidity problems.
4. Enhanced paper structure leading to a more readable paper overall.
5. More authoritative, more direct and more active writing style.

Novice writers already appreciate SWAN's functionalityand even senior writers, although evidence remains anecdotal. At this early stage, SWAN's capabilities are narrow in scope.We continue to enhance the existing evaluation metrics. And we are eager to include a new and already tested metric that reveals problems in how figures are used.

Acknowledgments

This works of T. Kinnunen and T. Kakkonen were supported by the Academy of Finland. The authors would like to thank Arttu Viljakainen, Teemu Turunen and Zhengzhe Wu in implementing various parts of SWAN.

References

[Aluisio et al.2001] S.M. Aluisio, I. Barcelos, J. Sampaio, and O.N. Oliveira Jr. 2001. How to learn the many "unwritten rules" of the game of the academic discourse: a hybrid approach based on critiques and cases to support scientific writing. In

[2] http://pdfbox.apache.org/

[3] http://tika.apache.org/

[4] http://www.jfree.org/jfreechart/

[5] http://xstream.codehaus.org/

Proc. IEEE International Conference on Advanced Learning Technologies, Madison, Wisconsin, USA.

[Chuck and Young2004] Jo-Anne Chuck and Lauren Young. 2004. A cohort-driven assessment task for scientific report writing. *Journal of Science, Education and Technology*, 13(3):367–376, September.

[Dale and Kilgarriff2010] R. Dale and A. Kilgarriff. 2010. Text massaging for computational linguistics as a new shared task. In *Proc. 6th Int. Natural Language Generation Conference*, Dublin, Ireland.

[Gopen and Swan1990] George D. Gopen and Judith A. Swan. 1990. The science of scientific writing. *American Scientist*, 78(6):550–558, November-December.

[Gopen2004] George D. Gopen. 2004. *Expectations: Teaching Writing From The Reader's perspective*. Longman.

[HOO2011] 2011. HOO - helping our own. Webpage, September. http://www.clt.mq.edu.au/research/projects/hoo/.

[Klein and Manning2003] Dan Klein and Christopher D. Manning. 2003. Accurate unlexicalized parsing. In *Proc. 41st Meeting of the Association for Computational Linguistics*, pages 423–430.

[Lebrun2011] Jean-Luc Lebrun. 2011. *Scientific Writing 2.0 – A Reader and Writer's Guide*. World Scientific Publishing Co. Pte. Ltd., Singapore.

[Page1966] E. Page. 1966. The imminence of grading essays by computer. In *Phi Delta Kappan*, pages 238–243.

[Paquot and Bestgen2009] M. Paquot and Y. Bestgen. 2009. Distinctive words in academic writing: A comparison of three statistical tests for keyword extraction. In A.H. Jucker, D. Schreier, and M. Hundt, editors, *Corpora: Pragmatics and Discourse*, pages 247–269. Rodopi, Amsterdam, Netherlands.

[Toutanova et al.2003] Kristina Toutanova, Dan Klein, Christopher Manning, and Yoram Singer. 2003. Feature-rich part-of-speech tagging with a cyclic dependency network. In *Proc. HLT-NAACL*, pages 252–259.

ONTS: "Optima" News Translation System

Marco Turchi*, **Martin Atkinson***, **Alastair Wilcox**+, **Brett Crawley**,
Stefano Bucci+, **Ralf Steinberger*** and **Erik Van der Goot***
European Commission - Joint Research Centre (JRC), IPSC - GlobeSec
Via Fermi 2749, 21020 Ispra (VA) - Italy
*[name].[surname]@jrc.ec.europa.eu
+[name].[surname]@ext.jrc.ec.europa.eu
brettcrawley@gmail.com

Abstract

We propose a real-time machine translation system that allows users to select a news category and to translate the related live news articles from Arabic, Czech, Danish, Farsi, French, German, Italian, Polish, Portuguese, Spanish and Turkish into English. The Moses-based system was optimised for the news domain and differs from other available systems in four ways: (1) News items are automatically categorised on the source side, before translation; (2) Named entity translation is optimised by recognising and extracting them on the source side and by re-inserting their translation in the target language, making use of a separate entity repository; (3) News titles are translated with a separate translation system which is optimised for the specific style of news titles; (4) The system was optimised for speed in order to cope with the large volume of daily news articles.

1 Introduction

Being able to read news from other countries and written in other languages allows readers to be better informed. It allows them to detect national news bias and thus improves transparency and democracy. Existing online translation systems such as *Google Translate* and *Bing Translator*[1] are thus a great service, but the number of documents that can be submitted is restricted (Google will even entirely stop their service in 2012) and submitting documents means disclosing the users' interests and their (possibly sensitive) data to the service-providing company.

For these reasons, we have developed our in-house machine translation system ONTS. Its translation results will be publicly accessible as part of the Europe Media Monitor family of applications, (Steinberger et al., 2009), which gather and process about 100,000 news articles per day in about fifty languages. ONTS is based on the open source phrase-based statistical machine translation toolkit Moses (Koehn et al., 2007), trained mostly on freely available parallel corpora and optimised for the news domain, as stated above. The main objective of developing our in-house system is thus not to improve translation quality over the existing services (this would be beyond our possibilities), but to offer our users a rough translation (a "gist") that allows them to get an idea of the main contents of the article and to determine whether the news item at hand is relevant for their field of interest or not.

A similar news-focused translation service is "Found in Translation" (Turchi et al., 2009), which gathers articles in 23 languages and translates them into English. "Found in Translation" is also based on Moses, but it categorises the news after translation and the translation process is not optimised for the news domain.

2 Europe Media Monitor

Europe Media Monitor (EMM)[2] gathers a daily average of 100,000 news articles in approximately 50 languages, from about 3,400 hand-selected web news sources, from a couple of hundred specialist and government websites, as well as from about twenty commercial news providers. It visits the news web sites up to every five minutes to

[1] `http://translate.google.com/` and `http://www.microsofttranslator.com/`

[2] `http://emm.newsbrief.eu/overview.html`

search for the latest articles. When news sites offer RSS feeds, it makes use of these, otherwise it extracts the news text from the often complex HTML pages. All news items are converted to Unicode. They are processed in a pipeline structure, where each module adds additional information. Independently of how files are written, the system uses UTF-8-encoded RSS format.

Inside the pipeline, different algorithms are implemented to produce monolingual and multilingual clusters and to extract various types of information such as named entities, quotations, categories and more. ONTS uses two modules of EMM: the named entity recognition and the categorization parts.

2.1 Named Entity Recognition and Variant Matching.

Named Entity Recognition (NER) is performed using manually constructed language-independent rules that make use of language-specific lists of trigger words such as titles (president), professions or occupations (tennis player, playboy), references to countries, regions, ethnic or religious groups (French, Bavarian, Berber, Muslim), age expressions (57-year-old), verbal phrases (deceased), modifiers (former) and more. These patterns can also occur in combination and patterns can be nested to capture more complex titles, (Steinberger and Pouliquen, 2007). In order to be able to cover many different languages, no other dictionaries and no parsers or part-of-speech taggers are used.

To identify which of the names newly found every day are new entities and which ones are merely variant spellings of entities already contained in the database, we apply a language-independent name similarity measure to decide which name variants should be automatically merged, for details see (Pouliquen and Steinberger, 2009). This allows us to maintain a database containing over 1,15 million named entities and 200,000 variants. The major part of this resource can be downloaded from `http://langtech.jrc.it/JRC-Names.html`

2.2 Category Classification across Languages.

All news items are categorized into hundreds of categories. Category definitions are multilingual, created by humans and they include geographic regions such as each country of the world, organizations, themes such as natural disasters or security, and more specific classes such as earthquake, terrorism or tuberculosis,

Articles fall into a given category if they satisfy the category definition, which consists of Boolean operators with optional vicinity operators and wild cards. Alternatively, cumulative positive or negative weights and a threshold can be used. Uppercase letters in the category definition only match uppercase words, while lowercase words in the definition match both uppercase and lowercase words. Many categories are defined with input from the users themselves. This method to categorize the articles is rather simple and user-friendly, and it lends itself to dealing with many languages, (Steinberger et al., 2009).

3 News Translation System

In this section, we describe our statistical machine translation (SMT) service based on the open-source toolkit Moses (Koehn et al., 2007) and its adaptation to translation of news items.

Which is the most suitable SMT system for our requirements? The main goal of our system is to help the user understand the content of an article. This means that a translated article is evaluated positively even if it is not perfect in the target language. Dealing with such a large number of source languages and articles per day, our system should take into account the translation speed, and try to avoid using language-dependent tools such as part-of-speech taggers.

Inside the Moses toolkit, three different statistical approaches have been implemented: *phrase based statistical machine translation* (PB-SMT) (Koehn et al., 2003), *hierarchical phrase based statistical machine translation* (Chiang, 2007) and *syntax-based statistical machine translation* (Marcu et al., 2006). To identify the most suitable system for our requirements, we run a set of experiments training the three models with Europarl V4 German-English (Koehn, 2005) and optimizing and testing on the News corpus (Callison-Burch et al., 2009). For all of them, we use their default configurations and they are run under the same condition on the same machine to better evaluate translation time. For the syntax model we use linguistic information only on the target side. According to our experiments, in terms of performance the hierarchical model performs better than PBSMT and syntax (18.31, 18.09, 17.62 Bleu points), but in terms of translation speed PBSMT is better than hierarchical and syntax (1.02, 4.5, 49 second per sentence). Although, the hierarchical model has the best Bleu score, we prefer to use the PBSMT system in our translation service, because it is four times faster.

Which training data can we use? It is known in statistical machine translation that more training data implies better translation. Although, the number of parallel corpora has been is growing in the last years, the amounts of training data vary from language pair to language pair. To train our models we use the freely available corpora (when possible): Europarl (Koehn, 2005), JRC-Acquis (Steinberger et al., 2006), DGT-TM[3], Opus (Tiedemann, 2009), SE-Times (Tyers and Alperen, 2010), Tehran English-Persian Parallel Corpus (Pilevar et al., 2011), News Corpus (Callison-Burch et al., 2009), UN Corpus (Rafalovitch and Dale, 2009), CzEng0.9 (Bojar and Žabokrtský, 2009), English-Persian parallel corpus distributed by ELRA[4] and two Arabic-English datasets distributed by LDC[5]. This results in some language pairs with a large coverage, (more than 4 million sentences), and other with a very small coverage, (less than 1 million). The language models are trained using 12 model sentences for the content model and 4.7 million for the title model. Both sets are extracted from English news.

For less resourced languages such as Farsi and Turkish, we tried to extend the available corpora. For Farsi, we applied the methodology proposed by (Lambert et al., 2011), where we used a large language model and an English-Farsi SMT model to produce new sentence pairs. For Turkish we added the Movie Subtitles corpus (Tiedemann, 2009), which allowed the SMT system to increase its translation capability, but included several slang words and spoken phrases.

How to deal with Named Entities in translation? News articles are related to the most important events. These names need to be efficiently translated to correctly understand the content of an article. From an SMT point of view, two main issues are related to Named Entity translation: (1) such a name is not in the training data or (2) part of the name is a common word in the target language and it is wrongly translated, e.g. the French name "Bruno Le Maire" which risks to be translated into English as "Bruno Mayor". To mitigate both the effects we use our multilingual named entity database. In the source language, each news item is analysed to identify possible entities; if an entity is recognised, its correct translation into English is retrieved from the database, and suggested to the SMT system enriching the source sentence using the xml markup option [6] in Moses. This approach allows us to complement the training data increasing the translation capability of our system.

How to deal with different language styles in the news? News title writing style contains more gerund verbs, no or few linking verbs, prepositions and adverbs than normal sentences, while content sentences include more preposition, adverbs and different verbal tenses. Starting from this assumption, we investigated if this phenomenon can affect the translation performance of our system.

We trained two SMT systems, $SMT_{content}$ and SMT_{title}, using the Europarl V4 German-English data as training corpus, and two different development sets: one made of content sentences, News Commentaries (Callison-Burch et al., 2009), and the other made of news titles in the source language which were translated into English using a commercial translation system. With the same strategy we generated also a Title test set. The SMT_{title} used a language model created using only English news titles. The News and Title test sets were translated by both the systems. Although the performance obtained translating the News and Title corpora are not comparable, we were interested in analysing how the same test set is translated by the two systems. We noticed that translating a test set with a system that was optimized with the same type of data resulted in almost 2 Blue score improvements: Title-TestSet: 0.3706 (SMT_{title}), 0.3511 ($SMT_{content}$); News-TestSet: 0.1768 (SMT_{title}), 0.1945 ($SMT_{content}$). This behaviour was present also in different language pairs. According to these results we decided to use two different translation systems for each language pair, one optimized using title data

[3]http://langtech.jrc.it/DGT-TM.html
[4]http://catalog.elra.info/
[5]http://www.ldc.upenn.edu/
[6]http://www.statmt.org/moses/?n=Moses.AdvancedFeatures#ntoc4

and the other using normal content sentences. Even though this implementation choice requires more computational power to run in memory two Moses servers, it allows us to mitigate the workload of each single instance reducing translation time of each single article and to improve translation quality.

3.1 Translation Quality

To evaluate the translation performance of ONTS, we run a set of experiments where we translate a test set for each language pair using our system and Google Translate. Lack of human translated parallel titles obliges us to test only the content based model. For German, Spanish and Czech we use the news test sets proposed in (Callison-Burch et al., 2010), for French and Italian the news test sets presented in (Callison-Burch et al., 2008), for Arabic, Farsi and Turkish, sets of 2,000 news sentences extracted from the Arabic-English and English-Persian datasets and the SE-Times corpus. For the other languages we use 2,000 sentences which are not news but a mixture of JRC-Acquis, Europarl and DGT-TM data. It is not guarantee that our test sets are not part of the training data of Google Translate.

Each test set is translated by Google Translate - Translator Toolkit, and by our system. Bleu score is used to evaluate the performance of both systems. Results, see Table 1, show that Google Translate produces better translation for those languages for which large amounts of data are available such as French, German, Italian and Spanish. Surprisingly, for Danish, Portuguese and Polish, ONTS has better performance, this depends on the choice of the test sets which are not made of news data but of data that is fairly homogeneous in terms of style and genre with the training sets.

The impact of the named entity module is evident for Arabic and Farsi, where each English suggested entity results in a larger coverage of the source language and better translations. For highly inflected and agglutinative languages such as Turkish, the output proposed by ONTS is poor. We are working on gathering more training data coming from the news domain and on the possibility of applying a linguistic pre-processing of the documents.

Source L.	ONTS	Google T.
Arabic	0.318	0.255
Czech	0.218	0.226
Danish	0.324	0.296
Farsi	0.245	0.197
French	0.26	0.286
German	0.205	0.25
Italian	0.234	0.31
Polish	0.568	0.511
Portuguese	0.579	0.424
Spanish	0.283	0.334
Turkish	0.238	0.395

Table 1: Automatic evaluation.

4 Technical Implementation

The translation service is made of two components: the connection module and the Moses server. The connection module is a servlet implemented in Java. It receives the RSS files, isolates each single news article, identifies each source language and pre-processes it. Each news item is split into sentences, each sentence is tokenized, lowercased, passed through a statistical compound word splitter, (Koehn and Knight, 2003), and the named entity annotator module. For language modelling we use the KenLM implementation, (Heafield, 2011).

According to the language, the correct Moses servers, title and content, are fed in a multi-thread manner. We use the multi-thread version of Moses (Haddow, 2010). When all the sentences of each article are translated, the inverse process is run: they are detokenized, recased, and untranslated/unknown words are listed. The translated title and content of each article are uploaded into the RSS file and it is passed to the next modules.

The full system including the translation modules is running in a 2xQuad-Core with Intel Hyper-threading Technology processors with 48GB of memory. It is our intention to locate the Moses servers on different machines. This is possible thanks to the high modularity and customization of the connection module. At the moment, the translation models are available for the following source languages: Arabic, Czech, Danish, Farsi, French, German, Italian, Polish, Portuguese, Spanish and Turkish.

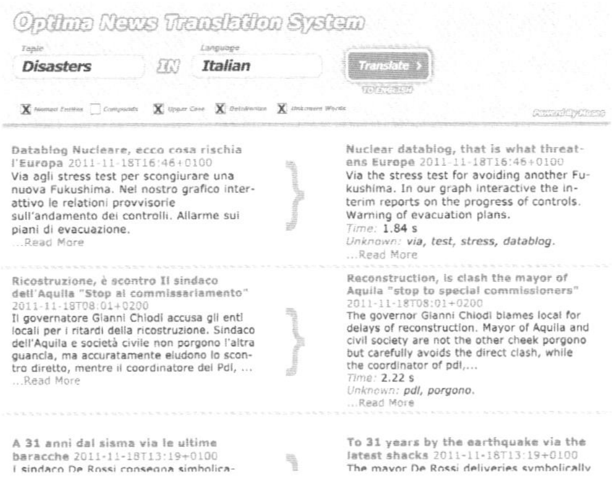

Figure 1: Demo Web site.

4.1 Demo

Our translation service is currently presented on a demo web site, see Figure 1, which is available at http://optima.jrc.it/Translate/. News articles can be retrieved selecting one of the topics and the language. All the topics are assigned to each article using the methodology described in 2.2. These articles are shown in the left column of the interface. When the button "Translate" is pressed, the translation process starts and the translated articles appear in the right column of the page.

The translation system can be customized from the interface enabling or disabling the named entity, compound, recaser, detokenizer and unknown word modules. Each translated article is enriched showing the translation time in milliseconds per character and, if enabled, the list of unknown words. The interface is linked to the connection module and data is transferred using RSS structure.

5 Discussion

In this paper we present the Optima News Translation System and how it is connected to Europe Media Monitor application. Different strategies are applied to increase the translation performance taking advantage of the document structure and other resources available in our research group. We believe that the experiments described in this work can result very useful for the development of other similar systems. Translations produced by our system will soon be available as part of the main EMM applications.

The performance of our system is encouraging, but not as good as the performance of web services such as Google Translate, mostly because we use less training data and we have reduced computational power. On the other hand, our in-house system can be fed with a large number of articles per day and sensitive data without including third parties in the translation process. Performance and translation time vary according to the number and complexity of sentences and language pairs.

The domain of news articles dynamically changes according to the main events in the world, while existing parallel data is static and usually associated to governmental domains. It is our intention to investigate how to adapt our translation system updating the language model with the English articles of the day.

Acknowledgments

The authors thank the JRC's OPTIMA team for its support during the development of ONTS.

References

O. Bojar and Z. Žabokrtský. 2009. *CzEng0.9: Large Parallel Treebank with Rich Annotation.* Prague Bulletin of Mathematical Linguistics, 92.

C. Callison-Burch and C. Fordyce and P. Koehn and C. Monz and J. Schroeder. 2008. *Further Meta-Evaluation of Machine Translation.* Proceedings of the Third Workshop on Statistical Machine Translation, pages 70–106. Columbus, US.

C. Callison-Burch, and P. Koehn and C. Monz and J. Schroeder. 2009. *Findings of the 2009 Workshop on Statistical Machine Translation.* Proceedings of the Fourth Workshop on Statistical Machine Translation, pages 1–28. Athens, Greece.

C. Callison-Burch, and P. Koehn and C. Monz and K. Peterson and M. Przybocki and O. Zaidan. 2009. *Findings of the 2010 Joint Workshop on Statistical Machine Translation and Metrics for Machine Translation.* Proceedings of the Joint Fifth Workshop on Statistical Machine Translation and MetricsMATR, pages 17–53. Uppsala, Sweden.

D. Chiang. 2005. *Hierarchical phrase-based translation.* Computational Linguistics, 33(2): pages 201–228. MIT Press.

B. Haddow. 2010. *Adding multi-threaded decoding to moses.* The Prague Bulletin of Mathematical Linguistics, 93(1): pages 57–66. Versita.

K. Heafield. 2011. *KenLM: Faster and smaller language model queries.* Proceedings of the Sixth Workshop on Statistical Machine Translation, Edinburgh, UK.

P. Koehn. 2005. *Europarl: A Parallel Corpus for Statistical Machine Translation.* Proceedings of the Machine Translation Summit X, pages 79-86. Phuket, Thailand.

P. Koehn and F. J. Och and D. Marcu. 2003. *Statistical phrase-based translation.* Proceedings of the 2003 Conference of the North American Chapter of the Association for Computational Linguistics on Human Language Technology, pages 48–54. Edmonton, Canada.

P. Koehn and K. Knight. 2003. *Empirical methods for compound splitting.* Proceedings of the tenth conference on European chapter of the Association for Computational Linguistics, pages 187–193. Budapest, Hungary.

P. Koehn and H. Hoang and A. Birch and C. Callison-Burch and M. Federico and N. Bertoldi and B. Cowan and W. Shen and C. Moran and R. Zens and C. Dyer and O. Bojar and A. Constantin and E. Herbst 2007. *Moses: Open source toolkit for statistical machine translation.* Proceedings of the Annual Meeting of the Association for Computational Linguistics, demonstration session, pages 177–180. Columbus, Oh, USA.

P. Lambert and H. Schwenk and C. Servan and S. Abdul-Rauf. 2011. *SPMT: Investigations on Translation Model Adaptation Using Monolingual Data.* Proceedings of the Sixth Workshop on Statistical Machine Translation, pages 284–293. Edinburgh, Scotland.

D. Marcu and W. Wang and A. Echihabi and K. Knight. 2006. *SPMT: Statistical machine translation with syntactified target language phrases.* Proceedings of the 2006 Conference on Empirical Methods in Natural Language Processing, pages 48–54. Edmonton, Canada.

M. Pilevar and H. Faili and A. Pilevar. 2011. *TEP: Tehran English-Persian Parallel Corpus.* Computational Linguistics and Intelligent Text Processing, pages 68–79. Springer.

B. Pouliquen and R. Steinberger. 2009. *Automatic construction of multilingual name dictionaries.* Learning Machine Translation, pages 59–78. MIT Press - Advances in Neural Information Processing Systems Series (NIPS).

A. Rafalovitch and R. Dale. 2009. *United nations general assembly resolutions: A six-language parallel corpus.* Proceedings of the MT Summit XIII, pages 292–299. Ottawa, Canada.

R. Steinberger and B. Pouliquen. 2007. *Cross-lingual named entity recognition.* Lingvisticæ Investigationes, 30(1) pages 135–162. John Benjamins Publishing Company.

R. Steinberger and B. Pouliquen and A. Widiger and C. Ignat and T. Erjavec and D. Tufiş and D. Varga. 2006. *The JRC-Acquis: A multilingual aligned parallel corpus with 20+ languages.* Proceedings of the 5th International Conference on Language Resources and Evaluation, pages 2142–2147. Genova, Italy.

R. Steinberger and B. Pouliquen and E. van der Goot. 2009. *An Introduction to the Europe Media Monitor Family of Applications.* Proceedings of the Information Access in a Multilingual World-Proceedings of the SIGIR 2009 Workshop, pages 1–8. Boston, USA.

J. Tiedemann. 2009. *News from OPUS-A Collection of Multilingual Parallel Corpora with Tools and Interfaces.* Recent advances in natural language processing V: selected papers from RANLP 2007, pages 309:237.

M. Turchi and I. Flaounas and O. Ali and T. DeBie and T. Snowsill and N. Cristianini. 2009. *Found in translation.* Proceedings of the European Conference on Machine Learning and Knowledge Discovery in Databases, pages 746–749. Bled, Slovenia.

F. Tyers and M.S. Alperen. 2010. *South-East European Times: A parallel corpus of Balkan languages.* Proceedings of the LREC workshop on Exploitation of multilingual resources and tools for Central and (South) Eastern European Languages, Valletta, Malta.

Just Title It! (by an Online Application)

Cédric Lopez, Violaine Prince, and Mathieu Roche
LIRMM, CNRS, University of Montpellier 2
161, rue Ada
Montpellier, France
{lopez,prince,mroche}@lirmm.fr

Abstract

This paper deals with an application of automatic titling. The aim of such application is to attribute a title for a given text. So, our application relies on three very different automatic titling methods. The first one extracts relevant noun phrases for their use as a heading, the second one automatically constructs headings by selecting words appearing in the text, and, finally, the third one uses nominalization in order to propose informative and catchy titles. Experiments based on 1048 titles have shown that our methods provide relevant titles.

1 Introduction

The important amount of textual documents is in perpetual growth and requires robust applications. Automatic titling is an essential task for several applications: Automatic titling of e-mails without subjects, text generation, summarization, and so forth. Furthermore, a system able to title HTML documents and so, to respect one of the W3C standards about Web site accessibility, is quite useful. The titling process goal is to provide a relevant representation of a document content. It might use metaphors, humor, or emphasis, thus separating a titling task from a summarization process, proving the importance of the rhetorical status in both tasks.

This paper presents an original application consisting in titling all kinds of texts. For that purpose, our application offers three main methods. The first one (called POSTIT) extracts noun phrases to be used as headings, the second one (called CATIT) automatically builds titles by selecting words appearing in the text, and, finally, the third one (called NOMIT) uses nominalization in order to propose relevant titles. Morphologic and semantic treatments are applied to obtain titles close to real titles. In particular, titles have to respect two characteristics: Relevance and catchiness.

2 Text Titling Application

The application presented in this paper was developed with PHP, and it is available on the Web[1]. It is based on several methods using Natural Language Processing (NLP) and Information Retrieval (IR) techniques. So, the input is a text and the output is a set of titles based on different kinds of strategies.

A single automatic titling method is not sufficient to title texts. Actually, it cannot respect diversity, noticed in real titles, which vary according to the writer's personal interests or/and his/her writing style. With the aim of getting closer to this variety, the user can choose the more relevant title according to his personal criteria among a list of titles automatically proposed by our system.

A few other applications have focused on titling: One of the most typical, (Banko, 2000), consists in generating coherent summaries that are shorter than a single sentence. These summaries are called "headlines". The main difficulty is to adjust the threshold (i.e, the headline length), in order to obtain syntactically correct titles. Whereas our methods create titles which are intrinsically correct, both syntactically and semantically.

In this section, we present the POSTIT, CATIT, and NOMIT methods. These three methods run

[1] https://www2.lirmm.fr/~lopez/Titrage_general/

in parallel, without interaction with each other. Three very different titles are thus determined for every text. For each of them, an example of the produced title is given on the following sample text: "*In her speech, Mrs Merkel has promised concrete steps towards a fiscal union - in effect close integration of the tax-and-spend polices of individual eurozone countries, with Brussels imposing penalties on members that break the rules. [...]*". Even if examples are in English, the application is actually in French (but easily reproducible in English). The POS tagging was performed by Sygfran (Chauché, 1984).

2.1 POSTIT

(Jin, 2001) implemented a set of title generation methods and evaluated them: The statistical approach based on the TF-IDF obtains the best results. In the same way, the POSTIT (Titling using Position and Statistical Information) method uses statistical information. Related works have shown that verbs are not as widely spread as nouns, named entities, and adjectives (Lopez, 2011a). Moreover, it was noticed that elements appearing in the title are often present in the body of the text (Zajic et al., 2002). (Zhou and Hovy, 2003) supports this idea and shows that the covering rate of those words present in titles, is very high in the first sentences of a text. So, the main idea is to extract noun phrases from the text and to select the more relevant for its use as title. The POSTIT approach is composed of the following steps:

1. *Candidate Sentence Determination.* We assume that any text contains only a few relevant sentences for titling. The goal of this step consists in recognizing them. Statistical analysis shows that, very often, terms useful for titling are located in the first sentences of the text.

2. *Extracting Candidate Noun Phrases for Titling.* This step uses syntactical filters relying on the statistical studies previously led. For that purpose, texts are tagged with Sygfran. Our syntactical patterns allowing noun phrase extraction are also inspired from (Daille, 1996).

3. *Selecting a Title.* Last, candidate noun phrases (t) are ranked according to a score based on the use of TF-IDF and information about noun phrase position (NP_{POS}) (see Lopez, 2011a). With $\lambda = 0.5$, this method obtains good results (see Formula 1).

$$NP_{score}(t) = \lambda \times NP_{POS}(t) + (1-\lambda) \times NP_{TF-IDF}(t) \quad (1)$$

Example of title with POSTIT: *Concrete steps towards a fiscal union.*

On one hand, this method proposes titles which are syntactically correct. But on the other hand, provided titles can not be considered as original. Next method, called CATIT, enables to generate more 'original' titles.

2.2 CATIT

CATIT (Automatic Construction of Titles) is an automatic process that constructs short titles. Titles have to show coherence with both the text and the Web, as well as with their dynamic context (Lopez, 2011b). This process is based on a global approach consisting in three main stages:

1. *Generation of Candidates Titles.* The purpose is to extract relevant nouns (using TF-IDF criterion) and adjectives (using TF criterion) from the text. Potential relevant couples (candidate titles) are built respecting the "Noun Adjective" and/or "Adjective Noun" syntactical patterns.

2. *Coherence of Candidate Titles.* Among the list of candidate titles, which ones are grammatically and semantically consistent ? The produced titles are supposed to be consistent with the text through the use of TF-IDF. To reinforce coherence, we set up a distance coefficient between a noun and an adjective which constitutes a new coherence criterion in candidate titles. Besides, the frequency of appearance of candidate titles on the Web (with Dice measure) is used in order to measure the dependence between the noun and the adjective composing a candidate title. This method thus automatically favors well-formed candidates.

3. *Dynamic Contextualization of Candidate Titles.* To determine the most relevant candidate title, the text context is compared with the context in which these candidates are met

on the Web. They are both modeled as vectors, according to Salton's vector model.

Example of title with CATIT: *Fiscal penalties.*

The automatic generation of titles is a complex task because titles have to be coherent, grammatically correct, informative, and catchy. These criteria are a brake in the generation of longer titles (being studied). That is why we suggest a new approach consisting in reformulating relevant phrases in order to determine informative and catchy "long" titles.

2.3 NOMIT

Based on statistical analysis, NOMIT (Nominalization for Titling) provides original titles relying on several rules to transform a verbal phrase in a noun phrase.

1. *Extracting Candidates.* First step consists in extracting segments of phrases which contain a past participle (in French). For example: *In her speech, Mrs Merkel* ***has promised*** *"concrete steps towards a fiscal union" - in effect close integration of the tax-and-spend polices of individual eurozone countries, with Brussels imposing penalties on members that break the rules.*

2. *Linguistic Treatment.* The linguistic treatment of the segments retained in the previous step consists of two steps aiming at nominalizing the "auxiliary + past participle" form (very frequent in French). First step consists in associating a noun for each past participle. Second step uses transforming rules in order to obtain nominalized segments. For example: *has promised* ⇒ *promise.*

3. *Selecting a Title.* Selection of the most relevant title relies on a Web validation. The interest of this validation is double. On one hand, the objective is to validate the connection between the nominalized past participle and the complement. On the other hand, the interest is to eliminate incorrect semantic constituents or not popular ones (e.g., "annunciation of the winners "), to prefer those which are more popular on Web (e.g. , "announcement of the winners").

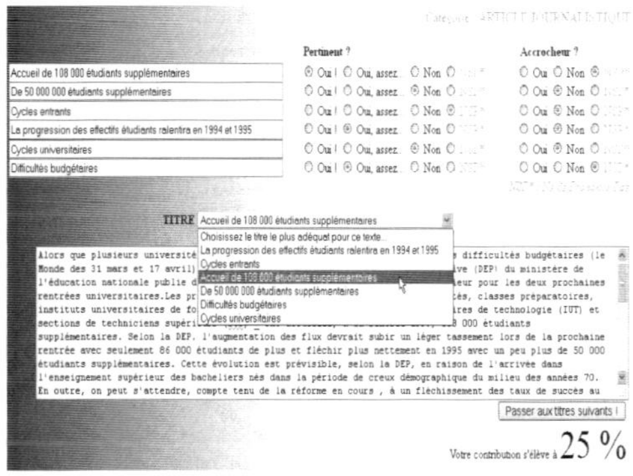

Figure 1: Screenshot of Automatic Titling Evaluation

Example of title with NOMIT: *Mrs Merkel: Promise of a concrete step towards a fiscal union.*

This method enables to obtain even more original titles than the previous one (i.e. CATIT). A positive aspect is that new transforming rules can be easily added in order to respect morpho-syntactical patterns of real titles.

3 Evaluations

3.1 Protocol Description

An online evaluation has been set up, accessible to all people (cf. Figure 1)[2]. The benefit of such evaluation is to compare different automatic methods according to several judgements. So, for each text proposed to the human user, several titles are presented, each one resulting from one of the automatic titling methods presented in this paper (POSTIT, CATIT, and NOMIT). Furthermore, random titles stemming from CATIT and POSTIT methods are evaluated (CATIT-R, and POSTIT-R), i.e., candidate titles built by our methods but not selected because of their bad score. The idea is to measure the efficiency of our ranking functions.

This evaluation is run on French articles stemming from the daily newspaper 'Le Monde'. We retained the first article published every day for the year 1994, up to a total of 200 journalistic articles. 190 people have participated to the online experiment, evaluating a total of 1048 titles. On average, every person has evaluated 41 titles. Every title has been evaluated by several people (between 2 and 10). The total number of obtained evaluations is 7764.

[2]URL: `http://www2.lirmm.fr/~lopez/Titrage_general/evaluation_web2/`

3.2 Results

Results of this evaluation indicate that the most adapted titling method for articles is NOMIT. This one enables to title 82.7% of texts in a relevant way (cf. Table 1). However, NOMIT does not determine titles for all the texts (in this evaluation, NOMIT determined a title for 58 texts). Indeed, if no past participle is present in the text, there is no title returned with this method. It is thus essential to consider the other methods which assure a title for every text. POSTIT enables to title 70% of texts in a relevant way. It is interesting to note that both gathered methods POSTIT and NOMIT provide at least one relevant title for 74 % of texts (cf. Table 2). Finally, even if CATIT obtains a weak score, this method provides a relevant title where POSTIT and NOMIT are silent. So, these three gathered methods propose at least one relevant title for 81% of journalistic articles.

Concerning catchiness, the three methods seem equivalent, proposing catchy titles for approximately 50% of texts. The three gathered methods propose at least one catchy title for 78% of texts. Real titles (RT) obtain close score (80.5%).

%	POSTIT	POSTIT-R	CATIT	CATIT-R	NOMIT	RT
Very relevant (VR)	39.1	16.4	15.7	10.3	60.3	71.4
Relevant (R)	30.9	22.3	21.3	14.5	22.4	16.4
(VR) and (R)	70.0	38.7	37.0	24.8	82.7	87.8
Not relevant	30.0	61.4	63.0	75.2	17.2	12.3
Catchy	49.1	30.9	47.2	32.2	53.4	80.5
Not catchy	50.9	69.1	52.8	67.8	46.6	19.5

Table 1: Average scores of our application.

%	POSTIT & NOMIT	POSTIT & CATIT	NOMIT & CATIT	POSTIT, CATIT, & NOMIT
(VR)	47	46	28	54
(R) or (VR)	74	78	49	81
Catchy	57	73	55	78

Table 2: Results of gathered methods.

Also, let us note that our ranking functions are relevant since CATIT-R and POSTIT-R obtain weak results compared with CATIT and POSTIT.

4 Conclusions

In this paper, we have compared the efficiency of three methods using various techniques. POSTIT uses noun phrases extracted from the text, CATIT consists in constructing short titles, and NOMIT uses nominalization. We proposed three different methods to approach the real context. Two persons can propose different titles for the same text, depending on personal criteria and on its own interests. That is why automatic titling is a complex task as much as evaluation of catchiness which remains subjective. Evaluation shows that our application provides relevant titles for 81% of texts and catchy titles for 78 % of texts. These results are very encouraging because real titles obtain close results.

A future work will consist in taking into account a context defined by the user. For example, the generated titles could depend on a political context if the user chooses to select a given thread. Furthermore, an "extended" context, automatically determined from the user's choice, could enhance or refine user's desiderata.

A next work will consist in adapting this application for English.

References

Michele Banko, Vibhu O. Mittal, and Michael J Witbrock. 1996. Headline generation based on statistical translation. *COLING'96.* p. 318–325.

Jacques Chauché. 1984. Un outil multidimensionnel de l'analyse du discours. *COLING'84.* p. 11-15.

Béatrice Daille. 1996. Study and implementation of combined techniques for automatic extraction of terminology. *The Balancing Act: Combining Symbolic and Statistical Approaches to language.* p. 29-36.

Rong Jin, and Alexander G. Hauptmann. 1996. Automatic title generation for spoken broadcast news. *Proceedings of the first international conference on Human language technology research.* p. 1–3.

Cédric Lopez, Violaine Prince, and Mathieu Roche. 2011. Automatic titling of Articles Using Position and Statistical Information. *RANLP'11.* p. 727-732.

Cédric Lopez, Violaine Prince, and Mathieu Roche. 2011. Automatic Generation of Short Titles. *LTC'11.* p. 461-465.

Gerard Salton and Christopher Buckley. 1988. Term-weighting approaches in automatic text retrieval. *Information Processing and Management 24.* p. 513-523.

Helmut Schmid. 1994. Probabilistic part-of-speech tagging using decision trees. *International Conference on New Methods in Language Processing.* p. 44-49.

Franck Smadja, Kathleen R. McKeown, and Vasileios Hatzivassiloglou. 1996. Translating collocations for bilingual lexicons: A statistical approach. *Computational linguistics, 22(1).* p. 1-38.

David Zajic, Bonnie Door, and Rich Schwarz. 2002. Automatic headline generation for newspaper stories. *ACL 2002.* Philadelphia.

Liang Zhou and Eduard Hovy. 2002. Headline summarization at ISI. *DUC 2003. Edmonton, Alberta, Canada.*

Folheador: browsing through Portuguese semantic relations

Hugo Gonçalo Oliveira
CISUC, University of Coimbra
Portugal
hroliv@dei.uc.pt

Hernani Costa
FCCN, Linguateca &
CISUC, University of Coimbra
Portugal
hpcosta@dei.uc.pt

Diana Santos
FCCN, Linguateca &
University of Oslo
Norway
d.s.m.santos@ilos.uio.no

Abstract

This paper presents Folheador, an online service for browsing through Portuguese semantic relations, acquired from different sources. Besides facilitating the exploration of Portuguese lexical knowledge bases, Folheador is connected to services that access Portuguese corpora, which provide authentic examples of the semantic relations in context.

1 Introduction

Lexical knowledge bases (LKBs) hold information about the words of a language and their interactions, according to their possible meanings. They are typically structured on word senses, which may be connected by means of semantic relations. Besides important resources for language studies, LKBs are key resources in the achievement of natural language processing tasks, such as word sense disambiguation (see e.g. Agirre et al. (2009)) or question answering (see e.g. Pasca and Harabagiu (2001)).

Regarding the complexity of most knowledge bases, their data formats are generally not suited for being read by humans. User interfaces have thus been developed for providing easier ways of exploring the knowledge base and assessing its contents. For instance, for LKBs, in addition to information on words and semantic relations, it is important that these interfaces provide usage examples where semantic relations hold, or at least where related words co-occur.

In this paper, we present Folheador[1], an online browser for Portuguese LKBs. Besides an interface for navigating through semantic relations acquired from different sources, Folheador is linked to two services that provide access to Portuguese corpora, thus allowing observation of related words co-occurring in authentic contexts of use, some of them even evaluated by humans.

After introducing several well-known LKBs and their interfaces, we present Folheador and its main features, also detailing the contents of the knowledge base currently browseable through this interface, which contains information acquired from public domain lexical resources of Portuguese. Then, before concluding, we discuss additional features planned for the future.

2 Related Work

Here, we mention a few interfaces that ease the exploration of well-known knowledge bases. Regarding the knowledge base structure, some of the interfaces are significantly different.

Princeton WordNet (Fellbaum, 1998) is the most widely used LKB to date. In addition to other alternatives, the creators of WordNet provide online access to their resource through the WordNet Search interface (Princeton University, 2010)[2]. As WordNet is structured around synsets (groups of synonymous lexical items), querying for a word prompts all synsets containing that word to be presented. For each synset, its part-of-speech (PoS), a gloss and a usage example are provided. Synsets can also be expanded to access the semantic relations they are involved in.

As a resource also organised in synsets, the

[1] See http://www.linguateca.pt/Folheador/

[2] http://wordnetweb.princeton.edu/perl/webwn

Brazilian Portuguese thesaurus TeP[3] has a similar interface (Maziero et al., 2008). Nevertheless, since TeP does not contain relations besides antonymy, its interface is simpler and provides only the synsets containing a queried word and their part-of-speech.

MindNet (Vanderwende et al., 2005) is a LKB extracted automatically, mainly from dictionaries, and structured on semantic relations connecting word senses to words. Its authors provide MNEX[4], an online interface for MindNet. After querying for a pair of words, MNEX provides all the semantic relation paths between them, established by a set of links that connect directly or indirectly one word to another. It is also possible to view the definitions that originated the path.

FrameNet (Baker et al., 1998) is a manually built knowledge base structured on semantic frames that describe objects, states or events. There are several means for exploring FrameNet easily, including FrameSQL (Sato, 2003)[5], which allows searching for frames, lexical units and relations in an integrated interface, and FrameGrapher[6], a graphical interface for the visualization of frame relations. For each frame, in both interfaces, a textual definition, annotated sentences of the frame elements, lists of the frame relations, and lists with the lexical units in the frame are provided.

ReVerb (Fader et al., 2011) is a Web-scale information extraction system that automatically acquires binary relations from text. Using ReVerb Search[7], a web interface for ReVerb extractions, it is possible to obtain sets of relational triples where the predicate and/or the arguments contain given strings. Regarding that each of the former is optional, it is possible, for instance, to search for all triples with the predicate *loves* and first argument *Portuguese*. Search results include the matching triples, organised according to the name of the predicate, as well as the number of times each triple was extracted. The sentences where each triple was extracted from are as well provided.

[3]http://www.nilc.icmc.usp.br/tep2

[4]http://stratus.research.microsoft.com/mnex/

[5]http://framenet2.icsi.berkeley.edu/frameSQL/fn2_15/notes/

[6]https://framenet.icsi.berkeley.edu/fndrupal/FrameGrapher

[7]http://www.cs.washington.edu/research/textrunner/reverbdemo.html

Finally, Visual Thesaurus (Huiping et al., 2006)[8] is a proprietary graphical interface that provides an alternative way of exploring a knowledge base structured on word senses, synonymy, antonymy and hypernymy relations. It presents a graph centered on a queried word, connected to its senses, as well as semantic relations between the senses and other words. Nodes and edges have a different color or look, respectively according to the PoS of the sense or to the type of semantic relation. If a word is clicked, a new graph, centered on that word, is drawn.

3 Folheador

Folheador, in figure 2, is an online service for browsing through instances of semantic relations, represented as relational triples.

Folheador was originally designed as an interface for PAPEL (Gonçalo Oliveira et al., 2010), a public domain lexical-semantic network, automatically extracted from a proprietary dictionary. It was soon expanded to other (public) resources for Portuguese as well (see Santos et al. (2010) for an overview of Portuguese LKBs).

The current version of Folheador browses through a LKB that, besides PAPEL, integrates semantic triples from the following sources: (i) synonymy acquired from two handcrafted thesauri of Portuguese[9], TeP (Dias-Da-Silva and de Moraes, 2003; da Silva et al., 2002) and OpenThesaurus.PT[10]; (ii) relations extracted automatically in the scope of the project Onto.PT (Gonçalo Oliveira and Gomes, 2010; Gonçalo Oliveira et al., 2011), which include triples extracted from Wiktionary.PT[11], and from Dicionário Aberto (Simões and Farinha, 2011), both public domain dictionaries.

Underlying relation triples in Folheador are thus in the form x RELATED-TO y, where x and y are lexical items and RELATED-TO is a predicate. Their interpretation is as follows: one sense of x is related to one sense of y, by means of a relation whose type is identified by RELATED-TO.

[8]http://www.visualthesaurus.com/

[9]We converted the thesauri to triples x synonym-of y, where x and y are lexical items in the same synset.

[10]http://openthesaurus.caixamagica.pt/

[11]http://pt.wiktionary.org/

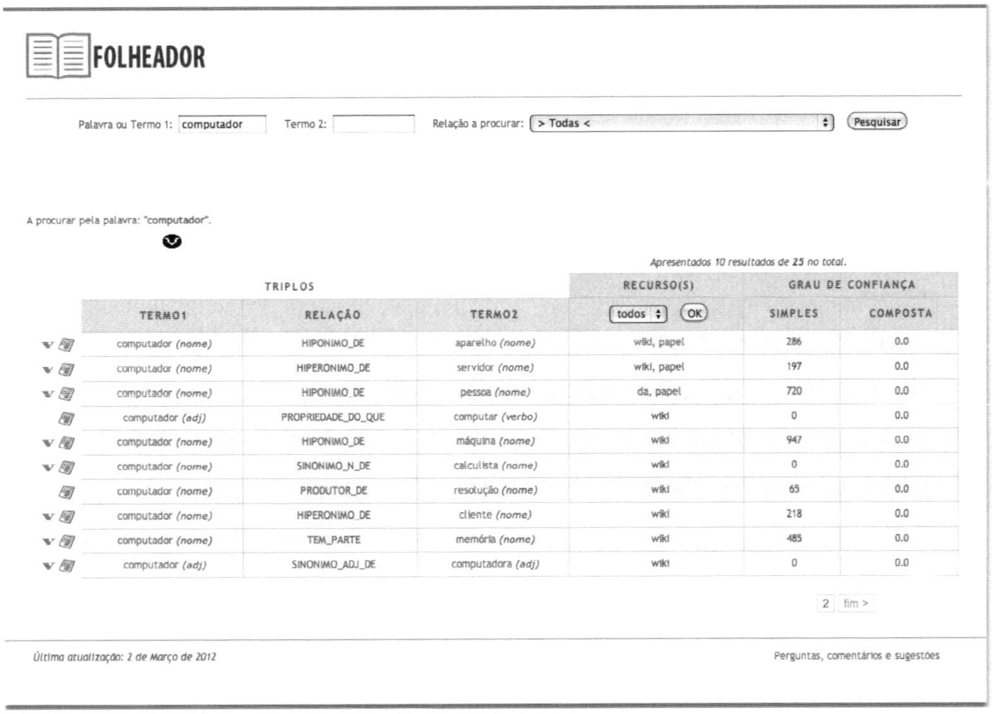

Figure 1: Folheador's interface.

3.1 Navigation

It is possible to use Folheador for searching for all relations with one, two, or no fixed arguments, and one or no types (relation names). Combining these options, Folheador can be used, for instance, to obtain: all lexical items related to a particular item; all relations between two lexical items; or a sample of relations involving a particular type.

The matching triples are listed and may be filtered according to the resource they were extracted from. For each triple, the PoS of the arguments is shown, as well as a list with the identification of the resources from where it was acquired. The arguments of each triple are also links that make navigation easier. When clicked, Folheador behaves the same way as if it had been queried with the clicked word as argument. Also, since the queried lexical item may occur in the first or in the second argument of a triple, when it occurs in the second, Folheador inverts the relation, so that the item appears always as the first argument. Therefore, there is no need to store both the direct and the inverse triples.

Consider the example in figure 2: it shows the triples retrieved after searching for the word *computador* (computer, in English). In most of the retrieved triples, *computador* is a noun (e.g. *computador* HIPONIMO_DE *máquina*), but there are relations where it is an adjective (e.g. *computador* PROPRIEDADE_DO_QUE *computar*). Moreover, as hypernymy relations are stored in the form *x* HIPERONIMO_DE *y*, some of the triples presented, such as *computador* HIPONIMO_DE *máquina* and *computador* HIPONIMO_DE *aparelho*, have been inverted on the fly.

Furthermore, for each triple, Folheador presents: a confidence value based on the mere co-occurrence of the words in corpora; and another based on the co-occurrence of the related words instantiating discriminating patterns of the particular relation.

3.2 Graph visualization

Currently, Folheador contains a very simple visualization tool, which draws the semantic relation graph established by the search results in a page, as in figure 3.2. In the future, we aim to provide an alternative for navigation based on textual links, which would be made through the graph.

3.3 The use of corpora

One of the problems of most lexical resources is that they do not integrate or contain frequency in-

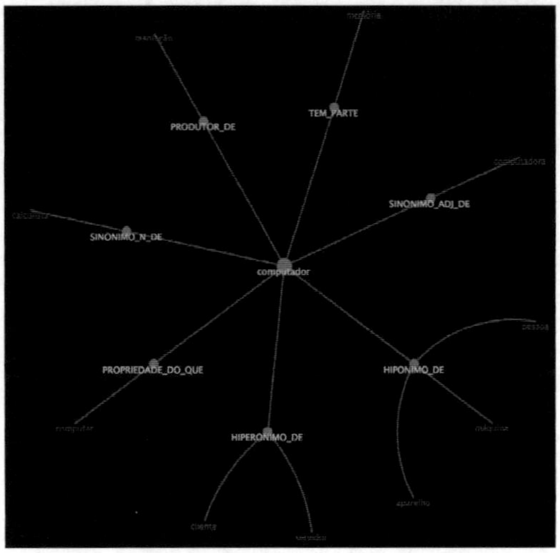

Figure 2: Graph for the results in figure 2.

formation. This is especially true when one is not simply listing words but going deeper into meaning, and listing semantic properties like word senses or relationships between senses.

So, a list of relations among words can conflate a number of highly specialized and obsolete words (or word senses) that co-occur with important and productive relations in everyday use, which is not a good thing for human and automatic users alike. On the other hand, using corpora allows one to add frequency information to both participants in the relation and the triples themselves, and thus provide another axis to the description of words.

In addition, it is always interesting to observe language use in context, especially in cases where the user is not sure whether the relation is correct or still in use (and the user can and should be fairly suspicious when s/he is browsing automatically compiled information). A corpus check therefore provides illustration, and confirmation, to a user facing an unusual or surprising relation, in addition to evaluation data for the relation curator or lexicographer. If these checks have been done before by a set of human beings (as is the case of VARRA (Freitas et al., forthcomming)), one can have much more confidence on the data browsed, something that is important for users.

Having this in mind, besides allowing to query for stored relational triples, Folheador is connected to AC/DC (Santos and Bick, 2000; Santos, 2011), an online service that provides access to a large set of Portuguese corpora. In just one click, it is possible to query for all the sentences in the AC/DC corpora connecting the arguments of a retrieved triple. Figure 3.3 shows some of the results for the words *computador* (computer) and *aparelho* (apparatus). While some of the returned sentences might contain the related words co-occurring almost by chance or without a clear semantic relation, other sentences validate the triple (e.g. sentence *par=saude16727* in figure 3.3). Sometimes, the sentences might as well invalidate the triple.

Furthermore, for some of the relation types, it is possible to connect to another online service, VARRA (Freitas et al., forthcomming), which is based on a set of patterns that express some of the relation types, in corpora text. After clicking on the VARRA link, this service is queried for occurrences of the corresponding triple in AC/DC. The presented sentences (a subset of those returned by the previous service) will thus contain the related words connected by a discriminating pattern for the relation they hold. Figure 3.3 shows two sentences returned for the relation *computador* HIPONIMO_DE *máquina*.

These patterns, as those proposed by Hearst (1992) and used in many projects since, may not be 100% reliable. So, VARRA was designed to allow human users to classify the sentences according to whether the latter validate the relation, are just compatible with it, or not even that.

In fact, people do not usually write definitions, especially when using common sense terms in ordinary discourse. Thus, co-occurrence of semantically-related terms frequently indicates a particular relation only implicitly. The choice of assessing sentences as good validators of a semantic relation is related to the task of automatically finding good illustrative examples for dictionaries, which is a surprisingly complex task (Rychlý et al., 2008).

This kind of information, amassed with the help of VARRA, is much more difficult to create, but is of great value to Folheador, since it provides good illustrative contexts for the related lexical items.

4 Further work and concluding remarks

We have shown that, as it is, Folheador is very useful, as it enables to browse for triples with fixed arguments, it identifies the source of the triples, and, in one click, it provides real sentences *par=2530*: Ela trazia irregularmente do Paraguai computadores, **aparelhos** eletrônicos e uísque .

par=2548: Em outubro, Wanderlei usou cerca de r $ 15 mil que Márcia havia juntado com os seus contrabandos para comprar duas televisões, dois videocassetes, um **aparelho** de som, uma filmadora e um computador .

: · Para você que quer ter uma coleção de músicas para seu computador ou mesmo para ouvir no seu novo **aparelho** de MP3, não perca essa oportunidade .

: Usando o CyberTracker, um software com o qual os ecologistas podem registrar suas observações em campo usando computadores portáteis conectados a **aparelhos** de posicionamento global (GPS) , os rastreadores puderam reunir dados que comprovam a degradação da população local da espécie .

: · Para você que quer ter uma coleção de músicas para seu computador ou mesmo para ouvir no seu novo **aparelho** de MP3, não perca essa oportunidade .

: Segundo a pesquisa, 16,6 % dos domicílios brasileiros têm computadores de mesa, contra 95,7 % que têm **aparelhos** de TV .

par=49126: O **aparelho** está equipado com modernos instrumentos de telecomunicações, primeiros-socorros, páraquedas e computador .

par=saude16727: Os avanços da ecografia, enquanto tecnologia, resultam da evolução da Infor mática, afinal, estes **aparelhos** são computadores que analisam o som e a imagem .

Figure 3: AC/DC: some sentences returned for the related words *computador* and *aparelho*.

Relação	Procura	Exemplo
máquina HIPERONIMO_DE computador	padrões usados	*par=Mais--94a-2*: E também de ensinar **máquinas** como **computadores** a identificarem 'ses objetos . (NSC)
máquina HIPERONIMO_DE computador	padrões usados	*par=ext328388-soc-95a-2*: **Máquinas** como os **computadores**, os faxes e os videofones devem poder comunicar entre si sem falhas, o que supõe um trabalho de programação importante . (CP)

Figure 4: VARRA: sentences that exemplify the relation *computador* hyponym-of *máquina*.

where related lexical items co-occur. Still, we are planning to implement new basic features, such as the suggestion of words, when the searched word is not in the LKB. Also, while currently Folheador only directly connects to AC/DC and VARRA, in order to increase its usability, we plan to connect it automatically to online definitions and other services available on the Web. We intend as well to crosslink Folheador from the AC/DC interface, in the sense that one can invoke Folheador also by just one click (Santos, forthcomming).

Currently, Folheador gives access to 169,385 lexical items: 93,612 nouns, 38,409 verbs, 33,497 adjectives and 3,867 adverbs, in a total of 722,589 triples, and it can browse through the following types of semantic relations: synonymy, hypernymy, part-of, member-of, causation, producer-of, purpose-of, place-of, and property-of. However, as the underlying resources, especially the ones created automatically, will continue to be updated, one important challenge is to create a service that does not get outdated, by accompanying the progress of these resources, ideally doing an automatic update every month. Furthermore, we believe that quantitative studies on the comparison and the aggregation of the integrated resources should be made, deeper than what is presented in Gonçalo Oliveira et al. (2011).

We would like to end by emphasizing that we are aware that the proper interpretation of the semantic relations may vary in the different resources, even disregarding possible mistakes in the automatic harvesting. It is enough to consider the (regular morphological) relation between a verb and an adjective/noun ended in *-dor* in Portuguese (and which can be paraphrased by one who Vs). For instance, in relations such as {sofrer - sofredor}, {correr - corredor}, {roer - roedor}, the kind of verb defines the kind of temporal relation conveyed: a rodent is essentially *roendo*, while a *sofredor* (sufferer) suffers hopefully in a particular situation and can stop suffering, and a *corredor* (runner) runs as job or as role.

The source code of Folheador is open source[12], so it may be used by other authors to explore their knowledge bases. Technical information about Folheador may be found in Costa (2011).

Acknowledgements

Folheador was developed under the scope of Linguateca, throughout the years jointly funded by the Portuguese Government, the European Union (FEDER and FSE), UMIC, FCCN and FCT. Hugo Gonçalo Oliveira is supported by the FCT grant SFRH/BD/44955/2008 co-funded by FSE.

References

Eneko Agirre, Oier Lopez De Lacalle, and Aitor Soroa. 2009. Knowledge-based WSD on specific domains: performing better than generic supervised WSD. In *Proceedings of 21st Interna-*

[12] Available from `http://code.google.com/p/folheador/`

tional Joint Conference on Artifical Intelligence, IJCAI'09, pages 1501–1506, San Francisco, CA, USA. Morgan Kaufmann Publishers Inc.

Collin F. Baker, Charles J. Fillmore, and John B. Lowe. 1998. The Berkeley FrameNet project. In *Proceedings of the 17th international conference on Computational linguistics*, pages 86–90, Morristown, NJ, USA. ACL Press.

Hernani Costa. 2011. O desenho do novo Folheador. Technical report, Linguateca.

Bento C. Dias da Silva, Mirna F. de Oliveira, and Helio R. de Moraes. 2002. Groundwork for the Development of the Brazilian Portuguese Wordnet. In Nuno Mamede and Elisabete Ranchhod, editors, *Advances in Natural Language Processing (PorTAL 2002)*, LNAI, pages 189–196, Berlin/Heidelberg. Springer.

Bento Carlos Dias-Da-Silva and Helio Roberto de Moraes. 2003. A construção de um thesaurus eletrônico para o português do Brasil. *ALFA*, 47(2):101–115.

Anthony Fader, Stephen Soderland, and Oren Etzioni. 2011. Identifying relations for open information extraction. In *Proceedings of the Conference of Empirical Methods in Natural Language Processing*, EMNLP '11, Edinburgh, Scotland, UK.

Christiane Fellbaum, editor. 1998. *WordNet: An Electronic Lexical Database (Language, Speech, and Communication)*. The MIT Press.

Cláudia Freitas, Diana Santos, Hugo Gonçalo Oliveira, and Violeta Quental. forthcomming. VARRA: Validação, Avaliação e Revisão de Relações semânticas no AC/DC. In *Atas do IX Encontro de Linguística de Corpus*, ELC 2010.

Hugo Gonçalo Oliveira and Paulo Gomes. 2010. Onto.PT: Automatic Construction of a Lexical Ontology for Portuguese. In *Proceedings of 5th European Starting AI Researcher Symposium (STAIRS 2010)*, pages 199–211. IOS Press.

Hugo Gonçalo Oliveira, Diana Santos, and Paulo Gomes. 2010. Extracção de relações semânticas entre palavras a partir de um dicionário: o PAPEL e sua avaliação. *Linguamática*, 2(1):77–93.

Hugo Gonçalo Oliveira, Leticia Antón Pérez, Hernani Costa, and Paulo Gomes. 2011. Uma rede léxico-semântica de grandes dimensões para o português, extraída a partir de dicionários electrónicos. *Linguamática*, 3(2):23–38.

Marti A. Hearst. 1992. Automatic acquisition of hyponyms from large text corpora. In *Proceedings of 14th Conference on Computational Linguistics*, pages 539–545, Morristown, NJ, USA. ACL Press.

Du Huiping, He Lin, and Hou Hanqing. 2006. Thinkmap visual thesaurus:a new kind of knowledge organization system. *Library Journal*, 12.

Erick G. Maziero, Thiago A. S. Pardo, Ariani Di Felippo, and Bento C. Dias-da-Silva. 2008. A Base de Dados Lexical e a Interface Web do TeP 2.0 - Thesaurus Eletrônico para o Português do Brasil. In *VI Workshop em Tecnologia da Informação e da Linguagem Humana*, TIL 2008, pages 390–392.

Marius Pasca and Sanda M. Harabagiu. 2001. The informative role of WordNet in open-domain question answering. In *Proceedings of NAACL 2001 Workshop on WordNet and Other Lexical Resources: Applications, Extensions and Customizations*, pages 138–143, Pittsburgh, USA.

Princeton University. 2010. Princeton university "About Wordnet". http://wordnet.princeton.edu.

Pavel Rychlý, Miloš Husák, Adam Kilgarriff, Michael Rundell, and Katy McAdam. 2008. GDEX: Automatically finding good dictionary examples in a corpus. In *Proceedings of the XIII EURALEX International Congress*, pages 425–432, Barcelona. Institut Universitari de Lingüística Aplicada.

Diana Santos and Eckhard Bick. 2000. Providing Internet access to Portuguese corpora: the AC/DC project. In *Proceedings of 2nd International Conference on Language Resources and Evaluation*, LREC'2000, pages 205–210. ELRA.

Diana Santos, Anabela Barreiro, Cláudia Freitas, Hugo Gonçalo Oliveira, José Carlos Medeiros, Luís Costa, Paulo Gomes, and Rosário Silva. 2010. Relações semânticas em português: comparando o TeP, o MWN.PT, o Port4NooJ e o PAPEL. In A. M. Brito, F. Silva, J. Veloso, and A. Fiéis, editors, *Textos seleccionados. XXV Encontro Nacional da Associação Portuguesa de Linguística*, pages 681–700. APL.

Diana Santos. 2011. Linguateca's infrastructure for Portuguese and how it allows the detailed study of language varieties. *OSLa: Oslo Studies in Language*, 3(2):113–128. Volume edited by J.B.Johannessen, Language variation infrastructure.

Diana Santos. forthcomming. Corpora at linguateca: vision and roads taken. In Tony Berber Sardinha and Telma S ao Bento Ferreira, editors, *Working with Portuguese corpora*.

Hiroaki Sato. 2003. FrameSQL: A software tool for FrameNet. In *Proceedings of Asialex 2003*, pages 251–258, Tokyo. Asian Association of Lexicography, Asian Association of Lexicography.

Alberto Simões and Rita Farinha. 2011. Dicionário Aberto: Um novo recurso para PLN. *Vice-Versa*, pages 159–171.

Lucy Vanderwende, Gary Kacmarcik, Hisami Suzuki, and Arul Menezes. 2005. Mindnet: An automatically-created lexical resource. In *Proceedings of HLT/EMNLP 2005 Interactive Demonstrations*, pages 8–9, Vancouver, British Columbia, Canada. ACL Press.

A Computer Assisted Speech Transcription System

Alejandro Revuelta-Martínez, Luis Rodríguez, Ismael García-Varea
Computer Systems Department
University of Castilla-La Mancha
Albacete, Spain
{Alejandro.Revuelta,Luis.RRuiz,Ismael.Garcia}@uclm.es

Abstract

Current automatic speech transcription systems can achieve a high accuracy although they still make mistakes. In some scenarios, high quality transcriptions are needed and, therefore, fully automatic systems are not suitable for them. These high accuracy tasks require a human transcriber. However, we consider that automatic techniques could improve the transcriber's efficiency. With this idea we present an interactive speech recognition system integrated with a word processor in order to assists users when transcribing speech. This system automatically recognizes speech while allowing the user to interactively modify the transcription.

1 Introduction

Speech has been the main mean of communication for thousands of years and, hence, is the most natural human interaction mode. For this reason, Automatic Speech Recognition (ASR) has been one of the major research interests within the Natural Language Processing (NLP) community.

Although current speech recognition approaches (which are based on statistical learning theory (Jelinek, 1998)) are speaker independent and achieve high accuracy, ASR systems are not perfect and transcription errors rise drastically when considering large vocabularies, dealing with noise environments or spontaneous speech. In those tasks (as for example, automatic transcription of parliaments proceedings) where perfect recognition results are required, ASR can not be fully reliable so far and, a human transcriber has to check and supervise the automatically generated transcriptions.

In the last years, cooperative systems, where a human user and an automatic system work together, have gain growing attention. Here we present a system that interactively assists a human transcriber when using an ASR software. The proposed tool is fully embedded into a widely used and open source word processor and it relies on an ASR system that is proposing suggestions to the user in the form of practical transcriptions for the input speech. The user is allowed to introduce corrections at any moment of the discourse and, each time an amendment is performed, the system will take it into account in order to propose a new transcription (always preserving the decision made by the user, as can be seen in Fig. 1). The rationale behind this idea is to reduce the human user's effort and increase efficiency.

Our proposal's main contribution is that it carries out an interactive ASR process, continually proposing new transcriptions that take into account user amendments to increase their usefulness. To our knowledge, no current transcription package provides such an interactive process.

2 Theoretical Background

Computer Assisted Speech Recognition (CAST) can be addressed by extending the statistical approach to ASR. Specifically, we have an input signal to be transcribed $\mathbf{x}$ and the user feedback in the form of a fully correct transcription prefix $\mathbf{p}$ (an example of a CAST session is shown in Fig. 1). From this, the recognition system has to search for the optimal completion (suffix) $\hat{\mathbf{s}}$ as:

$$\begin{aligned} \hat{\mathbf{s}} &= \arg\max_{\mathbf{s}} \Pr(\mathbf{s} \mid \mathbf{x}, \mathbf{p}) \\ &= \arg\max_{\mathbf{s}} \Pr(\mathbf{x} \mid \mathbf{p}, \mathbf{s}) \cdot \Pr(\mathbf{s} \mid \mathbf{p}) \quad (1) \end{aligned}$$

where, as in traditional ASR, we have an acoustic model $\Pr(\mathbf{x} \mid \mathbf{p}, \mathbf{s})$ and a language model $\Pr(\mathbf{s} \mid \mathbf{p})$. The main difference is that, here, part of the correct transcription is available (prefix) and we can use this information to improve the suffix recognition. This can be achieved by properly adapting the language model to account for the user validated prefix as it is detailed in (Rodríguez et al., 2007; Toselli et al., 2011).

As was commented before, the main goal of this approach is to improve the efficiency of the transcription process by saving user keystrokes. Off-line experiments have shown that this approach can save about 30% of typing effort when compared to the traditional approach of off-line post-editing results from an ASR system.

3 Prototype Description

A fully functional prototype, which implements the CAST techniques described in section 2, has been developed. The main goal is to provide a completely usable tool. To this end, we have implemented a tool that easily allows for organizing and accessing different transcription projects. Besides, the prototype has been embedded into a widely used office suite. This way, the transcribed document can be properly formatted since all the features provided by a word processor are available during the transcription process.

3.1 Implementation Issues

The system has been implemented following a modular architecture consisting of several components:

- *User interface*. Manages the graphical features of the prototype user interface.
- *Project management*: Allows the user to define and deal with transcription projects. These projects are stored in XML files containing parameters such as input files to be transcribed, output documents, etc.
- *System controller*. Manages communication among all the components.
- *OpenOffice integration*: This subsystem provides an appropriate integration between the CAST tool and the OpenOffice[1] software suite. The transcriber has, therefore, full access to a word processor functionality.
- *Speech manager*: Implements audio playback and synchronization with the ASR outcomes.
- *CAST engine*: Provides the interactive ASR suggestion mechanism.

This architecture is oriented to be flexible and portable so that different scenarios, word processor software or ASR engines can be adopted without requiring big changes in the current implementation. Although this initial prototype works as a standalone application the followed design should allow for a future "in the cloud" tool, where the CAST engine is located in a server and the user can employ a mobile device to carry out the transcription process.

With the purpose of providing a real-time system response, CAST is actually performed over a set of word lattices. A lattice, representing a huge set of hypotheses for the current utterance, is initially used to parse the user validated prefix and then to search for the best completion (suggestion).

3.2 System Interface and Usage

The prototype has been designed to be intuitive for professional speech transcribers and general users; we expect most users to quickly get used to the system without any previous experience or external assistance.

The prototype features and operation mode are described in the following items:

- The initial screen (Fig. 2) guides the user on how to address a transcription project. Here, the transcriber can select one of the three main tasks that have to be performed to obtain the final result.
- In the project management screen (Fig. 3), the user can interact with the current projects or create a new one. A project is a set of input audio files to be transcribed along with the partial transcription achieved and some other related parameters.
- Once the current project has been selected, a transcription session is started (Fig. 4). During this session, the application looks like a standard OpenOffice word processor incorporating CAST features. Specifically, the user can perform the following operations:

[1] www.openoffice.org

	utterance	
ITER-0	prefix	( )
ITER-1	suffix	(*Nine extra soul are planned half beam discovered these years*)
	validated	(**Nine**)
	correction	(extrasolar)
	prefix	(Nine extrasolar)
ITER-2	suffix	(*planets have been discovered these years*)
	validated	(**planets have been discovered**)
	correction	(this)
	prefix	(Nine extrasolar planets have been discovered this)
FINAL	suffix	(*year*)
	validated	(**#**)
	prefix	(**Nine** extrasolar **planets have been discovered** this **year**)

Figure 1: Example of a CAST session. In each iteration, the system suggests a suffix based on the input utterance and the previous prefix. After this, the user can validate part of the suggestion and type a correction to generate a new prefix that can be used in the next iteration. This process is iterated until the full utterance is transcribed.

The user can move between audio segments by pressing the "fast forward" and "rewind" buttons. Once the a segment to be transcribed has been chosen, the "play" button starts the audio replay and transcription. The system produces the text in synchrony with the audio so that the user can check in "real time" the proposed transcription. As soon as a mistake is produced, the transcriber can use the "pause" button to interrupt the process. Then, the error is corrected and by pressing "play" again the process is continued. At this point, the CAST engine will use the user amendment to improve the rest of the transcription.

- When all the segments have been transcribed, the final task in the initial screen allows the user to open the OpenOffice's PDF export dialog to generate the final document.

A video, showing the prototype operation mode, can be found on the following website: *www.youtube.com/watch?v=vc6bQCtYVR4*.

4 Conclusions and Future Work

In this paper we have presented a CAST system which has been fully implemented and integrated into the OpenOffice word processing software. The implemented techniques have been tested offline and the prototype has been presented to a reduced number of real users.

Preliminary results suggest that the system could be useful for transcribers when high quality transcriptions are needed. It is expected to save effort, increase efficiency and allow inexperienced users to take advantage of ASR systems all along the transcription process. However, these results should be corroborated by performing a formal usability evaluation.

Currently, we are in the process of carrying out a formal usability evaluation with real users that has been designed following the ISO/IEC 9126-4 (2004) standard according to the efficiency, effectiveness and satisfaction characteristics.

As future work, it will be interesting to consider concurrent collaborative work at both, project and transcription levels. Other promising line is to consider a multimodal user interface in order to allow users to control the playback and transcription features using their own speech. This has been explored in the literature (Rodríguez et al., 2010) and would allow the system to be used in devices with constrained interfaces such as mobile phones or tablet PCs.

Acknowledgments

Work supported by the EC (ERDF/ESF) and the Spanish government under the MIPRCV "Consolider Ingenio 2010" program (CSD2007-00018), and the Spanish *Junta de Comunidades de Castilla-La Mancha* regional government under projects PBI08-0210-7127 and PPII11-0309-6935.

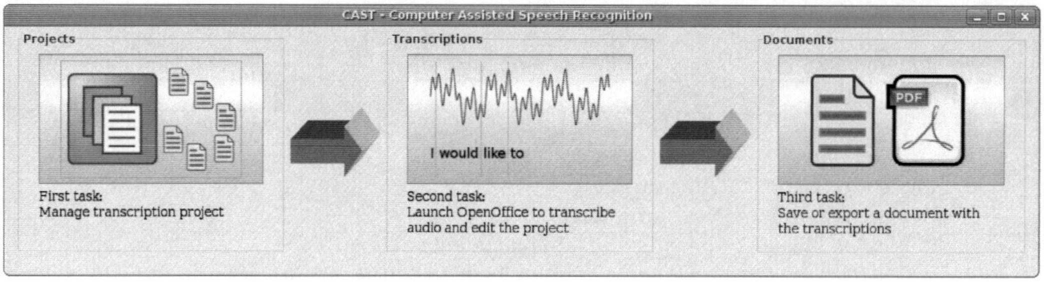

Figure 2: Main window prototype. The three stages of a transcription project are shown.

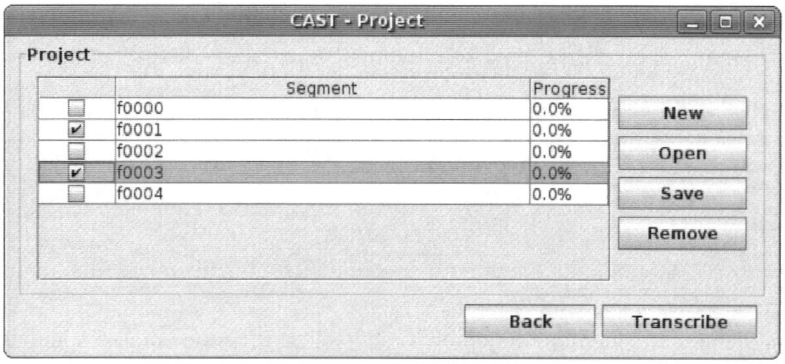

Figure 3: Screenshot of the project management window showing a loaded project. A project consists of several audio segments, each of them is stored in a file so that the user can easily add or remove files when needed. In this screen the user can choose the current working segments.

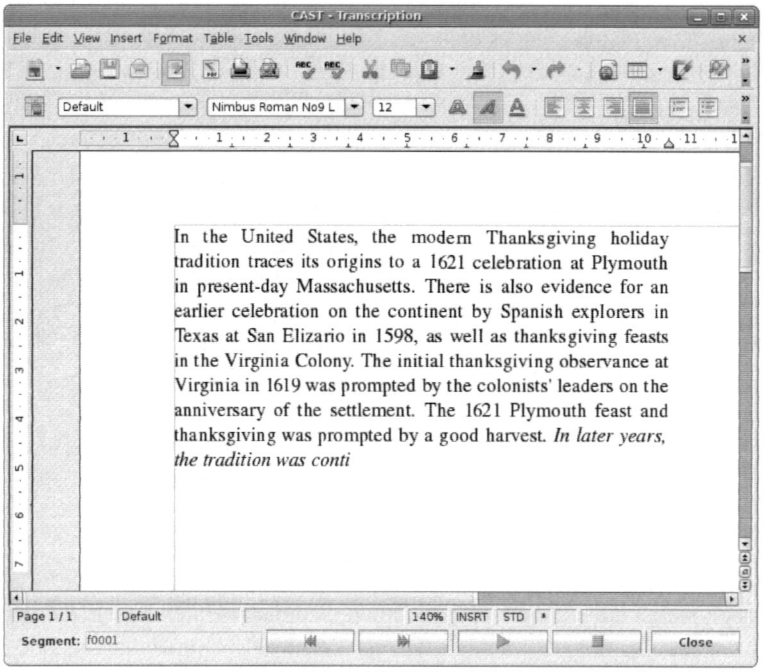

Figure 4: Screenshot of a transcription session. This shows the process of transcribing one audio segment. In this figure, all the text but the last incomplete sentence has already been transcribed and validated. The last partial sentence, shown in italics, is being produced by the ASR system while the transcriber listen to the audio. As soon as an error is detected the user momentarily interrupts the process to correct the mistake. Then, the system will continue transcribing the audio according to the new user feedback (prefix).

References

ISO/IEC 9126-4. 2004. Software engineering — Product quality — Part 4: Quality in use metrics.

F. Jelinek. 1998. *Statistical Methods for Speech Recognition*. The MIT Press, Cambridge, Massachusetts, USA.

Luis Rodríguez, Francisco Casacuberta, and Enrique Vidal. 2007. Computer assisted transcription of speech. In *Proceedings of the 3rd Iberian conference on Pattern Recognition and Image Analysis, Part I*, IbPRIA '07, pages 241–248, Berlin, Heidelberg. Springer-Verlag.

Luis Rodríguez, Ismael García-Varea, and Enrique Vidal. 2010. Multi-modal computer assisted speech transcription. In *Proceedings of the 12th International Conference on Multimodal Interfaces and the 7th International Workshop on Machine Learning for Multimodal Interaction, ICMI-MLMI*.

A.H. Toselli, E. Vidal, and F. Casacuberta. 2011. *Multimodal Interactive Pattern Recognition and Applications*. Springer.

A Statistical Spoken Dialogue System using Complex User Goals and Value Directed Compression

Paul A. Crook, Zhuoran Wang, Xingkun Liu and Oliver Lemon
Interaction Lab
School of Mathematical and Computer Sciences (MACS)
Heriot-Watt University, Edinburgh, UK
{p.a.crook, zhuoran.wang, x.liu, o.lemon}@hw.ac.uk

Abstract

This paper presents the first demonstration of a statistical spoken dialogue system that uses automatic belief compression to reason over complex user goal sets. Reasoning over the power set of possible user goals allows complex sets of user goals to be represented, which leads to more natural dialogues. The use of the power set results in a massive expansion in the number of belief states maintained by the Partially Observable Markov Decision Process (POMDP) spoken dialogue manager. A modified form of Value Directed Compression (VDC) is applied to the POMDP belief states producing a near-lossless compression which reduces the number of bases required to represent the belief distribution.

1 Introduction

One of the main problems for a spoken dialogue system (SDS) is to determine the user's goal (*e.g.* plan suitable meeting times or find a good Indian restaurant nearby) under uncertainty, and thereby to compute the optimal next system dialogue action (*e.g.* offer a restaurant, ask for clarification). Recent research in statistical SDSs has successfully addressed aspects of these problems through the application of Partially Observable Markov Decision Process (POMDP) approaches (Thomson and Young, 2010; Young et al., 2010). However POMDP SDSs are currently limited by the representation of user goals adopted to make systems computationally tractable.

Work in dialogue system evaluation, *e.g.* Walker et al. (2004) and Lemon et al. (2006), shows that real user goals are generally *sets of items*, rather than a single item. People like to explore possible trade offs between the attributes of items.

Crook and Lemon (2010) identified this as a central challenge for the field of spoken dialogue systems, proposing the use of automatic compression techniques to allow for extended accurate representations of user goals. This paper presents a proof of concept of these ideas in the form of a complete, working spoken dialogue system. The POMDP dialogue manager (DM) of this demonstration system uses a compressed belief space that was generated using a modified version of the Value Directed Compression (VDC) algorithm as originally proposed by Poupart (2005). This demonstration system extends work presented by Crook and Lemon (2011) in that it embeds the compressed complex user goal belief space into a working system *and* demonstrates planning (and acting) in the compressed space.

2 Complex User Goals

The type of SDS task that we focus on is a limited-domain query-dialogue, also known as a "slot filling" task. The spoken dialogue system has knowledge about some set of *objects* where these objects have *attributes* and these attributes can take several *values*. An object can thus be described by a conjunction of attribute-value pairs. A dialogue progresses with the system obtaining requirements from the user which are specified in terms of attribute values. The system should eventually present objects (search results) based upon its understanding of the user's requirement. The dialogue ends when the user accepts one of the domain objects.

Prior work on POMDP SDSs has assumed that a user has a narrowly constrained goal (as speci-

User goal: cheap central Thai or expensive French
S: Hello, how can I help you?
U: I'm looking for a cheap central Thai restaurant.
S: You're looking for budget, city centre, Thai restaurants. —
U: Or an expensive French restaurant anywhere.
S: You're looking for non-budget French restaurants. What —
U: And cheap, city centre, Thai.
S: You're looking for budget, city centre, Thai restaurants. What about —
U: (SIGH) And French.
S: You're looking for budget, city centre, French restaurants. What about —
U: (HANG UP)

Table 1: Example dialogue using simple user goals. S=System, U=User. '—' indicates the user barged in.

User goal: cheap central Thai or expensive French
S: Hello, how can I help you?
U: I'm looking for a cheap central Thai restaurant.
S: You're looking for budget, city centre, Thai restaurants. —
U: Or an expensive French restaurant anywhere.
S: You're looking for budget, city centre, Thai restaurants *or* non-budget French. What about Chang Thai in Old Town†? Chang Thai's set lunch price is £ 7.95 —
U: What alternatives do you have?
S: What about the Plumed Horse in Leith‡? The Plumed Horse is a Michelin starred French ...

Table 2: Example dialogue using complex user goals. S=System, U=User. †Old Town is part of the city centre. ‡Leith is outside the centre.

fied in terms of the domain objects) and thus the role of the DM is one of reducing uncertainty until its belief is strongly focused on a particular domain object. This has the unfortunate effect of forcing users to select one domain object in order to progress the dialogue, see Table 1. Note that the example given is problematic not only because the user wants two different food types but because they have different requirements associated with each, *i.e.* Thai restaurants should be in the centre and cheap, while any French restaurants should be expensive[1] and can be located anywhere. To our knowledge such a combination of goals with different attribute values cannot be straightforwardly handled by comparable state-of-the-art statistical SDSs which appear in the literature.

Crook and Lemon (2011) suggest that rather than the DM assuming that the user has a single narrowly constrained goal in mind, it should assume that they want any possible sub-set of the complete set of domain objects. Thus, instead of maintaining the POMDP belief over individual domain objects, it should be maintained over the *power set* of domain objects. As an example see Table 3 which is the power set for a domain with three objects that can take two attributes u, v with associated values $u1$, $u2$, $u3$ and $v1$ respectively.

The power set representation allows the demonstration system to straightforwardly handle previously problematic dialogues. See Table 2. Of course this approach significantly expands the state space of possible user goals, with the number of goal sets being equal to $2^{|domain\ objects|}$.

2.1 Automatic Compression

Even considering limited domains, POMDP state spaces for SDSs grow very quickly. Thus the current state-of-the-art in POMDP SDSs uses a variety of *handcrafted* compression techniques, such as making several types of independence assumption as discussed above.

Crook and Lemon (2010) propose replacing handcrafted compressions with automatic compression techniques. The idea is to use principled statistical methods for automatically reducing the dimensionality of belief spaces, but which preserve useful distributions from the full space, and thus can more accurately represent real user's goals.

2.2 VDC Algorithm

The VDC algorithm (Poupart, 2005) uses Krylov iteration to compute a reduced state space. It finds a set of linear basis vectors that can reproduce the *value*[2] of being in any of the original POMDP states. Where, if a lossless VDC compression is possible, the number of basis vectors is less than the original number of POMDP states.

The intuition here is that if the value of taking an action in a given state has been preserved then planning is equally as reliable in the compressed space as the in full space.

The VDC algorithm requires a fully specified POMDP, *i.e.* $\langle S, A, O, T, \Omega, \mathcal{R} \rangle$ where S is the set

[1] Interpreted as *non-budget* by the system since its database only classifies restaurants as budget or non-budget.

[2] The sum of discounted future rewards obtained through following some series of actions.

state	goal set	meaning: user's goal is
s_1	$\emptyset$ (empty set)	none of the domain objects
s_2	$u{=}u1 \wedge v{=}v1$	domain object 1
s_3	$u{=}u2 \wedge v{=}v1$	domain object 2
s_4	$u{=}u3 \wedge v{=}v1$	domain object 3
s_5	$(u{=}u1 \wedge v{=}v1) \vee (u{=}u2 \wedge v{=}v1)$	domain objects 1 or 2
s_6	$(u{=}u1 \wedge v{=}v1) \vee (u{=}u3 \wedge v{=}v1)$	domain objects 1 or 3
s_7	$(u{=}u2 \wedge v{=}v1) \vee (u{=}u3 \wedge v{=}v1)$	domain objects 2 or 3
s_8	$(u{=}u1 \wedge v{=}v1) \vee (u{=}u2 \wedge v{=}v1) \vee (u{=}u3 \wedge v{=}v1)$	any of the domain objects

Table 3: Example of complex user goal sets.

of states, A is the set of actions, O is the set of observations, T conditional transition probabilities, Ω conditional observation probabilities, and $\mathcal{R}$ is the reward function. Since it iteratively projects the rewards associated with each state and action using the state transition and observation probabilities, the compression found is dependent on structures and regularities in the POMDP model.

The set of basis vectors found can be used to project the POMDP reward, transition, and observation probabilities into the reduced state space allowing the policy to be learnt and executed in this state space.

Although the VDC algorithm (Poupart, 2005) produces compressions that are lossless in terms of the states' values, the set of basis vectors found (when viewed as a transformation matrix) can be ill-conditioned. This results in numerical instability and errors in the belief estimation. The compression used in this demonstration was produced using a modified VDC algorithm that improves the matrix condition by approximately selecting the most independent basis vectors, thus improving numerical stability. It achieves near-lossless state value compression while allowing belief estimation errors to be minimised and traded-off against the amount of compression. Details of this algorithm are to appear in a forthcoming publication.

3 System Description

3.1 Components

Input and output to the demonstration system is using standard open source and commercial components. FreeSWITCH (Minessale II, 2012) provides a platform for accepting incoming Voice over IP calls, routing them (using the Media Resource Control Protocol (MRCP)) to a Nuance 9.0 Automatic Speech Recogniser (Nuance, 2012). Output is similarly handled by FreeSWITCH routing system responses via a CereProc Text-to-Speech MRCP server (CereProc, 2012) in order to respond to the user.

The heart of the demonstration system consists of a State-Estimator server which estimates the current dialogue state using the compressed state space previously produced by VDC, a Policy-Executor server that selects actions based on the compressed estimated state, and a template based Natural Language Generator server. These servers, along with FreeSWITCH, use ZeroC's Internet Communications Engine (Ice) middleware (ZeroC, 2012) as a common communications platform.

3.2 SDS Domain

The demonstration system provides a restaurant finder system for the city of Edinburgh (Scotland, UK). It presents search results from a real database of over 600 restaurants. The search results are based on the attributes specified by the user, currently; location, food type and budget/non-budget.

3.3 Interface

The demonstration SDS is typically accessed over the phone network. For debugging and demonstration purposes it is possible to visualise the belief distribution maintained by the DM as dialogues progress. The compressed version of the belief distribution is not a conventional probability distribution[3] and its visualisation is uninformative. Instead we take advantage of the reversibility of the VDC compression and project the distribution back onto the full state space. For an example of the evolution of the belief distribution during a dialogue see Figure 1.

[3]The values associated with the basis vectors are not confined to the range $[0-1]$.

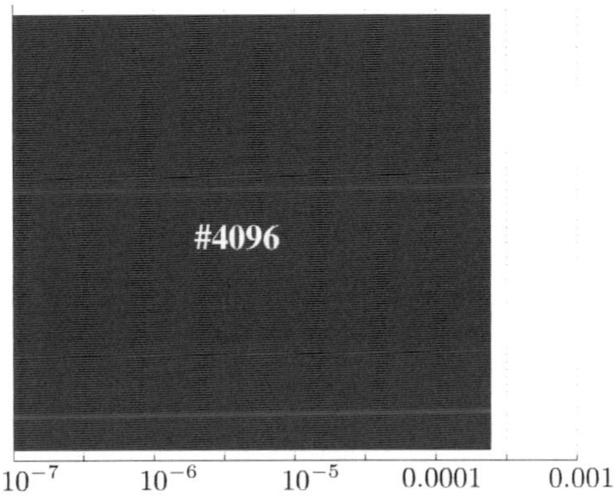

(a) Initial uniform distribution over the power set.

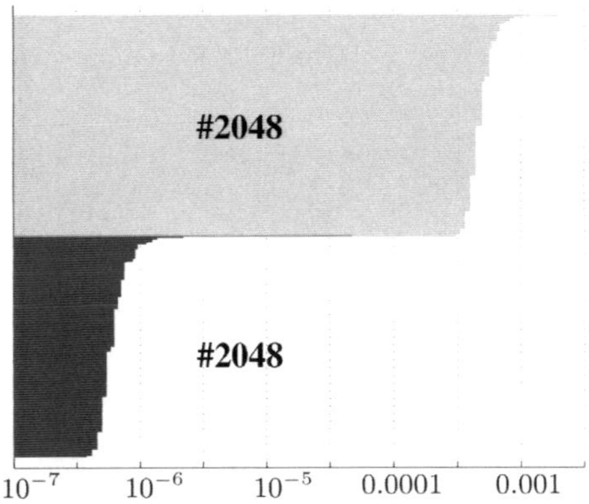

(b) Distribution after user responds to greet.

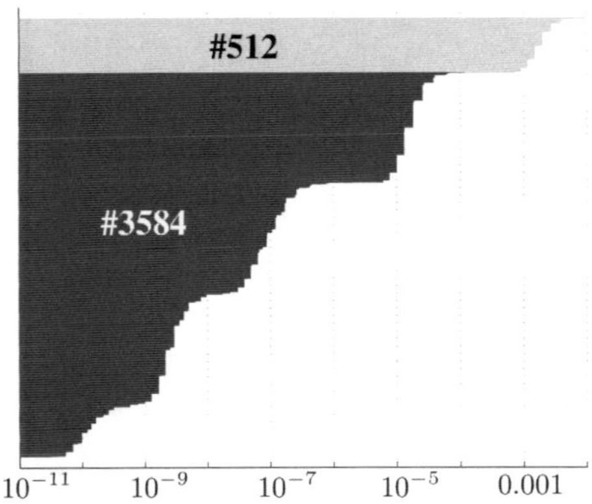

(c) Distribution after second user utterance.

Figure 1: Evolution of the belief distribution for the example dialogue in Table 2. The horizontal length of each bar corresponds to the probability of that complex user goal state. Note that the x-axis uses a logarithmic scale to allow low probability values to be seen. The y-axis is the set of complex user goals ordered by probability. Lighter shaded (green) bars indicate complex user goal states corresponding to "cheap, central Thai" and "cheap, central Thai or expensive French anywhere" in figures (b) and (c) respectively. The count '#' indicates the number of states in those groups.

4 Conclusions

We present a demonstration of a statistical SDS that uses automatic belief compression to reason over complex user goal sets. Using the power set of domain objects as the states of the POMDP DM allows complex sets of user goals to be represented, which leads to more natural dialogues. To address the massive expansion in the number of belief states, a modified form of VDC is used to generate a compression. It is this compressed space which is used by the DM for planning and acting in response to user utterances. This is the first demonstration of a statistical SDS that uses automatic belief compression to reason over complex user goal sets.

VDC and other automated compression techniques reduce the human design load by automating part of the current POMDP SDS design process. This reduces the knowledge required when building such statistical systems and should make them easier for industry to deploy.

Such compression approaches are not only applicable to SDSs but should be equally relevant for multi-modal interaction systems where several modalities are being combined in user-goal or state estimation.

5 Future Work

The current demonstration system is a proof of concept and is limited to a small number of attributes and attribute-values. Part of our ongoing work involves investigation of scaling. For example, increasing the number of attribute-values should produce more regularities across the POMDP space. Does VDC successfully exploit these?

We are in the process of collecting corpora for the Edinburgh restaurant domain mentioned above with the aim that the POMDP observation and transition statistics can be derived from data.

As part of this work we have launched a long term, public facing outlet for testing and data collection, see `http:\\www.edinburghinfo.co.uk`. It is planned to make future versions of the demonstration system discussed in this paper available via this public outlet.

Finally we are investigating the applicability of other automatic belief (and state) compression techniques for SDSs, *e.g.* E-PCA (Roy and Gordon, 2002).

Acknowledgments

The research leading to these results was funded by the Engineering and Physical Sciences Research Council, UK (EPSRC) under project no. EP/G069840/1 and was partially supported by the EC FP7 projects Spacebook (ref. 270019) and JAMES (ref. 270435).

References

CereProc. 2012. http://www.cereproc.com/.

Paul A. Crook and Oliver Lemon. 2010. Representing uncertainty about complex user goals in statistical dialogue systems. In *proceedings of SIGdial*.

Paul A. Crook and Oliver Lemon. 2011. Lossless Value Directed Compression of Complex User Goal States for Statistical Spoken Dialogue Systems. In *Proceedings of the Twelfth Annual Conference of the International Speech Communication Association (Interspeech)*.

Oliver Lemon, Kallirroi Georgila, and James Henderson. 2006. Evaluating Effectiveness and Portability of Reinforcement Learned Dialogue Strategies with real users: the TALK TownInfo Evaluation. In *IEEE/ACL Spoken Language Technology*.

Anthony Minessale II. 2012. FreeSWITCH. http://www.freeswitch.org/.

Nuance. 2012. Nuance Recognizer. http://www.nuance.com.

P. Poupart. 2005. *Exploiting Structure to Efficiently Solve Large Scale Partially Observable Markov Decision Processes*. Ph.D. thesis, Dept. Computer Science, University of Toronto.

N. Roy and G. Gordon. 2002. Exponential Family PCA for Belief Compression in POMDPs. In *NIPS*.

B. Thomson and S. Young. 2010. Bayesian update of dialogue state: A POMDP framework for spoken dialogue systems. *Computer Speech and Language*, 24(4):562–588.

Marilyn Walker, S. Whittaker, A. Stent, P. Maloor, J. Moore, M. Johnston, and G. Vasireddy. 2004. User tailored generation in the match multimodal dialogue system. *Cognitive Science*, 28:811–840.

S. Young, M. Gašić, S. Keizer, F. Mairesse, B. Thomson, and K. Yu. 2010. The Hidden Information State model: a practical framework for POMDP based spoken dialogue management. *Computer Speech and Language*, 24(2):150–174.

ZeroC. 2012. The Internet Communications Engine (Ice). http://www.zeroc.com/ice.html.

Automatically Generated Customizable Online Dictionaries

Enikő Héja
Dept. of Language Technology
Research Institute for Linguistics, HAS
P.O.Box. 360 H-1394, Budapest
eheja@nytud.hu

Dávid Takács
Dept. of Language Technology
Research Institute for Linguistics, HAS
P.O.Box. 360 H-1394, Budapest
takdavid@nytud.hu

Abstract

The aim of our software presentation is to demonstrate that corpus-driven bilingual dictionaries generated fully by automatic means are suitable for human use. Previous experiments have proven that bilingual lexicons can be created by applying word alignment on parallel corpora. Such an approach, especially the corpus-driven nature of it, yields several advantages over more traditional approaches. Most importantly, automatically attained translation probabilities are able to guarantee that the most frequently used translations come first within an entry. However, the proposed technique have to face some difficulties, as well. In particular, the scarce availability of parallel texts for medium density languages imposes limitations on the size of the resulting dictionary. Our objective is to design and implement a dictionary building workflow and a query system that is apt to exploit the additional benefits of the method and overcome the disadvantages of it.

1 Introduction

The work presented here is part of the pilot project EFNILEX [1] launched in 2008. The project objective was to investigate to what extent LT methods are capable of supporting the creation of bilingual dictionaries. Need for such dictionaries shows up specifically in the case of lesser used languages where it does not pay off for publishers to invest into the production of dictionaries due to the low demand. The targeted size of the dictionaries is between 15,000 and 25,000 entries. Since the completely automatic generation of clean bilingual resources is not possible according to the state of the art, we have decided to provide lexicographers with bilingual resources that can facilitate their work. These kind of lexical resources will be referred to as *proto-dictionaries* henceforward.

After investigating some alternative approaches e.g. hub-and-spoke model (Martin, 2007), alignment of WordNets, we have decided to use word alignment on parallel corpora. Former experiments (Héja, 2010) have proven that word alignment is not only able to help the dictionary creation process itself, but the proposed technique also yields some definite advantages over more traditional approaches. The main motivation behind our choice was that the corpus-driven nature of the method decreases the reliance on human intuition during lexicographic work. Although the careful investigation of large monolingual corpora might have the same effect, being tedious and time-cosuming it is not affordable in the case of lesser used languages.

In spite of the fact that word alignment has been widely used for more than a decade within the NLP community to produce bilingual lexicons e.g. Wu and Xia (1994) and several experts claimed that such resources might also be useful for lexicographic purposes e.g. Bertels et al. (2009), as far as we know, this technique has not been exploited in large-scale lexicographic projects yet e.g. Atkins and Rundell (2008).

Earlier experiments has shown that although word alignment has definite advantages over more traditional approaches, there are also some difficulties that have to be dealt with: The method in itself does not handle multi-word expressions and

[1] EFNILEX is financed by EFNIL

the proto-dictionaries comprise incorrect translation candidates, as well. In fact, in a given parallel corpus the number of incorrect translation candidates strongly depends on the size of the proto-dictionary, as there is a trade-off between precision and recall.

Accordingly, our objective is to design and implement a dictionary query system that is apt to exploit the benefits of the method and overcome the disadvantages of it. Hopefully, such a system renders the proto-dictionaries helpful for not only lexicographers, but also for ordinary dictionary users.

In Section 2 the basic generation process is introduced along with the difficulties we have to deal with. The various features of the Dictionary Query System are detailed in Section 3. Finally, a conclusion is given and future work is listed in Section 4.

The proto-dictionaries are available at: `http://efnilex.efnil.org`

2 Generating Proto-Dictionaries – One-Token Translation Pairs

2.1 Input data

Since the amount of available parallel data is crucial for this approach, in the first phase of the project we have experimented with two different language pairs. The Dutch-French language pair represents well-resourced languages while the Hungarian-Lithuaninan language pair represents medium density languages. As for the former, we have exploited the French-Dutch parallel corpus which forms subpart of the Dutch Parallel Corpus (Macken et al., 2007). It consists of 3,606,000 French tokens, 3,215,000 Dutch tokens and 186,945 translation units[2] (TUs). As for Hungarian and Lithuanian we have built a parallel corpus comprising 4,189,000 Hungarian and 3,544,000 Lithuanian tokens and 262,423 TUs. Because our original intention is to compile dictionaries covering every-day language, we have decided to focus on literature while collecting the texts. However, due to the scarce availability of parallel texts we made some concessions that might be questionable from a translation point of view. First, we did not confine ourselves purely to the literary domain: The parallel corpus comprises also philosophical works. Secondly, instead of focusing on direct translations between Lithuanian and Hungarian we have relied mainly on translations from a third language. Thirdly, we have treated every parallel text alike, regardless of the direction of the translation, although the DPC contains that information.

[2]The size of the parallel corpora is given in terms of translation units instead of in terms of sentence pairs, for many-to-many alignment was allowed, too.

2.2 The Generation Process

As already has been mentioned in Section 1, word alignment in itself deals only with one-token units. A detailed description of the generation process of such proto-dictionaries has been given in previous papers, e. g. Héja (2010). In the present paper we confine ourselves to a schematic overview. In the first step the lemmatized versions of each input text have been created by means of morhological analysis and disambiguation[3].

In the second step parallel corpora have been created. We used Hunalign (Varga et al., 2005) for sentence alignment.

In the next step word alignment has been performed with GIZA++ (Och and Ney, 2003). During word alignment GIZA++ builds a dictionary-file that stores translation candidates, i.e. source and target language lemmata along with their translation probabilities. We used this dictionary file as the starting point to create the proto-dictionaries.

In the fourth step the proto-dictionaries have been created. Only the most likely translation candidates were kept on the basis of some suitable heuristics, which has been developed while evaluating the results manually.

Finally, the relevant example sentences were provided in a concordance to give hints on the use of the translation candidates.

2.3 Trade-off between Precision and Recall

At this stage of the workflow some suitable heuristics need to be introduced to find the best translation candidates without the loss of too many correct pairs. Therefore, several evaluations were carried out.

[3]The analysis of the Lithuanian texts was performed by the Lithuanian Centre of Computational Linguistics (Zinkevičius et al., 2005). The Hungarian texts were annotated with the tool-chain of the Research Institute for Linguistics, HAS (Oravecz and Dienes, 2002).

It is important to note that throughout the manual evaluation we have focused on lexicographically useful translation candidates instead of perfect translations. The reason behind this is that translation synonymy is rare in general language e.g. Atkins and Rundell (2008, p. 467), thus other semantic relations, such as hyponymy or hyperonymy, were also considered. Moreover, since the word alignment method does not handle MWEs in itself, partial matching between SL and TL translation candidates occurs frequently. In either case, provided example sentences make possible to find the right translation.

We considered three parameters when searching for the best translations: *translational probability*, *source language lemma frequency* and *target language lemma frequency* (p_{tr}, F_s and F_t, respectively).

The lemma frequency had to be taken into account for at least two reasons. First, a minimal amount of data was necessary for the word alignment algorithm to be able to estimate the translational probability. Secondly, in the case of rarely used TL lemmas the alignment algorithm might assign high translational probabilities to incorrect lemma pairs if the source lemma occurs frequently in the corpus and both members of the lemma pair recurrently show up in aligned units.

Results of the first evaluation showed that translation pairs with relatively low frequency and with a relatively high translational probability yielded cc. 85% lexicographically useful translation pairs. Although the precision was rather convincing, it has also turned out that the size of the resulting proto-dictionaries might be a serious bottleneck of the method (Héja, 2010). Whereas the targeted size of the dictionaries is between 15,000 and 25,000 entries, the proto-dictionaries comprised only 5,521 Hungarian-Lithuanian and 7,007 French-Dutch translation candidates with the predefined parameters. Accordingly, the coverage of the proto-dictionaries should be augmented.

According to our hypothesis in the case of more frequent source lemmata even lower values of translation probability might yield the same result in terms of precision as in the case of lower frequency source lemmata. Hence, different evaluation domains need to be determined as a function of source lemma frequency. That is:

1. The refinement of the parameters yields approximately the same proportion of correct translation candidates as the basic parameter setting,

2. The refinement of the parameters ensures a greater coverage.

Detailed evaluation of the French-Dutch translation candidates confirmed the first part of our hypothesis. We have chosen a parameter setting in accordance with (1) (see Table 1). 6934 French-Dutch translation candidates met the given conditions. 10 % of the relevant pairs was manually evaluated. The results are presented in Table 1. 'OK' denotes the lexicographically useful translation candidates. For instance, the first evaluation range (1st row of Table 1) comprised translation candidates where the source lemma occurs at least 10 times and at most 20 times in the parallel corpus. With these parameters only those pairs were considered where the translation probability was at least 0.4. As the 1st and 2nd rows of Table 1 show, using different p_{tr} values as cut-off parameters give similar results (87%), if the two source lemma frequencies also differ.

F_s	p_{tr}	OK
$10 \leq LF \leq 20$	$p \geq 0.4$	83%
$100 \leq LF \leq 200$	$p \geq 0.06$	87%
$500 \leq LF$	$p \geq 0.02$	87.5%

Table 1: Evaluation results of the refined French-Dutch proto-dictionary.

The manual evaluation of the Hungarian-Lithuanian translation candidates yielded the same result. We have used this proto-dictionary to confirm the 2nd part of our hypothesis, i.e. that the refinement of these parameters may increase the size of the proto-dictionary. Table 2 presents the results. *Expected* refers to the expected number of correct translation candidates, estimated on the basis of the evaluation sample. 800 translation candidates were evaluated altogether, 200 from each evaluation domain. As Table 2 shows, it is possible to increase the size of the dictionary through refining the parameters: with fine-tuned parameters the estimated number of useful translation candidates was 13,605 instead of 5,521.

F_s	p_{tr}	OK	Expected
$5 \leq$ LF < 30	p > 0.3	64%	4,296
$30 \leq$ LF < 90	p > 0.1	80%	4,144
$90 \leq$ LF < 300	p > 0.07	89%	3,026
$300 \leq$ LF	p > 0.04	79%	2,139
			13,605

Table 2: Evaluation results of the refined Hungarian-Lithuanian proto-dictionary.

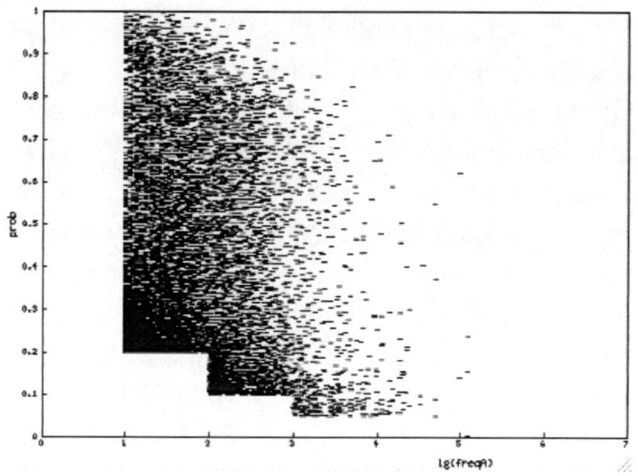

Figure 1: The customized dictionary: the distribution of the Lithuanian-Hungarian translation candidates. Logarithmic frequency of the source words on the x-axis, translation probability on the y-axis.

However, we should keep in mind when searching for the optimal values for these parameters that while we aim at including as many translation candidates as possible, we also expect the generated resource to be as clean as possible. That is, in the case of proto-dictionaries there is a trade-off between precision and recall: the size of the resulting proto-dictionaries can be increased only at the cost of more incorrect translation candidates.

This leads us to the question of what parameter settings are useful for what usage scenarios? We think that the proto-dictionaries generated by this method with various settings match well different user needs. For instance, when the settings are strict so that the minimal frequencies and probabilities are set high, the dictionary will contain less translation pairs, resulting in high precision and relatively low coverage, with only the most frequently used words and their most frequent translations. Such a dictionary is especially useful for a novice language learner. Professional translators are able to judge whether a translation is correct or not. They might be rather interested in special uses of words, lexicographically useful but not perfect translation candidates, and more subtle cross-language semantic relations, while at the same time, looking at the concordance provided along with the translation pairs, they can easily catch wrong translations which are the side-effect of the method. This kind of work may be supported by a proto-dictionary with increased recall even at the cost of a lower precision.

Thus, the Dictionary Query System described in Section 3 in more detail, should support various user needs.

However, user satisfaction has to be evaluated in order to confirm this hypothesis. It forms part of our future tasks.

3 Dictionary Query System

As earlier has been mentioned, the proposed method has several benefits compared to more traditional approaches:

1. A parallel corpus of appropriate size guarantees that the most relevant translations be included in the dictionary.
2. Based on the translational probabilities it is possible to rank translation candidates ensuring that the most likely used translation variants go first within an entry.
3. All the relevant example sentences from the parallel corpora are easily accessible facilitating the selection of the most appropriate translations from possible translation candidates.

Accordingly, the Dictionary Query System presents some novel features. On the one hand, users can select the best proto-dictionary for their purposes on the Cut Board Page. On the other hand, the innovative representation of the generated bilingual information helps to find the best translation for a specific user in the Dictionary Browser Window.

3.1 Customizable proto-dictionaries: the Cut Board Page

The dictionary can be customized on the Cut Board Page. Two different charts are displayed

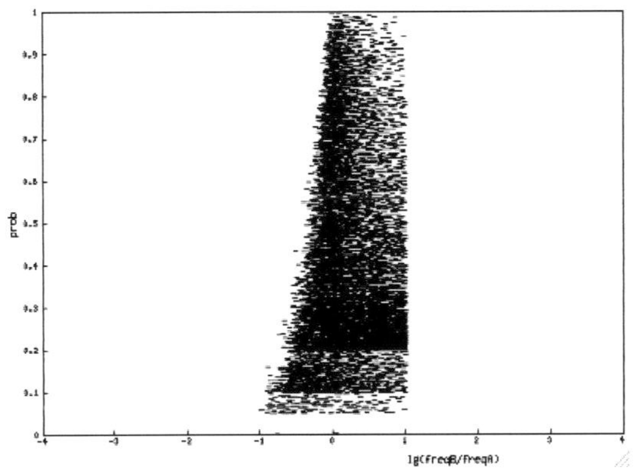

Figure 2: The customized dictionary: the distribution of the candidates. Logarithmic frequency ratio of the source and target words on the x-axis, translation probability on the y-axis.

here showing the distribution of all word pairs of the selected proto-dictionary.

1. Plot 1 visualizes the distribution of the logarithmic frequency of the source words and the relevant translation probability for each word pair, selected by the given custom criteria.

2. Plot 2 visualizes the distribution of the logarithmic frequency ratio of the target and source words and the corresponding translation probability for each word pair, selected by the given custom criteria..

Proto-dictionaries are customizable by the following criteria:

1. Maximum and minimum ratio of the relative frequencies of the source and target words (left and right boundary on Plot 1).

2. Overall minimum frequency of either the source and the target words (left boundary on Plot 2).

3. Overall minimum translation probability (bottom boundary on both plots).

4. Several more cut off intervals can be defined in the space represented by Plot 2: word pairs falling in rectangles given by their left, right and top boundaries are cut off.

After submitting the given parameters the charts are refreshed giving a feedback to the user and the parameters are stored for the session, i. e. the dictionary page shows only word pairs fitting the selected criteria.

3.2 Dictionary Browser

The Dictionary Browser displays four different types of information.

1. List of the translation candidates ranked by their translation probabilities. This guarantees that most often used translations come first in the list (from top to bottom). Absolute corpus frequencies are also displayed.

2. A plot displaying the distribution of the possible translations of the source word according to translation probability and the ratio of corpus ferquency between the source word and the corresponding translation candidate.

3. Word cloud reflecting semantic relations between source and target lemmata. Words in the word cloud vary in two ways.

   First, their *size* depends on their translation probabilities: the higher the probability of the target word, the bigger the font size is.

   Secondly, *colours* are assigned to target words according to their frequency ratios relative to the source word: less frequent target words are cool-coloured (dark blue and light blue) while more frequent target words are warm-coloured (red, orange). Target words with a frequency close to that of the source word get gray colour.

4. Provided example sentences with the source and target words highlighted, displayed by clicking one of the translation candidates.

According to our hypothesis the frequency ratios provide the user with hints about the semantic relations between source and target words which might be particularly important when creating texts in a foreign language. For instance, the Lithuanian lemma *karieta* has four Hungarian eqivalents: "kocsi" (word with general meaning, e.g. 'car', 'railway wagon', 'horse-drown vehicle'), "hintó" ('carriage'), "konflis" ('a horse-drawn vehicle for public hire'), "jármű" ('vehicle'). The various colours of the candidates indicate different semantic relations: the red colour of

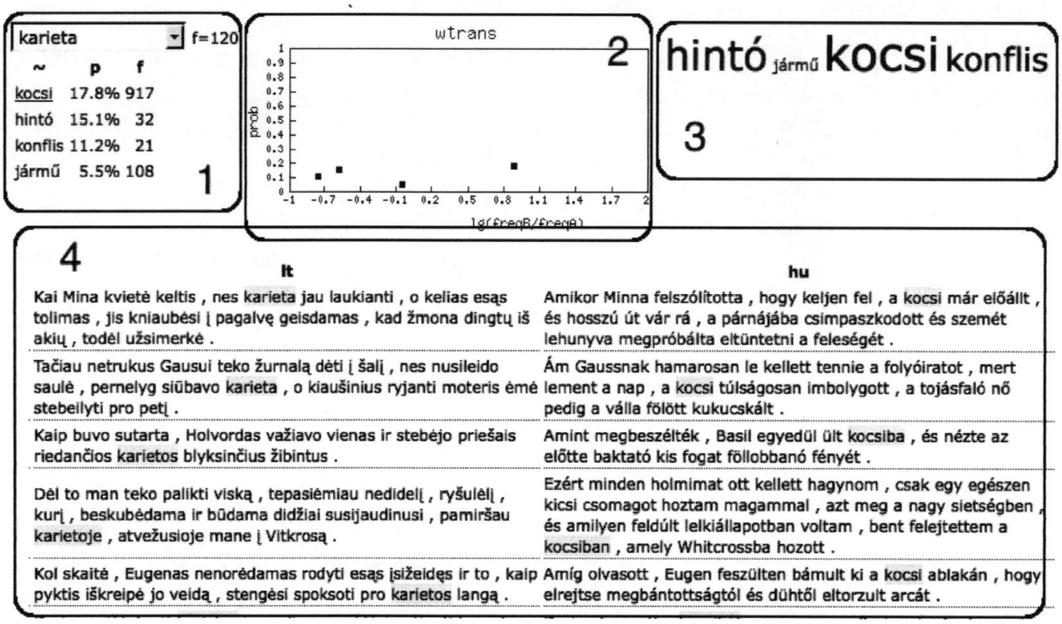

Figure 3: The Dictionary Browser

"kocsi" marks that the meaning of the target word is more general than that of the source word. Conversely, the dark blue colour of "konflis" shows that the meaning of the target word is more special. However, this hypothesis should be tested in the future which makes part of our future work.

3.3 Implementation

The online research tool is based on the LAMP web architecture. We use a relational database to store all the data: the multilingual corpus text, sentences and their translations, the word forms and lemmata and all the relations between them. The implementation of such a data structure and the formulation of the queries is straightforward and efficient. The data displayed in the dictionary browser as well as the distributional dataset presented on the charts is selected on-the-fly. The size of the database is log-linear with the size of the corpus and the dictionary.

4 Conclusions and Future Work

Previous experiments have proven that corpus-driven bilingual resources generated fully by automatic means are apt to facilitate lexicographic work when compiling bilingual dictionaries.

We think that the proto-dictionaries generated by this technique with various settings match well different user needs, and consequently, beside lexicographers, they might also be useful for end users, both for language learners and for professional translators. A possible future work is to further evaluate the dictionaries in real world use cases.

Some new assumptions can be formulated which connect the statistical properties of the translation pairs, e.g. their frequency ratios and the cross-language semantic relations between them. Based on the generated dictionaries such hypotheses may be further examined in the future.

In order to demonstrate the generated proto-dictionaries, we have designed and implemented an online dictionary query system, which exploits the advantages of the data-driven nature of the applied technique. It provides different visualizations of the possible translations based on their translation probabilities and frequencies, along with their relevant contexts in the corpus. By presetting different selection criteria the contents of the dictionaries are customizable to suit various usage scenarios.

The dictionaries are publicly available at `http://efnilex.efnil.org`.

References

Beryl T. Sue Atkins and Michael Rundell. 2008. *The Oxford Guide to Practical Lexicography*. OUP Oxford.

Ann Bertels, Cédrick Fairon, Jörg Tiedemann, and Serge Verlinde. 2009. Corpus parallèles et corpus ciblés au secours du dictionnaire de traduction. In *Cahiers de lexicologie*, number 94 in Revues, pages 199–219. Classiques Garnier.

Enikő Héja. 2010. The role of parallel corpora in bilingual lexicography. In Nicoletta Calzolari (Conference Chair), Khalid Choukri, Bente Maegaard, Joseph Mariani, Jan Odijk, Stelios Piperidis, Mike Rosner, and Daniel Tapias, editors, *Proceedings of the Seventh International Conference on Language Resources and Evaluation (LREC'10)*, Valletta, Malta, may. European Language Resources Association (ELRA).

Lieve Macken, Julia Trushkina, Hans Paulussen, Lidia Rura, Piet Desmet, and Willy Vandeweghe. 2007. Dutch parallel corpus : a multilingual annotated corpus. In *Proceedings of Corpus Linguistics 2007*.

Willy Martin. 2007. Government policy and the planning and production of bilingual dictionaries : The dutch approach as a case in point. *International Journal of Lexicography*, 20(3):221–237.

Franz Josef Och and Hermann Ney. 2003. A systematic comparison of various statistical alignment models. *Computational Linguistics*, 29(1):19–51.

Csaba Oravecz and Péter Dienes. 2002. Efficient stochastic part-of-speech tagging for hungarian. In *Proceedings of the Third International Conference on Language Resources and Evaluation*, pages 710–717, Las Palmas.

Dániel Varga, László Németh, Péter Halácsy, András Kornai, Viktor Trón, and Viktor Nagy. 2005. Parallel corpora for medium density languages. In *Recent Advances in Natural Language Processing (RANLP 2005)*, pages 590–596.

Dekai Wu and Xuanyin Xia. 1994. Learning an english-chinese lexicon from a parallel corpus. In *In Proceedings of the First Conference of the Association for Machine Translation in the Americas*, pages 206–213.

Vytautas Zinkevičius, Vidas Daudaravičius, and Erika Rimkutė. 2005. The Morphologically annotated Lithuanian Corpus. In *Proceedings of The Second Baltic Conference on Human Language Technologies*, pages 365–370.

MaltOptimizer: An Optimization Tool for MaltParser

Miguel Ballesteros
Complutense University of Madrid
Spain
miballes@fdi.ucm.es

Joakim Nivre
Uppsala University
Sweden
joakim.nivre@lingfil.uu.se

Abstract

Data-driven systems for natural language processing have the advantage that they can easily be ported to any language or domain for which appropriate training data can be found. However, many data-driven systems require careful tuning in order to achieve optimal performance, which may require specialized knowledge of the system. We present MaltOptimizer, a tool developed to facilitate optimization of parsers developed using MaltParser, a data-driven dependency parser generator. MaltOptimizer performs an analysis of the training data and guides the user through a three-phase optimization process, but it can also be used to perform completely automatic optimization. Experiments show that MaltOptimizer can improve parsing accuracy by up to 9 percent absolute (labeled attachment score) compared to default settings. During the demo session, we will run MaltOptimizer on different data sets (user-supplied if possible) and show how the user can interact with the system and track the improvement in parsing accuracy.

1 Introduction

In building NLP applications for new languages and domains, we often want to reuse components for tasks like part-of-speech tagging, syntactic parsing, word sense disambiguation and semantic role labeling. From this perspective, components that rely on machine learning have an advantage, since they can be quickly adapted to new settings provided that we can find suitable training data. However, such components may require careful feature selection and parameter tuning in order to give optimal performance, a task that can be difficult for application developers without specialized knowledge of each component.

A typical example is MaltParser (Nivre et al., 2006), a widely used transition-based dependency parser with state-of-the-art performance for many languages, as demonstrated in the CoNLL shared tasks on multilingual dependency parsing (Buchholz and Marsi, 2006; Nivre et al., 2007). MaltParser is an open-source system that offers a wide range of parameters for optimization. It implements nine different transition-based parsing algorithms, each with its own specific parameters, and it has an expressive specification language that allows the user to define arbitrarily complex feature models. Finally, any combination of parsing algorithm and feature model can be combined with a number of different machine learning algorithms available in LIBSVM (Chang and Lin, 2001) and LIBLINEAR (Fan et al., 2008). Just running the system with default settings when training a new parser is therefore very likely to result in suboptimal performance. However, selecting the best combination of parameters is a complicated task that requires knowledge of the system as well as knowledge of the characteristics of the training data.

This is why we present MaltOptimizer, a tool for optimizing MaltParser for a new language or domain, based on an analysis of the training data. The optimization is performed in three phases: data analysis, parsing algorithm selection, and feature selection. The tool can be run in "batch mode" to perform completely automatic optimization, but it is also possible for the user to manually tune parameters after each of the three phases. In this way, we hope to cater for users without specific knowledge of MaltParser, who can use the tool for black box optimization, as well as expert users, who can use it interactively to speed up optimization. Experiments on a number of data sets show that using MaltOptimizer for completely automatic optimization gives consistent and often substantial improvements over the default settings for MaltParser.

The importance of feature selection and parameter optimization has been demonstrated for many NLP tasks (Kool et al., 2000; Daelemans et al., 2003), and there are general optimization tools for machine learning, such as Paramsearch (Van den Bosch, 2004). In addition, Nilsson and Nugues (2010) has explored automatic feature selection specifically for MaltParser, but MaltOptimizer is the first system that implements a complete customized optimization process for this system.

In the rest of the paper, we describe the optimization process implemented in MaltOptimizer (Section 2), report experiments (Section 3), outline the demonstration (Section 4), and conclude (Section 5). A more detailed description of MaltOptimizer with additional experimental results can be found in Ballesteros and Nivre (2012).

2 The MaltOptimizer System

MaltOptimizer is written in Java and implements an optimization procedure for MaltParser based on the heuristics described in Nivre and Hall (2010). The system takes as input a training set, consisting of sentences annotated with dependency trees in CoNLL data format,[1] and outputs an optimized MaltParser configuration together with an estimate of the final parsing accuracy. The evaluation metric that is used for optimization by default is the labeled attachment score (LAS) excluding punctuation, that is, the percentage of non-punctuation tokens that are assigned the correct head and the correct label (Buchholz and Marsi, 2006), but other options are available. For efficiency reasons, MaltOptimizer only explores linear multiclass SVMs in LIBLINEAR.

2.1 Phase 1: Data Analysis

After validating that the data is in valid CoNLL format, using the official validation script from the CoNLL-X shared task,[2] the system checks the minimum Java heap space needed given the size of the data set. If there is not enough memory available on the current machine, the system informs the user and automatically reduces the size of the data set to a feasible subset. After these initial checks, MaltOptimizer checks the following characteristics of the data set:

1. Number of words/sentences.
2. Existence of "covered roots" (arcs spanning tokens with HEAD = 0).
3. Frequency of labels used for tokens with HEAD = 0.
4. Percentage of non-projective arcs/trees.
5. Existence of non-empty feature values in the LEMMA and FEATS columns.
6. Identity (or not) of feature values in the CPOSTAG and POSTAG columns.

Items 1–3 are used to set basic parameters in the rest of phase 1 (see below); 4 is used in the choice of parsing algorithm (phase 2); 5 and 6 are relevant for feature selection experiments (phase 3).

If there are covered roots, the system checks whether accuracy is improved by reattaching such roots in order to eliminate spurious non-projectivity. If there are multiple labels for tokens with HEAD=0, the system tests which label is best to use as default for fragmented parses.

Given the size of the data set, the system suggests different validation strategies during phase 1. If the data set is small, it recommends using 5-fold cross-validation during subsequent optimization phases. If the data set is larger, it recommends using a single development set instead. But the user can override either recommendation and select either validation method manually.

When these checks are completed, MaltOptimizer creates a baseline option file to be used as the starting point for further optimization. The user is given the opportunity to edit this option file and may also choose to stop the process and continue with manual optimization.

2.2 Phase 2: Parsing Algorithm Selection

MaltParser implements three groups of transition-based parsing algorithms:[3] (i) Nivre's algorithms (Nivre, 2003; Nivre, 2008), (ii) Covington's algorithms (Covington, 2001; Nivre, 2008), and (iii)

[1] http://ilk.uvt.nl/conll/#dataformat

[2] http://ilk.uvt.nl/conll/software.html#validate

[3] Recent versions of MaltParser contains additional algorithms that are currently not handled by MaltOptimizer.

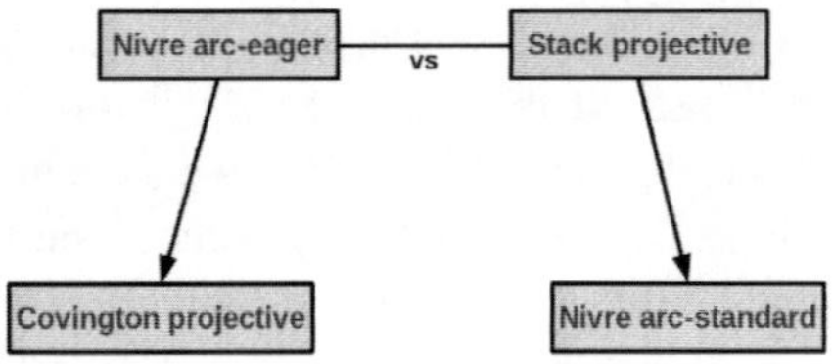

Figure 1: Decision tree for best projective algorithm.

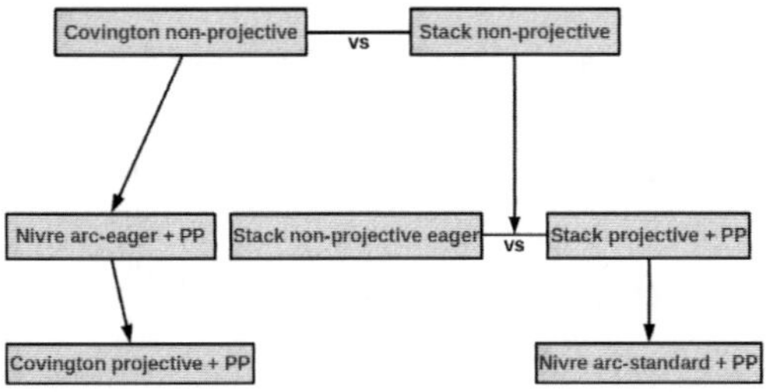

Figure 2: Decision tree for best non-projective algorithm (+PP for pseudo-projective parsing).

Stack algorithms (Nivre, 2009; Nivre et al., 2009) Both the Covington group and the Stack group contain algorithms that can handle non-projective dependency trees, and any projective algorithm can be combined with pseudo-projective parsing to recover non-projective dependencies in post-processing (Nivre and Nilsson, 2005).

In phase 2, MaltOptimizer explores the parsing algorithms implemented in MaltParser, based on the data characteristics inferred in the first phase. In particular, if there are no non-projective dependencies in the training set, then only projective algorithms are explored, including the arc-eager and arc-standard versions of Nivre's algorithm, the projective version of Covington's projective parsing algorithm and the projective Stack algorithm. The system follows a decision tree considering the characteristics of each algorithm, which is shown in Figure 1.

On the other hand, if the training set contains a substantial amount of non-projective dependencies, MaltOptimizer instead tests the non-projective versions of Covington's algorithm and the Stack algorithm (including a lazy and an eager variant), and projective algorithms in combination with pseudo-projective parsing. The system then follows the decision tree shown in Figure 2.

If the number of trees containing non-projective arcs is small but not zero, the system tests both projective algorithms and non-projective algorithms, following the decision trees in Figure 1 and Figure 2 and picking the algorithm that gives the best results after traversing both.

Once the system has finished testing each of the algorithms with default settings, MaltOptimizer tunes some specific parameters of the best performing algorithm and creates a new option file for the best configuration so far. The user is again given the opportunity to edit the option file (or stop the process) before optimization continues.

2.3 Phase 3: Feature Selection

In the third phase, MaltOptimizer tunes the feature model given all the parameters chosen so far (especially the parsing algorithm). It starts with backward selection experiments to ensure that all features in the default model for the given parsing algorithm are actually useful. In this phase, features are omitted as long as their removal does not decrease parsing accuracy. The system then proceeds with forward selection experiments, trying potentially useful features one by one. In this phase, a threshold of 0.05% is used to determine whether an improvement in parsing accuracy is sufficient for the feature to be added to the model. Since an exhaustive search for the best possible feature model is impossible, the system relies on a greedy optimization strategy using heuristics derived from proven experience (Nivre and Hall, 2010). The major steps of the forward selection experiments are the following:[4]

1. Tune the window of POSTAG n-grams over the parser state.
2. Tune the window of FORM features over the parser state.
3. Tune DEPREL and POSTAG features over the partially built dependency tree.
4. Add POSTAG and FORM features over the input string.
5. Add CPOSTAG, FEATS, and LEMMA features if available.
6. Add conjunctions of POSTAG and FORM features.

These six steps are slightly different depending on which algorithm has been selected as the best in phase 2, because the algorithms have different parsing orders and use different data structures,

[4]For an explanation of the different feature columns such as POSTAG, FORM, etc., see Buchholz and Marsi (2006) or see http://ilk.uvt.nl/conll/#dataformat

Language	Default	Phase 1	Phase 2	Phase 3	Diff
Arabic	63.02	63.03	63.84	65.56	2.54
Bulgarian	83.19	83.19	84.00	86.03	2.84
Chinese	84.14	84.14	84.95	84.95	0.81
Czech	69.94	70.14	72.44	78.04	8.10
Danish	81.01	81.01	81.34	83.86	2.85
Dutch	74.77	74.77	78.02	82.63	7.86
German	82.36	82.36	83.56	85.91	3.55
Japanese	89.70	89.70	90.92	90.92	1.22
Portuguese	84.11	84.31	84.75	86.52	2.41
Slovene	66.08	66.52	68.40	71.71	5.63
Spanish	76.45	76.45	76.64	79.38	2.93
Swedish	83.34	83.34	83.50	84.09	0.75
Turkish	57.79	57.79	58.29	66.92	9.13

Table 1: Labeled attachment score per phase and with comparison to default settings for the 13 training sets from the CoNLL-X shared task (Buchholz and Marsi, 2006).

but the steps are roughly equivalent at a certain level of abstraction. After the feature selection experiments are completed, MaltOptimizer tunes the cost parameter of the linear SVM using a simple stepwise search. Finally, it creates a complete configuration file that can be used to train MaltParser on the entire data set. The user may now continue to do further optimization manually.

3 Experiments

In order to assess the usefulness and validity of the optimization procedure, we have run all three phases of the optimization on all the 13 data sets from the CoNLL-X shared task on multilingual dependency parsing (Buchholz and Marsi, 2006). Table 1 shows the labeled attachment scores with default settings and after each of the three optimization phases, as well as the difference between the final configuration and the default.[5]

The first thing to note is that the optimization improves parsing accuracy for all languages without exception, although the amount of improvement varies considerably from about 1 percentage point for Chinese, Japanese and Swedish to 8–9 points for Dutch, Czech and Turkish. For most languages, the greatest improvement comes from feature selection in phase 3, but we also see significant improvement from phase 2 for languages with a substantial amount of non-projective dependencies, such as Czech, Dutch and Slovene, where the selection of parsing algorithm can be very important. The time needed to run the optimization varies from about half an hour for the smaller data sets to about one day for very large data sets like the one for Czech.

4 System Demonstration

In the demonstration, we will run MaltOptimizer on different data sets and show how the user can interact with the system while keeping track of improvements in parsing accuracy. We will also explain how to interpret the output of the system, including the final feature specification model, for users that are not familiar with MaltParser. By restricting the size of the input data set, we can complete the whole optimization procedure in 10–15 minutes, so we expect to be able to complete a number of cycles with different members of the audience. We will also let the audience contribute their own data sets for optimization, provided that they are in CoNLL format.[6]

5 Conclusion

MaltOptimizer is an optimization tool for MaltParser, which is primarily aimed at application developers who wish to adapt the system to a new language or domain and who do not have expert knowledge about transition-based dependency parsing. Another potential user group consists of researchers who want to perform comparative parser evaluation, where MaltParser is often used as a baseline system and where the use of suboptimal parameter settings may undermine the validity of the evaluation. Finally, we believe the system can be useful also for expert users of MaltParser as a way of speeding up optimization.

Acknowledgments

The first author is funded by the Spanish Ministry of Education and Science (TIN2009-14659-C03-01 Project), Universidad Complutense de Madrid and Banco Santander Central Hispano (GR58/08 Research Group Grant). He is under the support of the NIL Research Group (http://nil.fdi.ucm.es) from the same university.

[5] Note that these results are obtained using 80% of the training set for training and 20% as a development test set, which means that they are not comparable to the test results from the original shared task, which were obtained using the entire training set for training and a separate held-out test set for evaluation.

[6] The system is available for download under an open-source license at http://nil.fdi.ucm.es/maltoptimizer

References

Miguel Ballesteros and Joakim Nivre. 2012. MaltOptimizer: A System for MaltParser Optimization. In *Proceedings of the Eighth International Conference on Language Resources and Evaluation (LREC)*.

Sabine Buchholz and Erwin Marsi. 2006. CoNLL-X shared task on multilingual dependency parsing. In *Proceedings of the 10th Conference on Computational Natural Language Learning (CoNLL)*, pages 149–164.

Chih-Chung Chang and Chih-Jen Lin, 2001. *LIBSVM: A Library for Support Vector Machines*. Software available at http://www.csie.ntu.edu.tw/∼cjlin/libsvm.

Michael A. Covington. 2001. A fundamental algorithm for dependency parsing. In *Proceedings of the 39th Annual ACM Southeast Conference*, pages 95–102.

Walter Daelemans, Véronique Hoste, Fien De Meulder, and Bart Naudts. 2003. Combined optimization of feature selection and algorithm parameters in machine learning of language. In Nada Lavrac, Dragan Gamberger, Hendrik Blockeel, and Ljupco Todorovski, editors, *Machine Learning: ECML 2003*, volume 2837 of *Lecture Notes in Computer Science*. Springer.

R.-E. Fan, K.-W. Chang, C.-J. Hsieh, X.-R. Wang, and C.-J. Lin. 2008. LIBLINEAR: A library for large linear classification. *Journal of Machine Learning Research*, 9:1871–1874.

Anne Kool, Jakub Zavrel, and Walter Daelemans. 2000. Simultaneous feature selection and parameter optimization for memory-based natural language processing. In A. Feelders, editor, *BENELEARN 2000. Proceedings of the Tenth Belgian-Dutch Conference on Machine Learning*, pages 93–100. Tilburg University, Tilburg.

Peter Nilsson and Pierre Nugues. 2010. Automatic discovery of feature sets for dependency parsing. In *COLING*, pages 824–832.

Joakim Nivre and Johan Hall. 2010. A quick guide to MaltParser optimization. Technical report, maltparser.org.

Joakim Nivre and Jens Nilsson. 2005. Pseudo-projective dependency parsing. In *Proceedings of the 43rd Annual Meeting of the Association for Computational Linguistics (ACL)*, pages 99–106.

Joakim Nivre, Johan Hall, and Jens Nilsson. 2006. Maltparser: A data-driven parser-generator for dependency parsing. In *Proceedings of the 5th International Conference on Language Resources and Evaluation (LREC)*, pages 2216–2219.

Joakim Nivre, Johan Hall, Sandra Kübler, Ryan McDonald, Jens Nilsson, Sebastian Riedel, and Deniz Yuret. 2007. The CoNLL 2007 shared task on dependency parsing. In *Proceedings of the CoNLL Shared Task of EMNLP-CoNLL 2007*, pages 915–932.

Joakim Nivre, Marco Kuhlmann, and Johan Hall. 2009. An improved oracle for dependency parsing with online reordering. In *Proceedings of the 11th International Conference on Parsing Technologies (IWPT'09)*, pages 73–76.

Joakim Nivre. 2003. An efficient algorithm for projective dependency parsing. In *Proceedings of the 8th International Workshop on Parsing Technologies (IWPT)*, pages 149–160.

Joakim Nivre. 2008. Algorithms for deterministic incremental dependency parsing. *Computational Linguistics*, 34:513–553.

Joakim Nivre. 2009. Non-projective dependency parsing in expected linear time. In *Proceedings of the Joint Conference of the 47th Annual Meeting of the ACL and the 4th International Joint Conference on Natural Language Processing of the AFNLP (ACL-IJCNLP)*, pages 351–359.

Antal Van den Bosch. 2004. Wrapped progressive sampling search for optimizing learning algorithm parameters. In *Proceedings of the 16th Belgian-Dutch Conference on Artificial Intelligence*.

Fluid Construction Grammar: The New Kid on the Block

Remi van Trijp[1], Luc Steels[1,2], Katrien Beuls[3], Pieter Wellens[3]

[1]Sony Computer Science Laboratory Paris
6 Rue Amyot
75005 Paris (France)
`remi@csl.sony.fr`

[2]ICREA Institute for Evolutionary Biology (UPF-CSIC)
PRBB, Dr Aiguidar 88
08003 Barcelona (Spain)
`steels@ai.vub.ac.be`

[3] VUB AI Lab
Pleinlaan 2
1050 Brussels (Belgium)
`katrien|pieter@ai.vub.ac.be`

Abstract

Cognitive linguistics has reached a stage of maturity where many researchers are looking for an explicit formal grounding of their work. Unfortunately, most current models of deep language processing incorporate assumptions from generative grammar that are at odds with the cognitive movement in linguistics. This demonstration shows how Fluid Construction Grammar (FCG), a fully operational and bidirectional unification-based grammar formalism, caters for this increasing demand. FCG features many of the tools that were pioneered in computational linguistics in the 70s-90s, but combines them in an innovative way. This demonstration highlights the main differences between FCG and related formalisms.

1 Introduction

The "cognitive linguistics enterprise" (Evans et al., 2007) is a rapidly expanding research discipline that has so far avoided rigorous formalizations. This choice was wholly justified in the 70s-90s when the foundations of this scientific movement were laid (Rosch, 1975; Lakoff, 1987; Langacker, 1987), and it remained so during the past two decades while the enterprise worked on getting its facts straight through empirical studies in various subfields such as language acquisition (Tomasello, 2003; Goldberg et al., 2004; Lieven, 2009), language change and grammaticalization (Heine et al., 1991; Barðdal and Chelliah, 2009), and corpus research (Boas, 2003; Stefanowitsch and Gries, 2003). However, with numerous textbooks on the market (Lee, 2001; Croft and Cruse, 2004; Evans and Green, 2006), cognitive linguistics has by now established itself as a serious branch in the study of language, and many cognitive linguists are looking for ways of explicitly formalizing their work through computational models (McClelland, 2009).

Unfortunately, it turns out to be very difficult to adequately formalize a cognitive linguistic approach to grammar (or "construction grammar") using the tools for precision-grammars developed in the 70s-90s such as unification (Kay, 1979; Carpenter, 1992), because these tools are typically incorporated in a generative grammar (such as HPSG; Ginzburg and Sag, 2000) whose assumptions are incompatible with the foundations of construction grammar. First, cognitive linguistics blurs the distinction between 'competence' and 'performance', which means giving up the sharp distinction between declarative and procedural representations. Next, construction grammarians argue for a usage-based approach (Langacker, 2000), so the constraints on features may change and features may emerge or disappear from a grammar at any given time.

This demonstration introduces Fluid Construction Grammar (FCG; Steels, 2011, 2012a), a novel unification-based grammar formalism that addresses these issues, and which is available as open-source software at `www.fcg-net.org`. After more than a decade of development, FCG is now ready to handle sophisticated linguistic issues. FCG revisits many of the technologies developed by computational linguists and introduces several key innovations that are of interest to anyone working on deep language processing. The demonstration illustrates these innovations through FCG's interactive web interface.

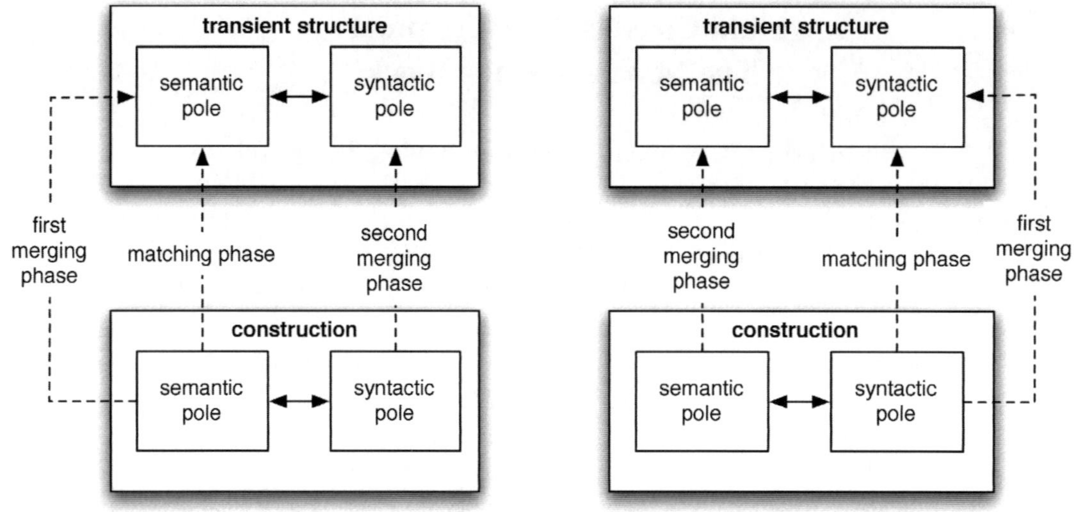

Figure 1: FCG allows the implementation of efficient and strongly reversible grammars. Left: In production, conditional units of the semantic pole of a construction are matched against a transient structure, before additional semantic constraints and the syntactic pole are merged with the structure. Right: In parsing, the same algorithm applies but in the opposite direction.

2 Strong and Efficient Reversibility

Reversible or bidirectional grammar formalisms can achieve both production and parsing (Strzalkowski, 1994). Several platforms, such as the LKB (Copestake, 2002), already achieve bidirectionality, but they do so through separate algorithms for parsing and production (mainly for efficiency reasons). One problem with this approach is that there may be a loss of coherence in grammar engineering. For instance, the LKB parser can handle a wider variety of structures than its generator.

FCG uses one core engine that handles both parsing and production with a single linguistic inventory (see Figure 1). When processing, the FCG-system builds a *transient structure* that contains all the information concerning the utterance that the system has to parse or produce, divided into a semantic and syntactic pole (both of whom are feature structures). Grammar rules or "constructions" are coupled feature structures as well and thus contain a semantic and syntactic pole.

When applying constructions, the FCG-system goes through three phases. In production, FCG first *matches* all feature-value pairs of the semantic pole of a construction with the semantic pole of the transient structure, except fv-pairs that are marked for being attributed by the construction (De Beule and Steels, 2005). Matching is a more strict form of unification that resembles a subsumption test (see Steels and De Beule, 2006). If matching is successful, all the marked fv-pairs of the semantic pole are merged with the transient structure in a first merge phase, after which the whole syntactic pole is merged in a second phase. FCG-merge is equivalent to "unification" in other formalisms. The same three-phase algorithm is applied in parsing as well, but this time in the opposite direction: if the syntactic pole of the construction matches with the transient structure, the attributable syntactic fv-pairs and the semantic pole are merged.

3 WYSIWYG Grammar Engineering

Most unification grammars use non-directional linguistic representations that are designed to be independent of any model of processing (Sag and Wasow, 2011). Whereas this may be desirable from a 'mathematical' point-of-view, it puts the burden of efficient processing on the shoulders of computational linguists, who have to find a balance between faithfulness to the hand-written theory and computational efficiency (Melnik, 2005). For instance, there is no HPSG implementation, but rather several platforms that support the implementation of 'HPSG-like' grammars: ALE (Carpenter and Penn, 1995), ALEP (Schmidt et al., 1996), CUF (Dörre and Dorna,

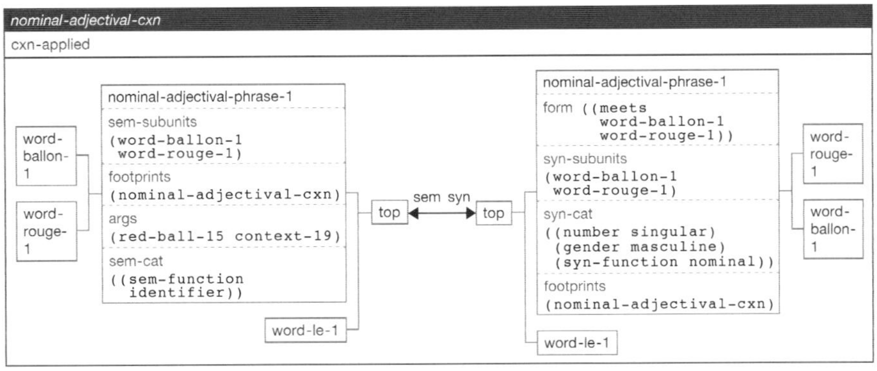

Figure 2: FCG comes equipped with an interactive web interface for inspecting the linguistic inventory, construction application and search. This Figure shows an example construction where two units are opened up for closer inspection of their feature structures.

1993), LIGHT (Ciortuz, 2002), LKB (Copestake, 2002), ProFIT (Erbach, 1995), TDL (Krieger and Schäfer, 1994), TFS (Emele, 1994), and others (see Bolc et al., 1996, for a survey). Unfortunately, the optimizations and technologies developed within these platforms are often considered by theoretical linguists as engineering solutions rather than scientific contributions.

FCG, on the other hand, adheres to the cognitive linguistics assumption that linguistic performance is equally important as linguistic competence, hence processing becomes a central notion in the formalism. FCG representations therefore offer a 'what you see is what you get' approach to grammar engineering where the representations have a direct impact on processing and vice versa. For instance, a construction's division between a semantic and syntactic pole is informative with respect to how the construction is applied.

Some grammarians may object that this design choice forces linguists to worry about processing, but that is entirely the point. It has already been demonstrated in other unification-based formalisms that different grammar representations have a significant impact on processing efficiency (Flickinger, 2000). Moreover, FCG-style representations can be directly implemented and tested without having to compromise on either faithfulness to a theory or computational efficiency.

Since writing grammars is highly complex, however, FCG also features a 'design level' on top of its operational level (Steels, 2012b). On this level, grammar engineers can use templates that build detailed constructions. The demonstration shows how to write a grammar in FCG, switching between its design level, its operational level and its interactive web interface (see Figure 2). The web interface allows FCG-users to inspect the linguistic inventory, the search tree in processing, and so on.

4 Robustness and Learning

Unification-based grammars have the reputation of being brittle when it comes to processing novelty or ungrammatical utterances (Tomuro, 1999). Since cognitive linguistics adheres to a usage-based view on language (Langacker, 2000), however, an adequate formalization must be robust and open-ended.

A first requirement is that there can be different degrees of 'entrenchment' in the grammar: while some features might still be emergent, others are already part of well-conventionalized linguistic patterns. Moreover, new features and constructions may appear (or disappear) from a grammar at any given time. These requirements are hard to reconcile with the *type hierarchy* approach of other formalisms, so FCG does not implement *typed* feature structures. The demonstration shows how FCG can nevertheless prevent over-licensing of linguistic structures through its matching phase and how it captures generalizations through its templates – two benefits typically associated with type hierarchies.

Secondly, FCG renders linguistic processing fluid and robust through a meta-level architecture, which consists of two layers of processing, as shown in Figure 3 (Beuls et al., 2012). There is a routine layer in which constructional processing takes place. At the same time, a meta-layer

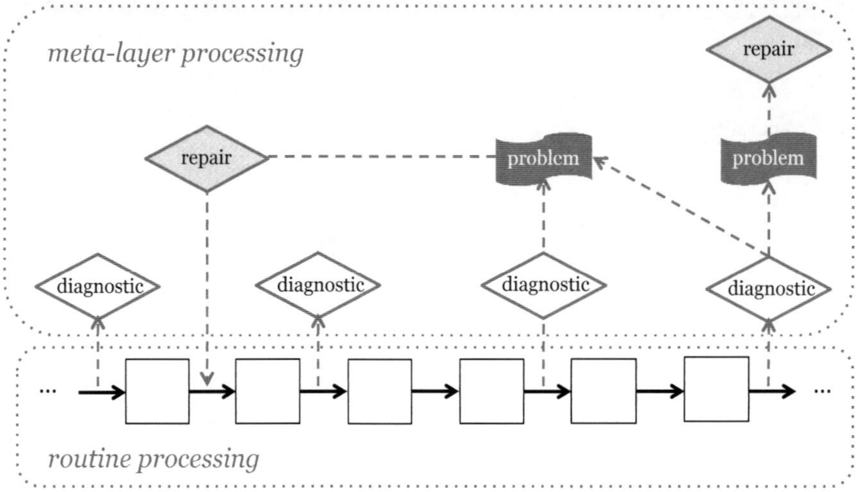

Figure 3: There are two layers of processing in FCG. On the routine level, constructional processing takes place. At the same time, a meta-layer of diagnostics and repairs try to detect and solve problems that occur in the routine layer.

is active that runs *diagnostics* for detecting problems in routine processing, and *repairs* for solving those problems. The demonstration shows how the meta-layer is used for solving common problems such as missing lexical entries and coercion (Steels and van Trijp, 2011), and how its architecture offers a uniform way of implementing the various solutions for robustness already pioneered in the aforementioned grammar platforms.

5 Efficiency

Unification is computationally expensive, and many technical solutions have been proposed for efficient processing of rich and expressive feature structures (Tomuro, 1999; Flickinger, 2000; Callmeier, 2001). In FCG, however, research on efficiency takes a different dimension because performance is considered to be an integral part of the linguistic theory that needs to be operationalized. The demonstration allows conference participants to inspect the following research results on the interplay between grammar and efficiency:

- In line with construction grammar, there is no distinction between the lexicon and the grammar. Based on language usage, the linguistic inventory can nevertheless organize itself in the form of *dependency networks* that regulate which construction should be considered when in processing (Wellens and De Beule, 2010; Wellens, 2011).
- There is abundant psycholinguistic evidence that language usage contains many ready-made language structures. FCG incorporates a chunking mechanism that is able to create such canned phrases for faster processing (Stadler, 2012).
- Morphological paradigms, such as the German case system, can be represented in the form of 'feature matrices', which reduce syntactic and semantic ambiguity and hence speed up processing efficiency and reliability (van Trijp, 2011).
- Many linguistic domains, such as spatial language, are known for their high degree of polysemy. By distinguishing between actual and potential values, such polysemous structures can be processed smoothly (Spranger and Loetzsch, 2011).

6 Conclusion

With many well-developed unification-based grammar formalisms available to the community, one might wonder whether any 'new kid on the block' can still claim relevance today. With this demonstration, we hope to show that Fluid Construction Grammar allows grammar engineers to unchart new territory, most notably in the relation between linguistic competence and performance, and in modeling usage-based approaches to language.

References

Johanna Barðdal and Shobhana Chelliah, editors. *The Role of Semantic, Pragmatic and Discourse Factors in the Development of Case*. John Benjamins, Amsterdam, 2009.

Katrien Beuls, Remi van Trijp, and Pieter Wellens. Diagnostics and repairs in Fluid Construction Grammar. In Luc Steels, editor, *Computational Issues in Fluid Construction Grammar*. Springer Verlag, Berlin, 2012.

Hans C. Boas. *A Constructional Approach to Resultatives*. Stanford Monograph in Linguistics. CSLI, Stanford, 2003.

Leonard Bolc, Krzysztof Czuba, Anna Kupść, Malgorzata Marciniak, Agnieszka Mykowiecka, and Adam Przepiórkowski. A survey of systems for implementing HPSG grammars. Research Report 814 of IPI PAN (Institute of Computer Science, Polish Academy of Sciences), 1996.

Ulrich Callmeier. Efficient parsing with large-scale unification grammars. Master's thesis, Universität des Saarlandes, 2001.

Bob Carpenter. *The Logic of Typed Feature Structures*. Cambridge UP, Cambridge, 1992.

Bob Carpenter and Gerald Penn. *The Attribute Logic Engine (Version 2.0.1)*. Pittsburgh, 1995.

Liviu Ciortuz. LIGHT – a constraint language and compiler system for typed-unification grammars. In *Proceedings of The 25th German Conferences on Artificial Intelligence (KI 2002)*, volume 2479 of *LNAI*, pages 3–17, Berlin, 2002. Springer-Verlag.

Ann Copestake. *Implementing Typed Feature Structure Grammars*. CSLI Publications, Stanford, 2002.

William Croft and D. Alan Cruse. *Cognitive Linguistics*. Cambridge Textbooks in Linguistics. Cambridge University Press, Cambridge, 2004.

J. De Beule and L. Steels. Hierarchy in fluid construction grammar. In U. Furbach, editor, *Proceedings of the 28th Annual German Conference on Artificial Intelligence*, volume 3698 of *Lecture Notes in Artificial Intelligence*, pages 1–15, Berlin, Germany, 2005. Springer Verlag.

Jochen Dörre and Michael Dorna. CUF – a formalism for linguistic knowledge representation. In Jochen Dörre, editor, *Computational Aspects of Constraint Based Linguistic Descriptions*, volume I, pages 1–22. DYANA-2 Project, Amsterdam, 1993.

Martin C. Emele. The typed feature structure representation formalism. In *Proceedings of the International Workshop on Sharable Natural Language Resources*, Ikoma, Nara, 1994.

Gregor Erbach. ProFIT: Prolog with features, inheritance and templates. In *Proceedings of EACL-95*, 1995.

Vyvyan Evans and Melanie Green. *Cognitive Linguistics: An Introduction*. Lawrence Erlbaum Associates / Edinburgh University Press, Hillsdale, NJ/Edinburgh, 2006.

Vyvyan Evans, Benjamin K. Bergen, and Jörg Zinken. The cognitive linguistics enterprise: An overview. In V. Evans, B.K. Bergen, and J. Zinken, editors, *The Cognitive Linguistics Reader*. Equinox Publishing, London, 2007.

Daniel P. Flickinger. On building a more efficient grammar by exploiting types. *Natural Language Engineering*, 6(1):15–28, 2000.

Jonathan Ginzburg and Ivan A. Sag. *Interrogative Investigations: the Form, the Meaning, and Use of English Interrogatives*. CSLI Publications, Stanford, 2000.

Adele E. Goldberg, Devin M. Casenhiser, and Nitya Sethuraman. Learning argument structure generalizations. *Cognitive Linguistics*, 15 (3):289–316, 2004.

Bernd Heine, Ulrike Claudi, and Friederike Hünnemeyer. *Grammaticalization: A Conceptual Framework*. University of Chicago Press, Chicago, 1991.

Martin Kay. Functional grammar. In *Proceedings of the Fifth Annual Meeting of the Berkeley Linguistics Society*, pages 142–158. Berkeley Linguistics Society, 1979.

Hans-Ulrich Krieger and Ulrich Schäfer. TDL – a type description language for HPSG. part 1: Overview. In *Proceedings of the 15th International Conference on Computational Linguistics*, pages 893–899, Kyoto, 1994.

George Lakoff. *Women, Fire, and Dangerous Things: What Categories Reveal about the Mind*. The University of Chicago Press, Chicago, 1987.

Ronald W. Langacker. *Foundations of Cognitive Grammar: Theoretical Prerequisites*. Stanford University Press, Stanford, 1987.

Ronald W. Langacker. A dynamic usage-based model. In Michael Barlow and Suzanne Kemmer, editors, *Usage-Based Models of Language*, pages 1–63. Chicago University Press, Chicago, 2000.

David Lee. *Cognitive Linguistics: An Introduction*. Oxford University Press, Oxford, 2001.

Elena Lieven. Developing constructions. *Cognitive Linguistics*, 20(1):191–199, 2009.

James L. McClelland. The place of modeling in cognitive science. *Topics in Cognitive Science*, 1:11–38, 2009.

Nurit Melnik. From "hand-written" to computationally implemented HPSG theories. In Stefan Müller, editor, *Proceedings of the HPSG05 Conference*, Stanford, 2005. CSLI Publications.

Eleanor Rosch. Cognitive representations of semantic categories. *Journal of Experimental Psychology: General*, 104:192–233, 1975.

Ivan A. Sag and Thomas Wasow. Performance-compatible competence grammar. In Robert D. Borsley and Kersti Börjars, editors, *Non-Transformational Syntax: Formal and Explicit Models of Grammar*, pages 359–377. Wiley-Blackwell, 2011.

Paul Schmidt, Sibylle Rieder, Axel Theofilidis, and Thierry Declerck. Lean formalisms, linguistic theory, and applications. grammar development in ALEP. In *Proceedings of the 16th International Conference on Computational Linguistics (COLING-96)*, pages 286–291, Copenhagen, 1996.

Michael Spranger and Martin Loetzsch. Syntactic indeterminacy and semantic ambiguity: A case study for German spatial phrases. In Luc Steels, editor, *Design Patterns in Fluid Construction Grammar*. John Benjamins, Amsterdam, 2011.

Kevin Stadler. Chunking constructions. In Luc Steels, editor, *Computational Issues in Fluid Construction Grammar*. Springer Verlag, Berlin, 2012.

Luc Steels, editor. *Design Patterns in Fluid Construction Grammar*. John Benjamins, Amsterdam, 2011.

Luc Steels, editor. *Computational Issues in Fluid Construction Grammar*. Springer, Berlin, 2012a.

Luc Steels. Design methods for Fluid Construction Grammar. In Luc Steels, editor, *Computational Issues in Fluid Construction Grammar*. Springer Verlag, Berlin, 2012b.

Luc Steels and Joachim De Beule. Unify and merge in Fluid Construction Grammar. In P. Vogt, Y. Sugita, E. Tuci, and C. Nehaniv, editors, *Symbol Grounding and Beyond.*, LNAI 4211, pages 197–223, Berlin, 2006. Springer.

Luc Steels and Remi van Trijp. How to make construction grammars fluid and robust. In Luc Steels, editor, *Design Patterns in Fluid Construction Grammar*, pages 301–330. John Benjamins, Amsterdam, 2011.

Anatol Stefanowitsch and Stefan Th. Gries. Collostructions: Investigating the interaction of words and constructions. *International Journal of Corpus Linguistics*, 2(8):209–243, 2003.

Tomek Strzalkowski, editor. *Reversible Grammar in Natural Language Processing*. Kluwer Academic Publishers, Boston, 1994.

Michael Tomasello. *Constructing a Language. A Usage Based Theory of Language Acquisition*. Harvard University Press, 2003.

Noriko Tomuro. *Left-Corner Parsing Algorithm for Unification Grammars*. PhD thesis, DePaul University, Chicago, 1999.

Remi van Trijp. Feature matrices and agreement: A case study for German case. In Luc Steels, editor, *Design Patterns in Fluid Construction Grammar*, pages 205–236. John Benjamins, Amsterdam, 2011.

Pieter Wellens. Organizing constructions in networks. In Luc Steels, editor, *Design Patterns in Fluid Construction Grammar*. John Benjamins, Amsterdam, 2011.

Pieter Wellens and Joachim De Beule. Priming through constructional dependencies: A case study in Fluid Construction Grammar. In A. Smith, M. Schouwstra, Bart de Boer, and K. Smith, editors, *The Evolution of Language (EVOLANG8)*, pages 344–351, Singapore, 2010. World Scientific.

A Support Platform for Event Detection using Social Intelligence

Timothy Baldwin, Paul Cook, Bo Han, Aaron Harwood, Shanika Karunasekera and **Masud Moshtaghi**
Department of Computing and Information Systems
The University of Melbourne
Victoria 3010, Australia

Abstract

This paper describes a system designed to support event detection over Twitter. The system operates by querying the data stream with a user-specified set of keywords, filtering out non-English messages, and probabilistically geolocating each message. The user can dynamically set a probability threshold over the geolocation predictions, and also the time interval to present data for.

1 Introduction

Social media and micro-blogs have entered the mainstream of society as a means for individuals to stay in touch with friends, for companies to market products and services, and for agencies to make official announcements. The attractions of social media include their reach (either targeted within a social network or broadly across a large user base), ability to selectively publish/filter information (selecting to publish certain information publicly or privately to certain groups, and selecting which users to follow), and real-time nature (information "push" happens immediately at a scale unachievable with, e.g., email). The serendipitous takeoff in mobile devices and widespread support for social media across a range of devices, have been significant contributors to the popularity and utility of social media.

While much of the content on micro-blogs describes personal trivialities, there is also a vein of high-value content ripe for mining. As such, organisations are increasingly targeting micro-blogs for monitoring purposes, whether it is to gauge product acceptance, detect events such as traffic jams, or track complex unfolding events such as natural disasters.

In this work, we present a system intended to support real-time analysis and geolocation of events based on Twitter. Our system consists of the following steps: (1) user selection of keywords for querying Twitter; (2) preprocessing of the returned queries to rapidly filter out messages not in a pre-selected set of languages, and optionally normalise language content; (3) probabilistic geolocation of messages; and (4) rendering of the data on a zoomable map via a purpose-built web interface, with facility for rich user interaction.

Our starting in the development of this system was the Ushahidi platform,[1] which has high uptake for social media surveillance and information dissemination purposes across a range of organisations. The reason for us choosing to implement our own platform was: (a) ease of integration of back-end processing modules; (b) extensibility, e.g. to visualise probabilities of geolocation predictions, and allow for dynamic thresholding; (c) code maintainability; and (d) greater logging facility, to better capture user interactions.

2 Example System Usage

A typical user session begins with the user specifying a disjunctive set of keywords, which are used as the basis for a query to the Twitter Streaming API.[2] Messages which match the query are dynamically rendered on an OpenStreetMap mash-up, indexed based on (grid cell-based) location. When the user clicks on a location marker, they are presented with a pop-up list of messages matching the location. The user can manipulate a time slider to alter the time period over which to present results (e.g. in the last 10 minutes, or over

[1] `http://ushahidi.com/`

[2] `https://dev.twitter.com/docs/streaming-api`

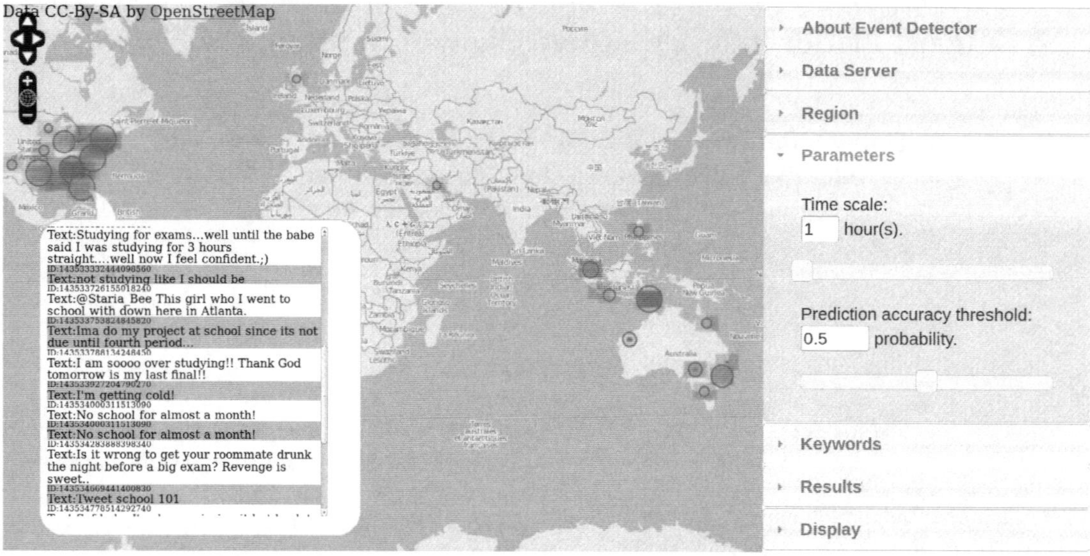

Figure 1: A screenshot of the system, with a pop-up presentation of the messages at the indicated location.

the last hour), to gain a better sense of report recency. The user can further adjust the threshold of the prediction accuracy for the probabilistic message locations to view a smaller number of messages with higher-confidence locations, or more messages that have lower-confidence locations.

A screenshot of the system for the following query is presented in Figure 1:

> *study studying exam "end of semester" examination test tests school exams university pass fail "end of term" snow snowy snowdrift storm blizzard flurry flurries ice icy cold chilly freeze freezing frigid winter*

3 System Details

The system is composed of a front-end, which provides a GUI interface for query parameter input, and a back-end, which computes a result for each query. The front-end submits the query parameters to the back-end via a servlet. Since the result for the query is time-dependent, the back-end regularly re-evaluates the query, generating an up-to-date result at regular intervals. The front-end regularly polls the back-end, via another servlet, for the latest results that match its submitted query. In this way, the front-end and back-end are loosely coupled and asynchronous.

Below, we describe details of the various modules of the system.

3.1 Twitter Querying

When the user inputs a set of keywords, this is issued as a disjunctive query to the Twitter Streaming API, which returns a streamed set of results in JSON format. The results are parsed, and piped through to the language filtering, lexical normalisation, and geolocation modules, and finally stored in a flat file, which the GUI interacts with.

3.2 Language Filtering

For language identification, we use `langid.py`, a language identification toolkit developed at The University of Melbourne (Lui and Baldwin, 2011).[3] `langid.py` combines a naive Bayes classifier with cross-domain feature selection to provide domain-independent language identification. It is available under a FOSS license as a stand-alone module pre-trained over 97 languages. `langid.py` has been developed specifically to be able to keep pace with the speed of messages through the Twitter "garden hose" feed on a single-CPU machine, making it particularly attractive for this project. Additionally, in an in-house evaluation over three separate corpora of Twitter data, we have found `langid.py` to be overall more accurate than other state-of-the-art language identification systems such as

[3] `http://www.csse.unimelb.edu.au/research/lt/resources/langid`

`lang-detect`[4] and the Compact Language Detector (CLD) from the Chrome browser.[5]

`langid.py` returns a monolingual prediction of the language content of a given message, and is used to filter out all non-English tweets.

3.3 Lexical Normalisation

The prevalence of noisy tokens in microblogs (e.g. *yr* "your" and *soooo* "so") potentially hinders the readability of messages. Approaches to lexical normalisation—i.e., replacing noisy tokens by their standard forms in messages (e.g. replacing *yr* with *your*)—could potentially overcome this problem. At present, lexical normalisation is an optional plug-in for post-processing messages.

A further issue related to noisy tokens is that it is possible that a relevant tweet might contain a variant of a query term, but not that query term itself. In future versions of the system we therefore aim to use query expansion to generate noisy versions of query terms to retrieve additional relevant tweets. We subsequently intend to perform lexical normalisation to evaluate the precision of the returned data.

The present lexical normalisation used by our system is the dictionary lookup method of Han and Baldwin (2011) which normalises noisy tokens only when the normalised form is known with high confidence (e.g. *you* for *u*). Ultimately, however, we are interested in performing context-sensitive lexical normalisation, based on a reimplementation of the method of Han and Baldwin (2011). This method will allow us to target a wider variety of noisy tokens such as typos (e.g. *earthquak* "earthquake"), abbreviations (e.g. *lv* "love"), phonetic substitutions (e.g. *b4* "before") and vowel lengthening (e.g. *goooood* "good").

3.4 Geolocation

A vital component of event detection is the determination of where the event is happening, e.g. to make sense of reports of traffic jams or floods. While Twitter supports device-based geotagging of messages, less than 1% of messages have geotags (Cheng et al., 2010). One alternative is to return the user-level registered location as the event location, based on the assumption that most users report on events in their local domicile. However, only about one quarter of users have registered locations (Cheng et al., 2010), and even when there is a registered location, there's no guarantee of its quality. A better solution would appear to be the automatic prediction of the geolocation of the message, along with a probabilistic indication of the prediction quality.[6]

Geolocation prediction is based on the terms used in a given message, based on the assumption that it will contain explicit mentions of local place names (e.g. *London*) or use locally-identifiable language (e.g. *jawn*, which is characteristic of the Philadelphia area). By including a probability with the prediction, we can give the system user control over what level of noise they are prepared to see in the predictions, and hopefully filter out messages where there is insufficient or conflicting geolocating evidence.

We formulate the geolocation prediction problem as a multinomial naive Bayes classification problem, based on its speed and accuracy over the task. Given a message m, the task is to output the most probable location $loc_{max} \in \{loc_i\}_1^n$ for m. User-level classification can be performed based on a similar formulation, by combining the total set of messages from a given user into a single combined message.

Given a message m, the task is to find $\arg\max_i P(loc_i|m)$ where each loc_i is a grid cell on the map. Based on Bayes' theorem and standard assumptions in the naive Bayes formulation, this is transformed into:

$$\arg\max_i P(loc_i) \prod_j^v P(w_j|loc_i)$$

To avoid zero probabilities, we only consider tokens that occur at least twice in the training data, and ignore unseen words. A probability is calculated for the most-probable location by normalising over the scores for each loc_i.

We employ the method of Ritter et al. (2011) to tokenise messages, and use token unigrams as features, including any hashtags, but ignoring twitter mentions, URLs and purely numeric tokens. We

[4] `http://code.google.com/p/language-detection/`

[5] `http://code.google.com/p/chromium-compact-language-detector/`

[6] Alternatively, we could consider a hybrid approach of user- and message-level geolocation prediction, especially for users where we have sufficient training data, which we plan to incorporate into a future version of the system.

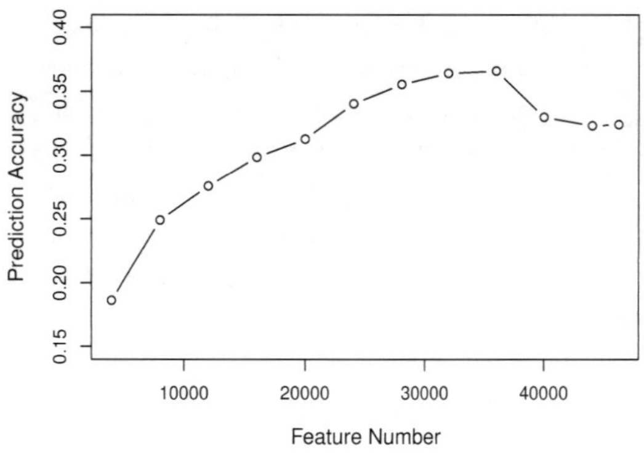

Figure 2: Accuracy of geolocation prediction, for varying numbers of features based on information gain

also experimented with included the named entity predictions of the Ritter et al. (2011) method into our system, but found that it had no impact on predictive accuracy. Finally, we apply feature selection to the data, based on information gain (Yang and Pedersen, 1997).

To evaluate the geolocation prediction module, we use the user-level geolocation dataset of Cheng et al. (2010), based on the lower 48 states of the USA. The user-level accuracy of our method over this dataset, for varying numbers of features based on information gain, can be seen in Figure 2. Based on these results, we select the top 36,000 features in the deployed version of the system.

In the deployed system, the geolocation prediction model is trained over one million geotagged messages collected over a 4 month period from July 2011, resolved to 0.1-degree latitude/longitude grid cells (covering the whole globe, excepting grid locations where there were less than 8 messages). For any geotagged messages in the test data, we preserve the geotag and simply set the probability of the prediction to 1.0.

3.5 System Interface

The final output of the various pre-processing modules is a list of tweets that match the query, in the form of an 8-tuple as follows:

- the Twitter user ID
- the Twitter message ID
- the geo-coordinates of the message (either provided with the message, or automatically predicted)
- the probability of the predicated geolocation
- the text of the tweet

In addition to specifying a set of keywords for a given session, system users can dynamically select regions on the map, either via the manual specification of a bounding box, or zooming the map in and out. They can additionally change the time scale to display messages over, specify the refresh interval and also adjust the threshold on the geolocation predictions, to not render any messages which have a predictive probability below the threshold. The size of each place marker on the map is rendered proportional to the number of messages at that location, and a square is superimposed over the box to represent the maximum predictive probability for a single message at that location (to provide user feedback on both the volume of predictions and the relative confidence of the system at a given location).

References

Zhiyuan Cheng, James Caverlee, and Kyumin Lee. 2010. You are where you tweet: a content-based approach to geo-locating twitter users. In *Proceedings of the 19th ACM international conference on Information and knowledge management*, CIKM '10, pages 759–768, Toronto, ON, Canada. ACM.

Bo Han and Timothy Baldwin. 2011. Lexical normalisation of short text messages: Makn sens a #twitter. In *Proceedings of the 49th Annual Meeting of the Association for Computational Linguistics: Human Language Technologies (ACL HLT 2011)*, pages 368–378, Portland, USA.

Marco Lui and Timothy Baldwin. 2011. Cross-domain feature selection for language identification. In *Proceedings of the 5th International Joint Conference on Natural Language Processing (IJCNLP 2011)*, pages 553–561, Chiang Mai, Thailand.

Alan Ritter, Sam Clark, Mausam, and Oren Etzioni. 2011. Named entity recognition in tweets: An experimental study. In *Proceedings of the 2011 Conference on Empirical Methods in Natural Language Processing*, pages 1524–1534, Edinburgh, Scotland, UK., July. Association for Computational Linguistics.

Yiming Yang and Jan O. Pedersen. 1997. A comparative study on feature selection in text categorization. In *Proceedings of the Fourteenth International Conference on Machine Learning*, ICML '97, pages 412–420, San Francisco, CA, USA. Morgan Kaufmann Publishers Inc.

NERD: A Framework for Unifying Named Entity Recognition and Disambiguation Extraction Tools

Giuseppe Rizzo
EURECOM / Sophia Antipolis, France
Politecnico di Torino / Turin, Italy
giuseppe.rizzo@eurecom.fr

Raphaël Troncy
EURECOM / Sophia Antipolis, France
raphael.troncy@eurecom.fr

Abstract

Named Entity Extraction is a mature task in the NLP field that has yielded numerous services gaining popularity in the Semantic Web community for extracting knowledge from web documents. These services are generally organized as pipelines, using dedicated APIs and different taxonomy for extracting, classifying and disambiguating named entities. Integrating one of these services in a particular application requires to implement an appropriate driver. Furthermore, the results of these services are not comparable due to different formats. This prevents the comparison of the performance of these services as well as their possible combination. We address this problem by proposing NERD, a framework which unifies 10 popular named entity extractors available on the web, and the NERD ontology which provides a rich set of axioms aligning the taxonomies of these tools.

1 Introduction

The web hosts millions of unstructured data such as scientific papers, news articles as well as forum and archived mailing list threads or (micro-)blog posts. This information has usually a rich semantic structure which is clear for the human being but that remains mostly hidden to computing machinery. Natural Language Processing (NLP) tools aim to extract such a structure from those free texts. They provide algorithms for analyzing atomic information elements which occur in a sentence and identify Named Entity (NE) such as name of people or organizations, locations, time references or quantities. They also classify these entities according to predefined schema increasing discoverability (e.g. through faceted search) and reusability of information.

Recently, research and commercial communities have spent efforts to publish NLP services on the web. Beside the common task of identifying POS and of reducing this set to NEs, they provide more and more disambiguation facility with URIs that describe web resources, leveraging on the web of real world objects. Moreover, these services classify such information using common ontologies (e.g. DBpedia ontology[1] or YAGO[2]) exploiting the large amount of knowledge available from the web of data. Tools such as AlchemyAPI[3], DBpedia Spotlight[4], Evri[5], Extractiv[6], Lupedia[7], OpenCalais[8], Saplo[9], Wikimeta[10], Yahoo! Content Extraction[11] and Zemanta[12] represent a clear opportunity for the web community to increase the volume of interconnected data. Although these extractors share the same purpose - extract NE from text, classify and disambiguate this information - they make use of different algorithms and provide different outputs.

This paper presents NERD (Named Entity Recognition and Disambiguation), a framework that unifies the output of 10 different NLP extrac-

[1] http://wiki.dbpedia.org/Ontology
[2] http://www.mpi-inf.mpg.de/yago-naga/yago
[3] http://www.alchemyapi.com
[4] http://dbpedia.org/spotlight
[5] http://www.evri.com/developer
[6] http://extractiv.com
[7] http://lupedia.ontotext.com/
[8] http://www.opencalais.com
[9] http://www.saplo.com/
[10] http://www.wikimeta.com
[11] http://developer.yahoo.com/search/content/V2/contentAnalysis.html
[12] http://www.zemanta.com

tors publicly available on the web. Our approach relies on the development of the NERD ontology which provides a common interface for annotating elements, and a web REST API which is used to access the unified output of these tools. We compare 6 different systems using NERD and we discuss some quantitative results. The NERD application is accessible online at `http://nerd.eurecom.fr`. It requires to input a URI of a web document that will be analyzed and optionally an identification of the user for recording and sharing the analysis.

2 Framework

NERD is a web application plugged on top of various NLP tools. Its architecture follows the REST principles and provides a web HTML access for humans and an API for computers to exchange content in JSON or XML. Both interfaces are powered by the NERD REST engine. The Figure 2 shows the workflow of an interaction among clients (humans or computers), the NERD REST engine and various NLP tools which are used by NERD for extracting NEs, for providing a type and disambiguation URIs pointing to real world objects as they could be defined in the Web of Data.

2.1 NERD interfaces

The web interface[13] is developed in HTML/-Javascript. It accepts any URI of a web document which is analyzed in order to extract its main textual content. Starting from the raw text, it drives one or several tools to extract the list of Named Entity, their classification and the URIs that disambiguate these entities. The main purpose of this interface is to enable a human user to assess the quality of the extraction results collected by those tools (Rizzo and Troncy, 2011a). At the end of the evaluation, the user sends the results, through asynchronous calls, to the REST API engine in order to store them. This set of evaluations is further used to compute statistics about precision scores for each tool, with the goal to highlight strengths and weaknesses and to compare them (Rizzo and Troncy, 2011b). The comparison aggregates all the evaluations performed and, finally, the user is free to select one or more evaluations to see the metrics that are computed for each service in real time. Finally, the application contains a help page that provides guidance and details about the whole evaluation process.

The API interface[14] is developed following the REST principles and aims to enable programmatic access to the NERD framework. GET, POST and PUT methods manage the requests coming from clients to retrieve the list of NEs, classification types and URIs for a specific tool or for the combination of them. They take as inputs the URI of the document to process and a user key for authentication. The output sent back to the client can be serialized in JSON or XML depending on the content type requested. The output follows the schema described below (in the JSON serialization):


```
entities: [{
    "entity":"Tim Berners-Lee",
    "type":"Person",
    "uri":"http://dbpedia.org/resource/
        Tim_berners_lee",
    "nerdType":"http://nerd.eurecom.fr/
        ontology#Person",
    "startChar": 30,
    "endChar": 45,
    "confidence": 1,
    "relevance": 0.5
}]
```


2.2 NERD REST engine

The REST engine runs on Jersey[15] and Grizzly[16] technologies. Their extensible framework allows to develop several components, so NERD is composed of 7 modules, namely: authentication, scraping, extraction, ontology mapping, store, statistics and web. The authentication enables to log in with an OpenID provider and subsequently attaches all analysis and evaluations performed by a user with his profile. The scraping module takes as input the URI of an article and extracts its main textual content. Extraction is the module designed to invoke the external service APIs and collect the results. Each service provides its own taxonomy of named entity types it can recognize. We therefore designed the NERD ontology which provides a set of mappings between these various classifications. The ontology mapping is the module in charge to map the classification type retrieved to the NERD ontology. The store module saves all evaluations according to the schema model we defined in the

[13] `http://nerd.eurecom.fr`

[14] `http://nerd.eurecom.fr/api/application.wadl`

[15] `http://jersey.java.net`

[16] `http://grizzly.java.net`

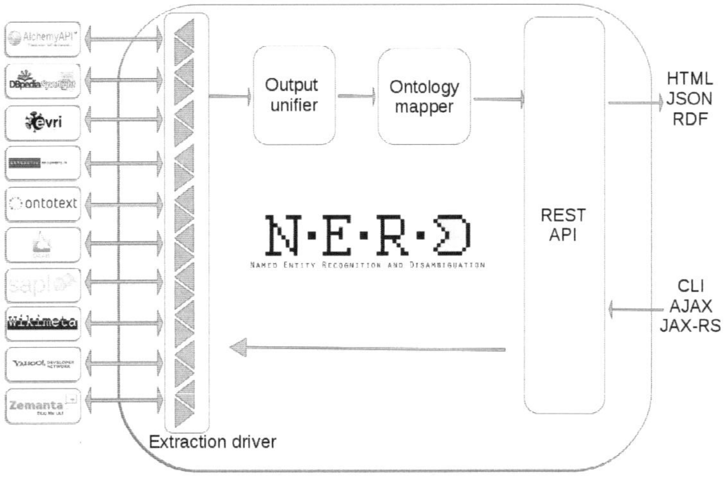

Figure 1: A user interacts with NERD through a REST API. The engine drives the extraction to the NLP extractor. The NERD REST engine retrieves the output, unifies it and maps the annotations to the NERD ontology. Finally, the output result is sent back to the client using the format reported in the initial request.

NERD database. The statistic module enables to extract data patterns from the user interactions stored in the database and to compute statistical scores such as Fleiss Kappa and precision/recall analysis. Finally, the web module manages the client requests, the web cache and generates the HTML pages.

3 NERD ontology

Although these tools share the same goal, they use different algorithms and their own classification taxonomies which makes hard their comparison. To address this problem, we have developed the NERD ontology which is a set of mappings established manually between the schemas of the Named Entity categories. Concepts included in the NERD ontology are collected from different schema types: ontology (for DBpedia Spotlight and Zemanta), lightweight taxonomy (for AlchemyAPI, Evri and Wikimeta) or simple flat type lists (for Extractiv, OpenCalais and Wikimeta). A concept is included in the NERD ontology as soon as there are at least two tools that use it. The NERD ontology becomes a reference ontology for comparing the classification task of NE tools. In other words, NERD is a set of axioms useful to enable comparison of NLP tools. We consider the DBpedia ontology exhaustive enough to represent all the concepts involved in a NER task. For all those concepts that do not appear in the NERD namespace, there are just sub-classes of parents that end-up in the NERD ontology. This ontology is available at `http://nerd.eurecom.fr/ontology`.

We provide the following example mapping among those tools which defines the `City` type: the `nerd:City` class is considered as being equivalent to `alchemy:City`, `dbpedia-owl:City`, `extractiv:CITY`, `opencalais:City`, `evri:City` while being more specific than `wikimeta:LOC` and `zemanta:location`.

```
nerd:City a rdfs:Class ;
  rdfs:subClassOf wikimeta:LOC ;
  rdfs:subClassOf zemanta:location ;
  owl:equivalentClass alchemy:City ;
  owl:equivalentClass dbpedia-owl:City ;
  owl:equivalentClass evri:City ;
  owl:equivalentClass extractiv:CITY ;
  owl:equivalentClass opencalais:City .
```

4 Ontology alignment results

We conducted an experiment to assess the alignment of the NERD framework according to the ontology we developed. For this experiment, we collected 1000 news articles of The New York Times from 09/10/2011 to 12/10/2011 and we performed the extraction of named entities with the tools supported by NERD. The goal is to explore the NE extraction patterns with this dataset and to assess commonalities and differences of the classification schema used. We propose the alignment of the 6 main types recognized by all tools using the NERD ontology. To conduct this experiment, we used the default configuration for all tools used. We define the following variables:

	AlchemyAPI	DBpedia Spotlight	Evri	Extractiv	OpenCalais	Zemanta
Person	6,246	14	2,698	5,648	5,615	1,069
Organization	2,479	-	900	81	2,538	180
Country	1,727	2	1,382	2,676	1,707	720
City	2,133	-	845	2,046	1,863	-
Time	-	-	-	123	1	-
Number	-	-	-	3,940	-	-

Table 1: Number of axioms aligned for all the tools involved in the comparison according to the NERD ontology for the sources collected from the *The New York Times* from 09/10/2011 to 12/10/2011.

the number n_d of evaluated documents, the number n_w of words, the total number n_e of entities, the total number n_c of categories and n_u URIs. Moreover, we compute the following metrics: word detection rate $r(w, d)$, i.e. the number of words per document, entity detection rate $r(e, d)$, i.e. the number of entities per document, entity detection rate per word, i.e. the ratio between entities and words $r(e, w)$, category detection rate, i.e. the number of categories per document $r(c, d)$ and URI detection rate, i.e. the number of URIs per document $r(u, d)$. The evaluation we performed concerned $n_d = 1000$ documents that amount to $n_w = 620, 567$ words. The word detection rate per document $r(w, d)$ is equal to 620.57 and the total number of recognized entities n_e is $164, 12$ with the $r(e, d)$ equal to 164.17. Finally $r(e, w)$ is 0.0264, $r(c, d)$ is 0.763 and $r(u, d)$ is 46.287.

Table 1 shows the classification comparison results. DBpedia Spotlight recognizes very few classes. Zemanta increases significantly classification performances with respect to DBpedia obtaining a number of recognized Person which is two magnitude order more important. AlchemyAPI has strong ability to recognize Person and City while obtaining significant scores for Organization and Country. OpenCalais shows good results to recognize the class Person and a strong ability to classify NEs with the label Organization. Extractiv holds the best score for classifying Country and it is the only extractor capable of extracting the classes Time and Number.

5 Conclusion

In this paper, we presented NERD, a framework developed following REST principles, and the NERD ontology, a reference ontology to map several NER tools publicly accessible on the web. We propose a preliminary comparison results where we investigate the importance of a reference ontology in order to evaluate the strengths and weaknesses of the NER extractors. We will investigate whether the combination of extractors may overcome the performance of a single tool or not. We will demonstrate more live examples of what NERD can achieve during the conference. Finally, with the increasing interest of interconnecting data on the web, a lot of research effort is spent to aggregate the results of NLP tools. The importance to have a system able to compare them is under investigation from the NIF[17] (NLP Interchange Format) project. NERD has recently been integrated with NIF (Rizzo and Troncy, 2012) and the NERD ontology is a milestone for creating a reference ontology for this task.

Acknowledgments

This paper was supported by the French Ministry of Industry (*Innovative Web* call) under contract 09.2.93.0966, “Collaborative Annotation for Video Accessibility” (ACAV).

References

Rizzo G. and Troncy R. 2011. *NERD: A Framework for Evaluating Named Entity Recognition Tools in the Web of Data.* 10th International Semantic Web Conference (ISWC'11), Demo Session, Bonn, Germany.

Rizzo G. and Troncy R. 2011. *NERD: Evaluating Named Entity Recognition Tools in the Web of Data.* Workshop on Web Scale Knowledge Extraction (WEKEX'11), Bonn, Germany.

Rizzo G., Troncy R, Hellmann S and Bruemmer M. 2012. *NERD meets NIF: Lifting NLP Extraction Results to the Linked Data Cloud.* 5th International Workshop on Linked Data on the Web (LDOW'12), Lyon, France.

[17] `http://nlp2rdf.org`

Automatic Analysis of Patient History Episodes in Bulgarian Hospital Discharge Letters

Svetla Boytcheva
State University of Library Studies
and Information Technologies
and IICT-BAS
svetla.boytcheva@gmail.com

Galia Angelova, Ivelina Nikolova
Institute of Information and
Communication Technologies (IICT),
Bulgarian Academy of Sciences (BAS)
{galia,iva}@lml.bas.bg

Abstract

This demo presents Information Extraction from discharge letters in Bulgarian language. The *Patient history* section is automatically split into episodes (clauses between two temporal markers); then drugs, diagnoses and conditions are recognised within the episodes with accuracy higher than 90%. The temporal markers, which refer to *absolute* or *relative* moments of time, are identified with precision 87% and recall 68%. The direction of time for the episode starting point: *backwards* or *forward* (with respect to certain moment orienting the episode) is recognised with precision 74.4%.

1 Introduction

Temporal information processing is a challenge in medical informatics (Zhou and Hripcsak, 2007) and (Hripcsak et al., 2005). There is no agreement about the features of the temporal models which might be extracted automatically from free texts. Some sophisticated approaches aim at the adaptation of TimeML-based tags to clinically-important entities (Savova et al., 2009) while others identify dates and prepositional phrases containing temporal expressions (Angelova and Boytcheva, 2011). Most NLP prototypes for automatic temporal analysis of clinical narratives deal with discharge letters.

This demo presents a prototype for automatic splitting of the *Patient history* into episodes and extraction of important patient-related events that occur within these episodes. We process Electronic Health Records (EHRs) of diabetic patients. In Bulgaria, due to centralised regulations on medical documentation (which date back to the 60's of the last century), hospital discharge letters have a predefined structure (Agreement, 2005). Using the section headers, our Information Extraction (IE) system automatically identifies the *Patient history* (Anamnesis). It contains a summary, written by the medical expert who hospitalises the patient, and documents the main phases in diabetes development, the main interventions and their effects. The splitting algorithm is based on the assumption that the *Patient history* texts can be represented as a structured sequence of adjacent clauses which are positioned between two temporal markers and report about some important events happening in the designated period. The temporal markers are usually accompanied by words signaling the direction of time (backward or forward). Thus we assume that the episodes have the following structure: *(i)* reference point, *(ii)* direction, *(iii)* temporal expression, *(iv)* diagnoses, *(v)* symptoms, syndromes, conditions, or complains; *(vi)* drugs; *(vii)* treatment outcome. The demo will show how our IE system automatically fills in the seven slots enumerated above. Among all symptoms and conditions, which are complex phrases and paraphrases, the extraction of features related to polyuria and polydipsia, weight change and blood sugar value descriptions will be demonstrated. Our present corpus contains 1,375 EHRs.

2 Recognition of Temporal Markers

Temporal information is very important in clinical narratives: there are 8,248 markers and 8,249 words/phrases signaling the direction backwards or forward in the corpus (while the drug name occurrences are 7,108 and the diagnoses are 7,565).

In the hospital information system, there are two explicitly fixed dates: the patient birth date and the hospitalisation date. Both of them are used as antecedents of temporal anaphora:

- the hospitalisation date is a reference point for 37.2% of all temporal expressions (e.g. '*since 5 years*', '*(since) last March*', '*3 years ago*', '*two weeks ago*', '*diabetes duration 22 years*', '*during the last 3 days*' etc.). For 8.46% of them, the expression allows for calculation of a particular date when the corresponding event has occurred;
- the age (calculated using the birth date) is a reference point for 2.1% of all temporal expressions (e.g. '*diabetes diagnosed in the age of 22 years*').

Some 28.96% of the temporal markers refer to an explicitly specified year which we consider as an *absolute* reference. Another 15.1% of the markers contain reference to day, month and year, and in this way 44.06% of the temporal expressions explicitly refer to dates. Adding to these 44.06% the above-listed referential citations of the hospitalization date and the birth date, we see that 83.36% of the temporal markers refer to explicitly specified moments of time and can be seen as *absolute* references. We note that diabetes is a chronicle disease and references like '*diabetes diagnosed 30 years ago*' are sufficiently precise to be counted as explicit temporal pointers.

The anaphoric expressions refer to events described in the *Patient history* section: these expressions are 2.63% of the temporal markers (e.g. '*20 days after the operation*', '*3 years after diagnosing the diabetes*', '*about 1 year after that*', '*with the same duration*' etc.). We call these expressions *relative temporal markers* and note that much of our temporal knowledge is relative and cannot be described by a date (Allen, 1983).

The remaining 14% of the temporal markers are undetermined, like '*many years ago*', '*before the puberty*', '*in young age*', '*long-duration diabetes*'. About one third of these markers refer to periods e.g. '*for a period of 3 years*', '*with duration of 10-15 years*' and need to be interpreted inside the episode where they occur.

Identifying a temporal expression in some sentence in the *Patient history*, we consider it as a signal for a new episode. Thus it is very important to recognise automatically the time anchors of the events described in the episode: whether they happen *at* the moment, designated by the marker, *after* or *before* it. The temporal markers are accompanied by words signaling time direction *backwards* or *forward* as follows:

- the preposition '*since*' (от) unambiguously designates the episode startpoint and the time interval when the events happen. It occurs in 46.78% of the temporal markers;

- the preposition '*in*' (през) designates the episode startpoint with probability 92.14%. It points to a moment of time and often marks the beginning of a new period. But the events happening after '*in*' might refer backwards to past moments, like e.g. '*diabetes diagnosed in 2004, (as the patient) lost 20 kg in 6 months with reduced appetite*'. So there could be past events embedded in the '*in*'-started episodes which should be considered as separate episodes (but are really difficult for automatic identification);

- the preposition '*after*' (след) unambiguously identifies a relative time moment oriented to the immediately preceding event e.g. '*after that*' with synonym '*later*' e.g. '*one year later*'. Another kind of reference is explicit event specification e.g. '*after the Maninil has been stopped*';

- the preposition '*before*' or '*ago*' (преди) is included in 11.2% of all temporal markers in our corpus. In 97.4% of its occurrences it is associated to a number of years/months/days and refers to the hospitalisation date, e.g. '*3 years ago*', '*two weeks ago*'. In 87.6% of its occurrences it denotes starting points in the past after which some events happen. However, there are cases when '*ago*' marks an endpoint, e.g. '*Since 1995 the hypertony 150/100 was treated by Captopril 25mg, later by Enpril 10mg but two years ago the therapy has been stopped because of hypotony*';

- the preposition '*during, throughout*' (в продължение на) occurs relatively rarely, only in 1.02% of all markers. It is usually associated with explicit time period.

3 Recognition of Diagnoses and Drugs

We have developed high-quality extractors of diagnoses, drugs and dosages from EHRs in Bulgarian language. These two extracting components are integrated in our IE system which processes *Patient history* episodes.

Phrases designating diagnoses are juxtaposed to ICD-10 codes (ICD, 10). Major difficulties in matching ICD-10 diseases to text units are due to *(i)* numerous Latin terms written in Latin or Cyrillic alphabets; *(ii)* a large variety of abbreviations; *(iii)* descriptions which are hard to associate to ICD-10 codes, and *(iv)* various types of ambiguity e.g. text fragments that might be juxtaposed to many ICD-10 labels.

The drug extractor finds in the EHR texts 1,850 brand names of drugs and their daily dosages. Drug extraction is based on algorithms using regular expressions to describe linguistic patterns. The variety of textual expressions as well as the absent or partial dosage descriptions impede the extraction performance. Drug names are juxtaposed to ATC codes (ATC, 11).

4 IE of symptoms and conditions

Our aim is to identify diabetes symptoms and conditions in the free text of *Patient history*. The main challenge is to recognise automatically phrases and paraphrases for which no "canonical forms" exist in any dictionary. Symptom extraction is done over a corpus of 1,375 discharge letters. We analyse certain dominant factors when diagnosing with diabetes - values of blood sugar, body weight change and polyuria, polydipsia descriptions. Some examples follow:

(i) *Because of polyuria-polydipsia syndrome, blood sugar was - 19 mmol/l.*
(ii) *... on the background of obesity - 117 kg...*

The challenge in the task is not only to identify sentences or phrases referring to such expressions but to determine correctly the borders of the description, recognise the values, the direction of change - increased or decreased value and to check whether the expression is negated or not.

The extraction of symptoms is a hybrid method which includes document classification and rule-based pattern recognition. It is done by a 6-steps algorithm as follows: *(i)* manual selection of symptom descriptions from a training corpus; *(ii)* compiling a list of keyterms per each symptom; *(iii)* compiling probability vocabularies for left- and right-border tokens per each symptom description according to the frequencies of the left- and right-most tokens in the list of symptom descriptions; *(iv)* compiling a list of features per each symptom (these are all tokens available in the keyterms list without the stop words); *(v)* performing document classification for selecting the documents containing the symptom of interest based on the feature selection in the previous step and *(vi)* selection of symptom descriptions by applying consecutively rules employing the keyterms vocabulary and the left- and right-border tokens vocabularies. For overcoming the inflexion of Bulgarian language we use stemming.

The last step could be actually segmented into five subtasks such as: focusing on the expressions which contain the terms; determining the scope of the expressions; deciding on the condition worsening - increased, decreased values; identifying the values - interval values, simple values, measurement units etc. The final subtask is to determine whether the expression is negated or not.

5 Evaluation results

The evaluation of all linguistic modules is performed in close cooperation with medical experts who assess the methodological feasibility of the approach and its practical usefulness.

The temporal markers, which refer to *absolute* or *relative* moments of time, are identified with precision 87% and recall 68%. The direction of time for the episode events: backwards or forward (with respect to certain moment orienting the episode) is recognised with precision 74.4%.

ICD-10 codes are associated to phrases with precision 84.5%. Actually this component has been developed in a previous project where it was run on 6,200 EHRs and has extracted 26,826 phrases from the EHR section *Diagnoses*; correct ICD-10 codes were assigned to 22,667 phrases. In this way the ICD-10 extractor uses a dictionary of 22,667 phrases which designate 478 ICD-10 disease names occurring in diabetic EHRs (Boytcheva, 2011a).

Drug names are juxtaposed to ATC codes with f-score 98.42%; the drug dosage is recognised with f-score 93.85% (Boytcheva, 2011b). This result is comparable to the accuracy of the best systems e.g. MedEx which extracts medication events with 93.2% f-score for drug names, 94.5% for dosage, 93.9% for route and 96% for frequency (Xu et al., 2010). We also identify the drugs taken by the patient at the moment of hospitalisation. This is evaluated on 355 drug names occurring in the EHRs of diabetic patients. The extraction is done with f-score 94.17% for drugs in *Patient history* (over-generation 6%) (Boytcheva et al., 2011).

In the separate phases of symptom description extraction the f-score goes up to 96%. The complete blood sugar descriptions are identified with 89% f-score; complete weight change descriptions - with 75% and complete polyuria and polydipsia descriptions with 90%. These figures are comparable to the success of extracting conditions, reported in (Harkema et al., 2009).

6 Demonstration

The demo presents: *(i)* the extractors of diagnoses, drugs and conditions within episodes and *(ii)* their integration within a framework for temporal segmentation of the *Patient history* into episodes with identification of temporal markers and time direction. Thus the prototype automatically recognises the time period, when some events of interest have occurred.

Example 1. (April 2004) Diabetes diagnosed last August with blood sugar values 14mmol/l. Since then put on a diet but without following it too strictly. Since December follows the diet but the blood sugar decreases to 12mmol/l. This makes it necessary to prescribe Metfodiab in the morning and at noon 1/2t. since 15.I. Since then the body weight has been reduced with about 6 kg. Complains of fornication in the lower limbs.

This history is broken down into the episodes, imposed by the time markers (table 1). Please note that we suggest no order for the episodes. This should be done by a temporal reasoner.

However, it is hard to cope with expressions like the ones in Examples 2-5, where more than one temporal marker occurs in the same sentence with possibly diverse orientation. This requires semantic analysis of the events happening within the sentences. *Example 2*: Since 1,5 years with growing swelling of the feet which became permanent and massive since the summer of 2003. *Example 3*: Diabetes type 2 with duration 2 years, diagnosed due to gradual body weight reduction during the last 5-6 years. *Example 4*: Secondary amenorrhoea after a childbirth 12 months ago, after the birth with ceased menstruation and without lactation. *Example 5*: Now hospitalised 3 years after a radioiodine therapy of a nodular goiter which has been treated before that by thyreostatic medication for about a year.

Ep	reference	August 2003
	direction	forward
	expression	last August
	condition	blood sugar 14mmol/l
Ep	reference	August 2003
	direction	forward
	expression	Since then
Ep	reference	December 2003
	direction	forward
	expression	Since December
	condition	blood sugar 12mmol/l
Ep	reference	15.I
	direction	forward
	expression	since 15.I
	treatment	Metfodiab A10BA02
		1/2t. morning and noon
Ep	reference	15.I
	direction	forward
	expression	Since then
	condition	body weight reduced 6 kg.

Table 1: A patient history broken down into episodes.

In conclusion, this demo presents one step in the temporal analysis of clinical narratives: decomposition into fragments that could be considered as happening in the same period of time. The system integrates various components which extract important patient-related entities. The relative success is partly due to the very specific text genre. Further effort is needed for ordering the episodes in timelines, which is in our research agenda for the future. These results will be integrated into a research prototype extracting conceptual structures from EHRs.

Acknowledgments

This work is supported by grant DO/02-292 EVTIMA funded by the Bulgarian National Science Fund in 2009-2012. The anonymised EHRs are delivered by the University Specialised Hospital of Endocrinology, Medical University - Sofia.

References

Allen, J. *Maintaining Knowledge about Temporal Intervals*. Comm. ACM, 26(11), 1983, pp. 832-843.

Angelova G. and S. Boytcheva. *Towards Temporal Segmentation of Patient History in Discharge Letters*. In Proceedings of the Second Workshop on Biomedical Natural Language Processing, associated to RANLP-2011. September 2011, pp. 11-18.

Boytcheva, S. *Automatic Matching of ICD-10 Codes to Diagnoses in Discharge Letters*. In Proceedings of the Second Workshop on Biomedical Natural Language Processing, associated to RANLP-2011. September 2011, pp. 19-26.

Boytcheva, S. *Shallow Medication Extraction from Hospital Patient Records*. In Patient Safety Informatics - Adverse Drug Events, Human Factors and IT Tools for Patient Medication Safety, IOS Press, Studies in Health Technology and Informatics series, Volume 166. May 2011, pp. 119-128.

Boytcheva, S., D. Tcharaktchiev and G. Angelova. *Contextualization in automatic extraction of drugs from Hospital Patient Records*. In A. Moen at al. (Eds) User Centred Networked Health Case, Proceedings of MIE-2011, IOS Press, Studies in Health Technology and Informatics series, Volume 169. August 2011, pp. 527-531.

Harkema, H., J. N. Dowling, T. Thornblade, and W. W. Chapman. 2009. *ConText: An algorithm for determining negation, experiencer, and temporal status from clinical reports*. J. Biomedical Informatics, 42(5), 2009, pp. 839-851.

Hripcsak G., L. Zhou, S. Parsons, A. K. Das, and S. B. Johnson. *Modeling electronic dis-charge summaries as a simple temporal con-straint satisfaction problem*. JAMIA (J. of Amer. MI Assoc.) 2005, 12(1), pp. 55-63.

Savova, G., S. Bethard, W. Styler, J. Martin, M. Palmer, J. Masanz, and W. Ward. *Towards Temporal Relation Discovery from the Clinical Narrative*. In Proc. AMIA Annual Sympo-sium 2009, pp. 568-572.

Xu.H., S. P Stenner, S. Doan, K. Johnson, L. Waitman, and J. Denny. *MedEx: a medication information extraction system for clinical narratives*. JAMIA 17 (2010), pp. 19-24.

Zhou L. and G. Hripcsak. *Temporal reasoning with medical data - a review with emphasis on medical natural language processing*. J. Biom. Informatics 2007, 40(2), pp. 183-202.

Agreement fixing the sections of Bulgarian hospital discharge letters. Bulgarian Parliament, Official State Gazette 106 (2005), Article 190(3).

ICD v.10: International Classification of Diseases http://www.nchi.government.bg/download.html.

ATC (Anatomical Therapeutic Chemical Classification System), http://who.int/classifications/atcddd/en.

ElectionWatch: Detecting Patterns in News Coverage of US Elections

Saatviga Sudhahar, Thomas Lansdall-Welfare, Ilias Flaounas, Nello Cristianini
Intelligent Systems Laboratory
University of Bristol
(saatviga.sudhahar, Thomas.Lansdall-Welfare,
ilias.flaounas, nello.cristianini)@bristol.ac.uk

Abstract

We present a web tool that allows users to explore news stories concerning the 2012 US Presidential Elections via an interactive interface. The tool is based on concepts of "narrative analysis", where the key actors of a narration are identified, along with their relations, in what are sometimes called "semantic triplets" (one example of a triplet of this kind is "Romney Criticised Obama"). The network of actors and their relations can be mined for insights about the structure of the narration, including the identification of the key players, of the network of political support of each of them, a representation of the similarity of their political positions, and other information concerning their role in the media narration of events. The interactive interface allows the users to retrieve news report supporting the relations of interest.

1 Introduction

U.S presidential elections are major media events, following a fixed calendar, where two or more public relation "machines" compete to send out their message. From the point of view of the media, this event is often framed as a race, with contenders, front runners, and complex alliances. By the end of the campaign, which lasts for about one year, two line-ups are created in the media, one for each major party. This event provides researchers an opportunity to analyse the narrative structures found in the news coverage, the amounts of media attention that is devoted to the main contenders and their allies, and other patterns of interest.

We propose to study the U.S Presidential Elections with the tools of (quantitative) narrative analysis, identifying the key actors and their political relations, and using this information to infer the overall structure of the political coalitions. We are also interested in how the media covers such event that is which role is attributed to each actor within this narration.

Quantitative Narrative Analysis (QNA) is an approach to the analysis of news content that requires the identification of the key actors, and of the kind of interactions they have with each other (Franzosi, 2010). It usually requires a significant amount of manual labour, for "coding" the news articles, and this limits the analysis to small samples. We claim that the most interesting relations come from analysing large networks resulting from tens of thousands of articles, and therefore that QNA needs to be automated.

Our approach is to use a parser to extract simple SVO triplets, forming a semantic graph to identify the noun phrases with actors, and to classify the verbal links between actors in three simple categories: those expressing political support, those expressing political opposition, and the rest. By identifying the most important actors and triplets, we form a large weighted and directed network which we analyse for various types of patterns.

In this paper we demonstrate an automated system that can identify articles relative to the 2012 US Presidential Election, from 719 online news outlets, and can extract information about the key players, their relations, and the role they play in the electoral narrative. The system refreshes its information every 24 hours, and has already analysed tens of thousands of news articles. The tool allows the user to browse the growing set of news articles by the relations between actors, for example retrieving all articles where Mitt Romney praises Obama[1].

A set of interactive plots allows users to explore the news data by following specific candidates and also specific types of relations, to see a spectrum of all key actors sorted by their political affinity, a network representing relations of political support between actors, and a two-dimensional space where proximity again represents political affinity, but also they can access information about the role mostly played by a given actor in the media narrative: that of a subject or that of an object.

The ElectionWatch system is built on top of our infrastructure for news content analysis, which has been described elsewhere. It has also access to named entities information, with which it can generate timelines and activity-maps. These are also available through the web interface.

2 Data Collection

Our system collects news articles from 719 English language news outlets. We monitor both U.S and International media. A detailed description of the underlying infrastructure has been presented in our previous work (Flaounas, 2011).

In this demo we use only articles related to US Elections. We detect those articles using a topic detector based on Support Vector Machines (Chang, 2011). We trained and validated our classifier using the specialised Election news feed from Yahoo!. The performance of the classifier reached 83.46% precision, 73.29% recall, validated on unseen articles.

While the main focus of the paper is to present Narrative patterns in elections stories, the system presents also timelines and activity maps generated by detected Named Entities associated with the election process.

3 Methodology

We perform a series of methodologies for narrative analysis. Figure 1 illustrates the main components that are used to analyse news and create the website.

Preprocessing. First, we perform co-reference and anaphora resolution on each U.S Election article. This is based on the ANNIE plugin in GATE (Cunningham, 2002). Next, we extract Subject-Verb-Object (SVO) triplets using the Minipar parser output (Lin, 1998). An extracted triplet is denoted for example like "Obama(S)–Accuse(V)–Republicans(O)". We found that news media contains less than 5% of passive sentences and therefore it is ignored. We store each triplet in a database annotated with a reference to the article from which it was extracted. This allows us to track the background information of each triplet in the database.

Key Actors. From triplets extracted, we make a list of actors which are defined as subjects and objects of triplets. We rank actors according to their frequencies and consider the top 50 subjects and objects as the key actors.

Polarity of Actions. The verb element in triplets are defined as actions. We map actions to two specific action types which are endorsement and opposing. We obtained the endorsement/opposing polarity of verbs using the Verbnet data (Kipper et al, 2006)).

Extraction of Relations. We retain all triplets that have a) the key actors as subjects or objects; and b) an endorse/oppose verb. To extract relations we introduced a weighting scheme. Each endorsement-relation between actors a, b is weighted by $w_{a,b}$:

$$w_{a,b} = \frac{f_{a,b}(+) - f_{a,b}(-)}{f_{a,b}(+) + f_{a,b}(-)} \quad (1)$$

where $f_{a,b}(+)$ denotes the number of triplets between a, b with positive relation and $f_{a,b}(-)$ with negative relation. This way, actors who had equal number of positive and negative relations are eliminated.

Endorsement Network. We generate a triplet network with the weighted relations where actors are the nodes and weights calculated by Eq. 1 are the links. This network reveals endorse/oppose relations between key actors. The network in the main page of ElectionWatch website, illustrated in Fig. 2, is a typical example of such a network.

Network Partitioning. By using graph partitioning methods we can analyse the allegiance of actors to a party, and therefore their role in the political discourse. The Endorsement Network is a directed graph. To perform its partitioning we first omit directionality by calculating graph $B = A + A^T$, where A is the adjacency matrix of the Endorsement Network. We computed eigenvectors of the B and selected the eigenvector that

[1]Barack Obama and Mitt Romney are the two main opposing candidates in 2012 U.S Presidential Elections.

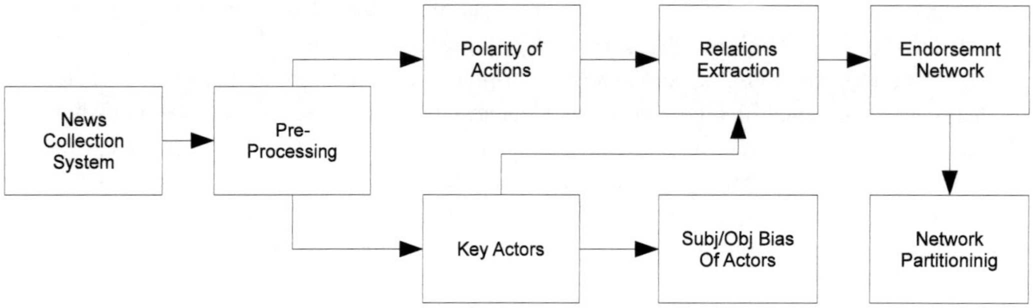

Figure 1: The Pipeline

correspond to the highest eigenvalue. The elements of the eigenvector represent actors. We sort them by their magnitude and we obtain a sorted list of actors. In the website we display only actors that are very polarised politically in the sides of the list. These two sets of actors correlate well with the left-right political ordering in our experiments on past US Elections. Since in the first phase of the campaign there are more than two sides, we added a scatter plot using the first two eigenvectors.

Subject/Object Bias of Actors. The Subject/Object bias S_a of actor a reveals the role it plays in the news narrative. It is computed as:

$$\mathrm{S_a} = \frac{f_{Subj}(a) - f_{Obj}(a)}{f_{Subj}(a) + f_{Obj}(a)} \quad (2)$$

A positive value of S for actor a indicates that the actor is used more often as a subject and a negative value indicates that the actor is used more often as an object.

4 The Website

We analyse news related to U.S Elections 2012 every day, automatically, and the results of our analysis are presented integrated under a publicly available website[2]. Figure 2 illustrates the homepage of ElectionWatch. Here, we list the key features of the site:

Triplet Graph – The main network in Fig. 2 is created using the weighted relations. A positive sign for the edge indicates an endorsement relation and a negative sign indicates an opposition relation in the network. By clicking on each edge in the network, we display triplets and articles that support the relation.

[2]ElectionWatch: http://electionwatch.enm.bris.ac.uk

Actor Spectrum – The left side of Fig. 2 shows the Actor Spectrum, coloured from blue for Democrats to red for Republicans. Actor spectrum was obtained by applying spectral graph partitioning methods to the triplet network.Note, that currently there are more than two campaigns that run in parallel between key actors that dominate the elections news coverage. Nevertheless, we still find that the two main opposing candidates in each party were in either sides of the list.

Relations – On the right hand side of the website we show the endorsement/opposition relations between key actors. For example, "Republicans Oppose Democrats". When clicking on a relation the webpage displays the news articles that support the relation.

Actor Space – The tab labelled 'Actor Space' plots the first and second eigenvector values for all actors in the actor spectrum.

Actor Bias The tab labelled 'Actor Bias' plots the subject/object bias of actors against the first eigenvector in a two dimensional space.

Pie Chart – Pie Chart on the left bottom in the webpage shows the share of each actor with regard to the total number of articles mentioning an endorse/oppose relation.

Map – The map geo-locates articles related to US Elections and refer to US locations.

Bar Chart – The bar chart tab, illustrated in Fig. 3, plots the number of articles in which actors were involved in a endorse/oppose relation. The height of each column reveals the frequency of it. The default plot focuses on only the first five actors in the actor spectrum.

Timelines & Activity Map – We track the activity of each named entity in the actor spectrum within the United States and present it in a timeline. The activity map monitors the media atten-

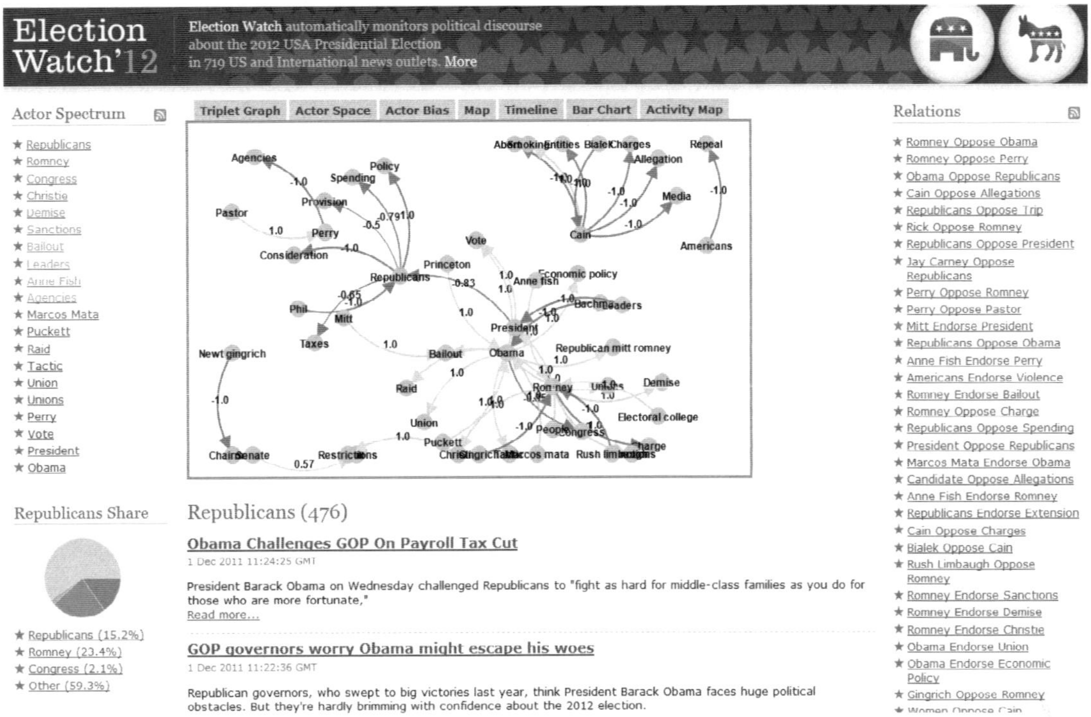

Figure 2: Screenshot of the home page of ElectionWatch

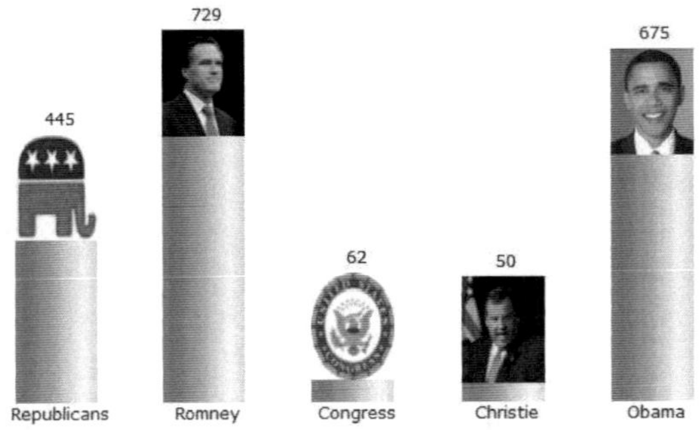

Figure 3: Barchart showing endorse/oppose article frequencies for actor "Obama" with other top actors.

tion for Presidential candidates in each state in the Unites States. At present we monitor this activity for Mitt Romney, Rick Perry, Michele Bachmann, Herman Cain and Barack Obama.

5 Discussion

We have demonstrated the system ElectionWatch that presents key actors in U.S election news articles and their role in political discourse. This builds on various recent contributions from the field of Pattern Analysis, such as (Trampus, 2011), augmenting them with multiple analysis tools that respond to the needs of social sciences investigations.

We agree on the fact that the triplets extracted by the system are not very clean. This noise can be ignored since we perform analysis on only filtered triplets containing key actors and specific type of actions, and also it's extracted from huge amount of data.

We have tested this system on data from all previous six elections, using the New York Times corpus as well as our own database. We use only support/criticism relations revealing a strong polarisation among actors and this seems to correspond to the left/right political dimension. Evaluation is an issue due to lack of data but results on the past six election cycles on New York Times always seperated the two competing candidates along the eigenvector spectrum. This is not so easy in the primary part of the elections, when multiple candidates compete with each other for the role of contender. To cover this case, we generate also a two-dimensional plot using the first two eigenvalues of the adjacency matrix, which seems to capture the main groupings in the political narrative.

Future work will include making better use of the information coming from the parser, which goes well beyond the simple SVO structure of sentences, and developing more sophisticated methods for the analysis of large and complex networks that can be inferred with the methodology we have developed.

Acknowledgments

I. Flaounas and N. Cristianini are supported by FP7 CompLACS; N. Cristianini is supported by a Royal Society Wolfson Merit Award; The members of the Intelligent Systems Laboratory are supported by the 'Pascal2' Network of Excellence. Authors would like to thank Omar Ali and Roberto Franzosi.

References

Chang C.C., and Lin C.J. 2011. *LIBSVM: a library for support vector machines*. ACM Transactions on Intelligent Systems and Technology 2(3):1–27

Cunningham H., Maynard D., Bontcheva K. and Tablan V. 2002. *GATE: A Framework and Graphical Development Environment for Robust NLP Tools and Applications*. Proc. of the 40th Anniversary Meeting of the Association for Computational Linguistics 168–175.

Earl J., Martin A., McCarthy J.D., Soule S.A. 2004. *The Use of Newspaper Data in the Study of Collective Action*. Annual Review of Sociology, 30:65–80.

Flaounas I., Ali O., Turchi M., Snowsill T., Nicart F., De Bie T., Cristianini N. 2011. *NOAM:News Outlets Analysis and Monitoring system*. Proc. of the 2011 ACM SIGMOD international conference on Management of data, 1275–1278.

Franzosi R. 2010. *Quantitative Narrative Analysis*. Sage Publications Inc, Quantitative Applications in the Social Sciences, 162–200.

Kipper K., Korhonen A., Ryant N., Palmer M. 2006. *Extensive Classifications of English verbs*. 12th EURALEX International Congress, Turin, Italy.

Lin D. 1998. *Dependency-Based Evaluation of Minipar*. Text, Speech and Language Technology 20:317–329.

Sandhaus, E. 2008. *The New York Times Annotated Corpus*. Linguistic Data Consortium

Trampus M., Mladenic D. 2011. *Learning Event Patterns from Text*. Informatica 35

Query log analysis with GALATEAS LangLog

Marco Trevisan and **Luca Dini**
CELI
trevisan@celi.it
dini@celi.it

Eduard Barbu
Università di Trento
eduard.barbu@unitn.it

Igor Barsanti
Gonetwork
i.barsanti@gonetwork.it

Nikolaos Lagos
Xerox Research Centre Europe
Nikolaos.Lagos@xrce.xerox.com

Frédérique Segond and **Mathieu Rhulmann**
Objet Direct
fsegond@objetdirect.com
mruhlmann@objetdirect.com

Ed Vald
Bridgeman Art Library
ed.vald@bridgemanart.co.uk

Abstract

This article describes GALATEAS LangLog, a system performing Search Log Analysis. LangLog illustrates how NLP technologies can be a powerful support tool for market research even when the source of information is a collection of queries each one consisting of few words. We push the standard Search Log Analysis forward taking into account the semantics of the queries. The main innovation of LangLog is the implementation of two highly customizable components that cluster and classify the queries in the log.

1 Introduction

Transaction logs become increasingly important for studying the user interaction with systems like Web Searching Engines, Digital Libraries, Intranet Servers and others (Jansen, 2006). Various service providers keep log files recording the user interaction with the searching engines. Transaction logs are useful to understand the user search strategy but also to improve query suggestions (Wen and Zhang, 2003) and to enhance the retrieval quality of search engines (Joachims, 2002). The process of analyzing the transaction logs to understand the user behaviour and to assess the system performance is known as Transaction Log Analysis (TLA). Transaction Log Analysis is concerned with the analysis of both browsing and searching activity inside a website. The analysis of transaction logs that focuses on search activity only is known as Search Log Analysis (SLA). According to Jansen (2008) both TLA and SLA have three stages: data collection, data preparation and data analysis. In the data collection stage one collects data describing the user interaction with the system. Data preparation is the process of loading the collected data in a relational database. The data loaded in the database gives a transaction log representation independent of the particular log syntax. In the final stage the data prepared at the previous step is analyzed. One may notice that the traditional three levels log analyses give a syntactic view of the information in the logs. Counting terms, measuring the logical complexity of queries or the simple procedures that associate queries with the sessions in no way accesses the semantics of queries. LangLog system addreses the semantic problem performing clustering and classification for real query logs. Clustering the queries in the logs allows the identification of meaningful groups of queries. Classifying the queries according to a relevant list of categories permits the assessment of how well the searching engine meets the user needs. In addition the LangLog system address problems like automatic language identification, Name Entity Recognition, and automatic query translation. The rest of the paper is organized as follows: the next section briefly reviews some systems performing SLA. Then we present the data sources the architecture and the analysis process of the LangLog system. The conclusion section concludes the article summarizing the work and presenting some new possible enhancements of the LangLog.

2 Related work

The information in the log files is useful in many ways, but its extraction raises many challenges and issues. Facca and Lanzi (2005) offer a survey of the topic. There are several commercial systems to extract and analyze this information, such as Adobe web analytics[1], SAS Web Analytics[2], Infor Epiphany[3], IBM SPSS[4]. These products are often part of a customer relation management (CRM) system. None of those showcases include any form of linguistic processing. On the other hand, Web queries have been the subject of linguistic analysis, to improve the performance of information retrieval systems. For example, a study (Monz and de Rijke, 2002) experimented with shallow morphological analysis, another (Li et al., 2006) analyzed queries to remove spelling mistakes. These works encourage our belief that linguistic analysis could be beneficial for Web log analysis systems.

3 Data sources

LangLog requires the following information from the Web logs: the time of the interaction, the query, click-through information and possibly more. LangLog processes log files which conform to the W3C extended log format. No other formats are supported. The system prototype is based on query logs spanning one month of interactions recorded at the Bridgeman Art Library[5]. Bridgeman Art library contains a large repository of images coming from 8000 collections and representing more than 29.000 artists.

4 Analyses

LangLog organizes the search log data into units called queries and hits. In a typical searching scenario a user submits a query to the content provider's site-searching engine and clicks on some (or none) of the search results. From now on we will refer to a clicked item as a hit, and we will refer to the text typed by the user as the query. This information alone is valuable to the content provider because it allows to discover which queries were served with results that satisfied the user, and which queries were not.

LangLog extracts queries and hits from the log files, and performs the following analyses on the queries:

- language identification
- tokenization and lemmatization
- named entity recognition
- classification
- cluster analysis

Language information may help the content provider decide whether to translate the content into new languages.

Lemmatization is especially important in languages like German and Italian that have a rich morphology. Frequency statistics of keywords help understand what users want, but they are biased towards items associated with words with lesser ortographic and morpho-syntactic variation. For example, two thousand queries for "trousers", one thousand queries for "handbag" and another thousand queries for "handbags" means that handbags are twice as popular as trousers, although statistics based on raw words would say otherwise.

Named entities extraction helps the content provider for the same reasons lemmatization does. Named entities are especially important because they identify real-world items that the content provider can relate to, while lemmas less often do so. The name entities and the most important concepts can be linked afterwards with resources like Wikipedia which offer a rich specification of their properties.

Both classification and clustering allow the content provider to understand what kind of the users look for and how this information is targeted by means of queries.

Classification consists of classifying queries into categories drawn from a classification schema. When the schema used to classify is different from the schema used in the content provider's website, classification may provide hints as to what kind of queries are not matched by items in the website. In a similar way, cluster analysis can be used to identify new market segments or new trends in the user's behaviour. Clus-

[1] http://www.omniture.com/en/products/analytics

[2] http://www.sas.com/solutions/webanalytics/index.html

[3] http://www.infor.com

[4] http://www-01.ibm.com/software/analytics/spss/

[5] http://www.bridgemanart.com

ter analysis provide more flexybility than classification, but the information it produces is less precise. Many trials and errors may be necessary before finding interesting results. One hopes that the final clustering solution will give insights into the patterns of users' searches. For example an online book store may discover that one cluster contains many software-related terms, altough none of those terms is popular enough to be noticeable in the statistics.

5 Architecture

LangLog consists of three subsystems: log acquisition, log analysis, log disclosure. Periodically the log acquisition subsystem gathers new data which it passes to the log analyses component. The results of the analyses are then available through the log disclosure subsystem.

Log acquisition deals with the acquisition and normalization and anonymization of the data contained in the content provider's log files. The data flows from the content provider's servers to LangLog's central database. This process is carried out by a series of Pentaho Data Integration[6] procedures.

Log analysis deals with the anaysis of the data. The analyses proper are executed by NLP systems provided by third parties and accessible as Web services. LangLog uses NLP Web services for language identification, morpho-syntactic analysis, named entity recognition, classification and clustering. The analyses are stored in the database along with the original data.

Log disclosure is actually a collection of independent systems that allow the content providers to access their information and the analyses. Log disclosure systems are also concerned with access control and protection of privacy. The content provider can access the output of LangLog using AWStats, QlikView, or JPivot.

- AWStats[7] is a widely used log analysis system for websites. The logs gathered from the websites are parsed by AWStats, which generates a complete report about visitors, visits duration, visitor's countries and other data to disclose useful information about the visitor's behavior.

[6]http://kettle.pentaho.com

[7]http://awstats.sourceforge.net

- QlikView[8] is a business intelligence (BI) platform. A BI platform provides historical, current, and predictive views of business operations. Usually such tools are used by companies to have a clear view of their business over time. In LangLog, QlickView does not display sales or costs evolution over time. Instead, it displays queries on the content provider's website over time. A dashboard with many elements (input selections, tables, charts, etc.) provides a wide range of tools to visualize the data.

- JPivot[9] is a front-end for Mondrian. Mondrian[10] is an Online Analytical Processing (OLAP) engine, a system capable of handling and analyzing large quantities of data. JPivot allows the user to explore the output of LangLog, by slicing the data along many dimensions. JPivot allows the user to display charts, export results to Microsoft Excel or CSV, and use custom OLAP MDX queries.

Log analysis deals with the anaysis of the data. The analyses proper are executed by NLP systems provided by third parties and accessible as Web services. LangLog uses NLP Web services for language identification, morpho-syntactic analysis, named entity recognition, classification and clustering. The analyses are stored in the database along with the original data.

5.1 Language Identification

The system uses a language identification system (Bosca and Dini, 2010) which offers language identification for English, French, Italian, Spanish, Polish and German. The system uses four different strategies:

- N-gram character models: uses the distance between the character based models of the input and of a reference corpus for the language (Wikipedia).

- Word frequency: looks up the frequency of the words in the query with respect to a reference corpus for the language.

- Function words: searches for particles highly connoting a specific language (such as prepositions, conjunctions).

[8]http://www.qlikview.com

[9]http://jpivot.sourceforge.net

[10]http://mondrian.pentaho.com

- Prior knowledge: provides a default guess based on a set of hypothesis and heuristics like region/browser language.

5.2 Lemmatization

To perform lemmatization, Langlog uses general-purpose morpho-syntactic analysers based on the Xerox Incremental Parser (XIP), a deep robust syntactic parser (Ait-Mokhtar et al., 2002). The system has been adapted with domain-specific part of speech disambiguation grammar rules, according to the results a linguistic study of the development corpus.

5.3 Named entity recognition

LangLog uses the Xerox named entity recognition web service (Brun and Ehrmann, 2009) for English and French. XIP includes also a named entity detection component, based on a combination of lexical information and hand-crafted contextual rules. For example, the named entity recognition system was adapted to handle titles of portraits, which were frequent in our dataset. While for other NLP tasks LangLog uses the same system for every content provider, named entity recognition is a task that produces better analyses when it is tailored to the domain of the content. Because LangLog uses a NER Web service, it is easy to replace the default NER system with a different one. So if the content provider is interested in the development of a NER system tailored for a specific domain, LangLog can accomodate this.

5.4 Clustering

We developed two clustering systems: one performs hierarchical clustering, another performs soft clustering.

- CLUTO: the hierarchical clustering system relies on CLUTO4[11], a clustering toolkit. To understand the main ideas CLUTO is based on one might consult Zhao and Karypis (2002). The clustering process proceeds as follows. First, the set of queries to be clustered is partitioned in k groups where k is the number of desired clusters. To do so, the system uses a partitional clustering algorithm which finds the k-way clustering solution making repeated bisections. Then the system arranges the clusters in a hierarchy by successively merging the most similar clusters in a tree.

- MALLET: the soft clustering system we developed relies on MALLET (McCallum, 2002), a Latent Dirichlet Allocation (LDA) toolkit (Steyvers and Griffiths, 2007).

  Our MALLET-based system considers that each query is a document and builds a topic model describing the documents. The resulting topics are the clusters. Each query is associated with each topic according to a certain strenght. Unlike the system based on CLUTO, this system produces soft clusters, i.e. each query may belong to more than one cluster.

5.5 Classification

LangLog allows the same query to be classified many times using different classification schemas and different classification strategies. The result of the classification of an input query is always a map that assigns each category a weight, where the higher the weight, the more likely the query belongs to the category. If NER performs better when tailored to a specific domain, classification is a task that is hardly useful without any customization. We need a different classification schema for each content provider. We developed two classification system: an unsupervised system and a supervised one.

- Unsupervised: this system does not require any training data nor any domain-specific corpus. The output weight of each category is computed as the cosine similarity between the vector models of the most representative Wikipedia article for the category and the collection of Wikipedia articles most relevant to the input query. Our evaluation in the KDD-Cup 2005 dataset results in 19.14 precision and 22.22 F-measure. For comparison, the state of the art in the competition achieved a 46.1 F-measure. Our system could not achieve a similar score because it is unsupervised, and therefore it cannot make use of the KDD-Cup training dataset. In addition, it uses only the query to perform classification, whereas KDD-Cup systems were also able to access the result sets associated to the queries.

[11] http://glaros.dtc.umn.edu/gkhome/views/cluto

- Supervised: this system is based on the Weka framework. Therefore it can use any machine learning algorithm implemented in Weka. It uses features derived from the queries and from Bridgeman metadata. We trained a Naive Bayes classifier on a set of 15.000 queries annotated with 55 categories and hits and obtained a F-measure of 0.26. The results obtained for the classification are encouraging but not yet at the level of the state of the art. The main reason for this is the use of only in-house meta-data in the feature computation. In the future we will improve both components by providing them with features from large resources like Wikipedia or exploiting the results returned by Web Searching engines.

6 Demonstration

Our demonstration presents:

- The setting of our case study: the Bridgeman Art Library website, a typical user search, and what is recorded in the log file.
- The conceptual model of the results of the analyses: search episodes, queries, lemmas, named entities, classification, clustering.
- The data flow across the parts of the system, from content provider's servers to the front-end through databases, NLP Web services and data marts.
- The result of the analyses via QlikView.

7 Conclusion

In this paper we presented the LangLog system, a customizable system for analyzing query logs. The LangLog performs language identification, lemmatization, NER, classification and clustering for query logs. We tested the LangLog system on queries in Bridgeman Library Art. In the future we will test the system on query logs in different domains (e.g. pharmaceutical, hardware and software, etc.) thus increasing the coverage and the significance of the results. Moreover we will incorporate in our system the session information which should increase the precision of both clustering and classification components.

References

Salah Ait-Mokhtar, Jean-Pierre Chanod and Claude Roux 2002. *Robustness Beyond Shallowness: Incremental Deep Parsing. Journal of Natural Language Engineering* 8, 2-3, 121-144.

Alessio Bosca and Luca Dini. 2010. *Language Identification Strategies for Cross Language Information Retrieval. CLEF 2010 Working Notes.*

C. Brun and M. Ehrmann. 2007. *Adaptation of a Named Entity Recognition System for the ESTER 2 Evaluation Campaign.* In proceedings of *the IEEE International Conference on Natural Language Processing and Knowledge Engineering.*

F. M. Facca and P. L. Lanzi. 2005. *Mining interesting knowledge from weblogs: a survey. Data Knowl. Eng.* 53(3):225241.

Jansen, B. J. 2006. *Search log analysis: What is it; what's been done; how to do it. Library and Information Science Research* 28(3):407-432.

Jansen, B. J. 2008. *The methodology of search log analysis.* In B. J. Jansen, A. Spink and I. Taksa (eds) *Handbook of Web log analysis* 100-123. Hershey, PA: IGI.

Joachims T. 2002. *Optimizing search engines using clickthrough data.* In proceedings of *the 8th ACM SIGKDD international conference on Knowledge discovery and data mining* 133-142.

M. Li, Y. Zhang, M. Zhu, and M. Zhou. 2006. *Exploring distributional similarity based models for query spelling correction.* In proceedings of *In ACL 06: the 21st International Conference on Computational Linguistics and the 44th annual meeting of the ACL* 10251032, 2006.

Andrew Kachites McCallum. 2002. *MALLET: A Machine Learning for Language Toolkit. http://mallet.cs.umass.edu.*

C. Monz and M. de Rijke. 2002. *Shallow Morphological Analysis in Monolingual Information Retrieval for Dutch, German and Italian. In Proceedings of CLEF 2001.* Springer

M. Steyvers and T. Griffiths. 2007. *Probabilistic Topic Models.* In T. Landauer, D McNamara, S. Dennis and W. Kintsch (eds), *Handbook of Latent Semantic Analysis,* Psychology Press.

J. R. Wen and H.J. Zhang 2003. *Query Clustering in the Web Context.* In Wu, Xiong and Shekhar (eds) *Information Retrieval and Clustering* 195-226. Kluwer Academic Publishers.

Y. Zhao and G. Karypis. 2002. *Evaluation of hierarchical clustering algorithms for document datasets.* In proceedings of *the ACM Conference on Information and Knowledge Management.*

A platform for collaborative semantic annotation

Valerio Basile and **Johan Bos** and **Kilian Evang** and **Noortje Venhuizen**
{v.basile,johan.bos,k.evang,n.j.venhuizen}@rug.nl
Center for Language and Cognition Groningen (CLCG)
University of Groningen, The Netherlands

Abstract

Data-driven approaches in computational semantics are not common because there are only few semantically annotated resources available. We are building a large corpus of public-domain English texts and annotate them semi-automatically with syntactic structures (derivations in Combinatory Categorial Grammar) and semantic representations (Discourse Representation Structures), including events, thematic roles, named entities, anaphora, scope, and rhetorical structure. We have created a wiki-like Web-based platform on which a crowd of expert annotators (i.e. linguists) can log in and adjust linguistic analyses in real time, at various levels of analysis, such as boundaries (tokens, sentences) and tags (part of speech, lexical categories). The demo will illustrate the different features of the platform, including navigation, visualization and editing.

1 Introduction

Data-driven approaches in computational semantics are still rare because there are not many large annotated resources that provide empirical information about anaphora, presupposition, scope, events, tense, thematic roles, named entities, word senses, ellipsis, discourse segmentation and rhetorical relations in a single formalism. This is not surprising, as it is challenging and time-consuming to create such a resource from scratch.

Nevertheless, our objective is to develop a large annotated corpus of Discourse Representation Structures (Kamp and Reyle, 1993), comprising most of the aforementioned phenomena: the Groningen Meaning Bank (GMB). We aim to reach this goal by:

1. Providing a wiki-like platform supporting collaborative annotation efforts;
2. Employing state-of-the-art NLP software for bootstrapping semantic analysis;
3. Giving real-time feedback of annotation adjustments in their resulting syntactic and semantic analysis;
4. Ensuring kerfuffle-free dissemination of our semantic resource by considering only public-domain texts for annotation.

We have developed the wiki-like platform from scratch simply because existing annotation systems, such as GATE (Dowman et al., 2005), NITE (Carletta et al., 2003), or UIMA (Hahn et al., 2007), do not offer the functionality required for deep semantic annotation combined with crowdsourcing.

In this description of our platform, we motivate our choice of data and explain how we manage it (Section 2), we describe the complete toolchain of NLP components employed in the annotation-feedback process (Section 3), and the Web-based interface itself is introduced, describing how linguists can adjust boundaries of tokens and sentences, and revise tags of named entities, parts of speech and lexical categories (Section 4).

2 Data

The goal of the Groningen Meaning Bank is to provide a widely available corpus of texts, with deep semantic annotations. The GMB only comprises texts from the public domain, whose distribution isn't subject to copyright restrictions. Moreover, we include texts from various genres and sources, resulting in a rich, comprehensive corpus appropriate for use in various disciplines within NLP.

The documents in the current version of the GMB are all in English and originate from four main sources: (i) *Voice of America* (VOA), an online newspaper published by the US Federal Government; (ii) the *Manually Annotated Sub-Corpus* (MASC) from the Open American National Corpus (Ide et al., 2010); (iii) country descriptions from the *CIA World Factbook* (CIA) (Central Intelligence Agency, 2006), in particular the Background and Economy sections, and (iv) a collection of Aesop's fables (AF). All these documents are in the public domain and are thus redistributable, unlike for example the WSJ data used in the Penn Treebank (Miltsakaki et al., 2004).

Each document is stored with a separate file containing metadata. This may include the language the text is written in, the genre, date of publication, source, title, and terms of use of the document. This metadata is stored as a simple feature-value list.

The documents in the GMB are categorized with different statuses. Initially, newly added documents are labeled as *uncategorized*. As we manually review them, they are relabeled as either *accepted* (document will be part of the next stable version, which will be released in regular intervals), *postponed* (there is some difficulty with the document that can possibly be solved in the future) or *rejected* (something is wrong with the document form, i.e., character encoding, or with the content, e.g., it contains offensive material).

Currently, the GMB comprises 70K English text documents (Table 1), corresponding to 1,3 million sentences and 31,5 million tokens.

Table 1: Documents in the GMB, as of March 5, 2012

Documents	VOA	MASC	CIA	AF	All
Accepted	4,651	34	515	0	5,200
Uncategorized	61,090	0	0	834	61,924
Postponed	2,397	339	3	1	2,740
Rejected	184	27	4	0	215
Total	68,322	400	522	835	70,079

3 The NLP Toolchain

The process of building the Groningen Meaning Bank takes place in a bootstrapping fashion. A chain of software is run, taking the raw text documents as input. The output of this automatic process is in the form of several layers of stand-off annotations, i.e., files with links to the original, raw documents.

We employ a chain of NLP components that carry out, respectively, tokenization and sentence boundary detection, POS tagging, lemmatization, named entity recognition, supertagging, parsing using the formalism of Combinatory Categorial Grammar (Steedman, 2001), and semantic and discourse analysis using the framework of Discourse Representation Theory (DRT) (Kamp and Reyle, 1993) with rhetorical relations (Asher, 1993).

The lemmatizer used is morpha (Minnen et al., 2001), the other steps are carried out by the C&C tools (Curran et al., 2007) and Boxer (Bos, 2008).

3.1 Bits of Wisdom

After each step in the toolchain, the intermediate result may be automatically adjusted by auxiliary components that apply annotations provided by expert users or other sources. These annotations are represented as "Bits of Wisdom" (BOWs): tuples of information regarding, for example, token and sentence boundaries, tags, word senses or discourse relations. They are stored in a MySQL database and can originate from three different sources: (i) explicit annotation changes made by experts using the Explorer Web interface (see Section 4); (ii) an annotation game played by non-experts, similar to 'games with a purpose' like Phrase Detectives (Chamberlain et al., 2008) and Jeux de Mots (Artignan et al., 2009); and (iii) external NLP tools (e.g. for word sense disambiguation or co-reference resolution).

Since BOWs come from various sources, they may contradict each other. In such cases, a judge component resolves the conflict, currently by preferring the most recent expert BOW. Future work will involve the application of different judging techniques.

3.2 Processing Cycle

The widely known open-source tool *GNU make* is used to orchestrate the toolchain while avoiding unnecessary reprocessing. The need to rerun the toolchain for a document arises in three situations: a new BOW for that document is available; a new, improved version of one of the components is available; or reprocessing is forced by a user via the "reprocess" button in the Web interface. A continually running program, the 'updat-

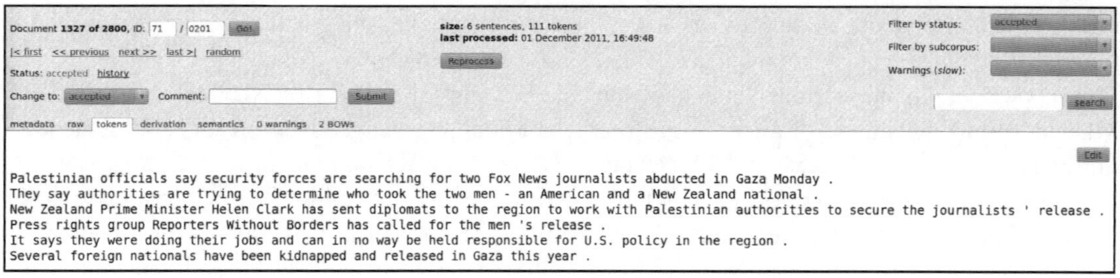

Figure 1: A screenshot of the web interface, displaying a tokenised document.

ing daemon', is responsible for calling *make* for the right document at the right time. It checks the database for new BOWs or manual reprocessing requests in very short intervals to ensure immediate response to changes experts make via the Web interface. It also updates and rebuilds the components in longer intervals and continuously loops through all documents, remaking them with the newest versions of the components. The number of *make* processes that can run in parallel is configurable; standard techniques of concurrent programming are used to prevent more than one *make* process from working simultaneously on the same document.

4 The Expert Interface

We developed a wiki-like Web interface, called the GMB Explorer, that provides users access to the Groningen Meaning Bank. It fulfills three main functions: navigation and search through the documents, visualization of the different levels of annotation, and manual correction of the annotations. We will discuss these functions below.

4.1 Navigation and Search

The GMB Explorer allows navigation through the documents of the GMB with their stand-off annotations (Figure 1). The default order of documents is based on their size in terms of number of tokens. It is possible to apply filters to restrict the set of documents to be shown: showing only documents from a specific subcorpus, or specifically showing documents with/without warnings generated by the NLP toolchain.

The Explorer interface comes with a built-in search engine. It allows users to pose single- or multi-word queries. The search results can then be restricted further by looking for a specific lexical category or part of speech. A more advanced search system that is based on a *semantic lexicon* with lexical information about all levels of annotation is currently under development.

4.2 Visualization

The different visualization options for a document are placed in tabs: each tab corresponds to a specific layer of annotation or additional information. Besides the raw document text, users can view its tokenized version, an interactive derivation tree per sentence, and the semantic representation of the entire discourse in graphical DRS format. There are three further tabs in the Explorer: a tab containing the warnings produced by the NLP pipeline (if any), one containing the Bits of Wisdom that have been collected for the document, and a tab with the document metadata.

The *sentences* view allows the user to show or hide sub-trees per sentence and additional information such as POS-tags, word senses, supertags and partial, unresolved semantics. The derivations are shown using the CCG notation, generated by XSLT stylesheets applied to Boxer's XML output. An example is shown in Figure 2.

The *discourse* view shows a fully resolved semantic representation in the form of a DRS with

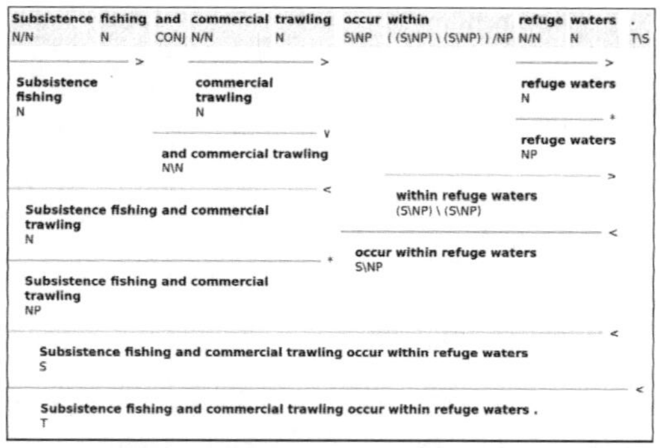

Figure 2: An example of a CCG derivation as shown in GMB Explorer.

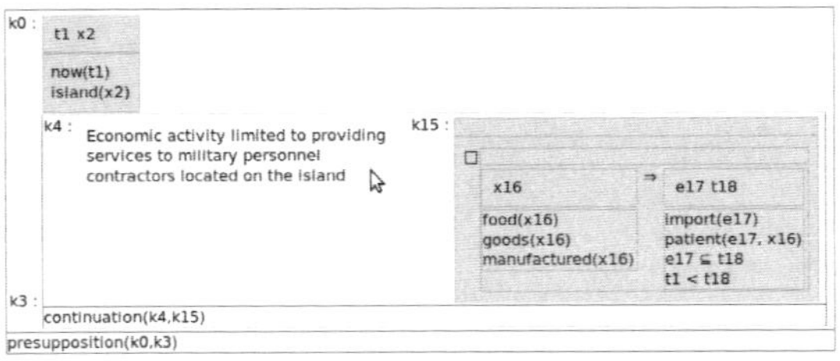

Figure 3: An example of the semantic representations in the GMB, with DRSs representing discourse units.

rhetorical relations. Clicking on discourse units switches the visualization between text and semantic representation. Figure 3 shows how DRSs are visualized in the Web interface.

4.3 Editing

Some of the tabs in the Explorer interface have an "edit" button. This allows registered users to manually correct certain types of annotations. Currently, the user can edit the tokenization view and on the derivation view. Clicking "edit" in the tokenization view gives an annotator the possibility to add and remove token and sentence boundaries in a simple and intuitive way, as Figure 4 illustrates. This editing is done in real-time, following the WYSIWYG strategy, with tokens separated by spaces and sentences separated by new lines. In the derivation view, the annotator can change part-of-speech tags and named entity tags by selecting a tag from a drop-down list (Figure 5).

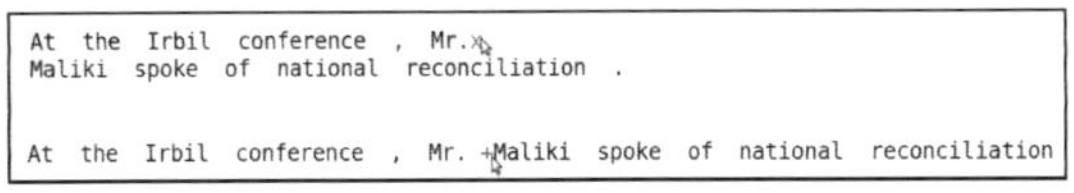

Figure 4: Tokenization edit mode. Clicking on the red '×' removes a sentence boundary after the token; clicking on the green '+' adds a sentence boundary.

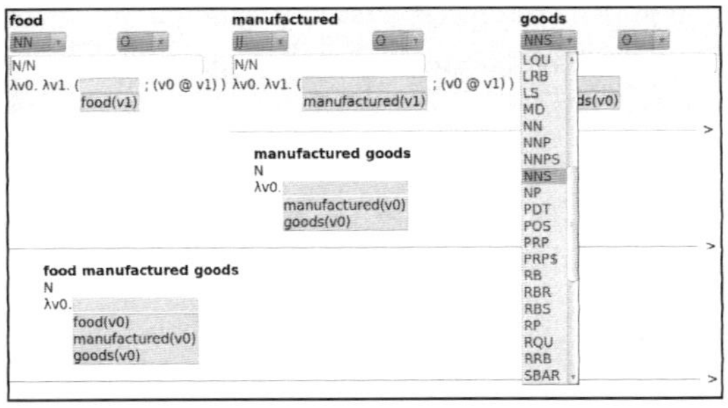

Figure 5: Tag edit mode, showing derivation with partial DRSs and illustrating how to adjust a POS tag.

As the updating daemon is running continually, the document is immediately reprocessed after editing so that the user can directly view the new annotation with his BOW taken into account. Re-analyzing a document typically takes a few seconds, although for very large documents it can take longer. It is also possible to directly rerun the NLP toolchain on a specific document via the "reprocess" button, in order to apply the most recent version of the software components involved. The GMB Explorer shows a timestamp of the last processing for each document.

We are currently working on developing new editing options, which allow users to change different aspects of the semantic representation, such as word senses, thematic roles, co-reference and scope.

5 Demo

In the demo session we show the functionality of the various features in the Web-based user interface of the GMB Explorer, which is available online via: `http://gmb.let.rug.nl`.

We show (i) how to navigate and search through all the documents, including the refinement of search on the basis of the lexical category or part of speech, (ii) the operation of the different view options, including the raw, tokenized, derivation and semantics view of each document, and (iii) how adjustments to annotations can be realised in the Web interface. More concretely, we demonstrate how boundaries of tokens and sentences can be adapted, and how different types of tags can be changed (and how that affects the syntactic, semantic and discourse analysis).

In sum, the demo illustrates innovation in the way changes are made and how they improve the linguistic analysis in real-time. Because it is a web-based platform, it paves the way for a collaborative annotation effort. Currently it is actively in use as a tool to create a large semantically annotated corpus for English texts: the Groningen Meaning Bank.

References

Guillaume Artignan, Mountaz Hascoët, and Mathieu Lafourcade. 2009. Multiscale visual analysis of lexical networks. In *13th International Conference on Information Visualisation*, pages 685–690, Barcelona, Spain.

Nicholas Asher. 1993. *Reference to Abstract Objects in Discourse*. Kluwer Academic Publishers.

Johan Bos. 2008. Wide-Coverage Semantic Analysis with Boxer. In J. Bos and R. Delmonte, editors, *Semantics in Text Processing. STEP 2008 Conference Proceedings*, volume 1 of *Research in Computational Semantics*, pages 277–286. College Publications.

J. Carletta, S. Evert, U. Heid, J. Kilgour, J. Robertson, and H. Voormann. 2003. The NITE XML toolkit: flexible annotation for multi-modal language data. *Behavior Research Methods, Instruments, and Computers*, 35(3):353–363.

Central Intelligence Agency. 2006. *The CIA World Factbook*. Potomac Books.

John Chamberlain, Massimo Poesio, and Udo Kruschwitz. 2008. Addressing the Resource Bottleneck to Create Large-Scale Annotated Texts. In Johan Bos and Rodolfo Delmonte, editors, *Semantics in Text Processing. STEP 2008 Conference Proceedings*, volume 1 of *Research in Computational Semantics*, pages 375–380. College Publications.

James Curran, Stephen Clark, and Johan Bos. 2007. Linguistically Motivated Large-Scale NLP with C&C and Boxer. In *Proceedings of the 45th Annual Meeting of the Association for Computational Linguistics Companion Volume Proceedings of the Demo and Poster Sessions*, pages 33–36, Prague, Czech Republic.

Mike Dowman, Valentin Tablan, Hamish Cunningham, and Borislav Popov. 2005. Web-assisted annotation, semantic indexing and search of television and radio news. In *Proceedings of the 14th International World Wide Web Conference*, pages 225–234, Chiba, Japan.

U. Hahn, E. Buyko, K. Tomanek, S. Piao, J. McNaught, Y. Tsuruoka, and S. Ananiadou. 2007. An annotation type system for a data-driven NLP pipeline. In *Proceedings of the Linguistic Annotation Workshop*, pages 33–40, Prague, Czech Republic, June. Association for Computational Linguistics.

Nancy Ide, Christiane Fellbaum, Collin Baker, and Rebecca Passonneau. 2010. The manually annotated sub-corpus: a community resource for and by the people. In *Proceedings of the ACL 2010 Conference Short Papers*, pages 68–73, Stroudsburg, PA, USA.

Hans Kamp and Uwe Reyle. 1993. *From Discourse to Logic; An Introduction to Modeltheoretic Semantics of Natural Language, Formal Logic and DRT*. Kluwer, Dordrecht.

Eleni Miltsakaki, Rashmi Prasad, Aravind Joshi, and Bonnie Webber. 2004. The Penn Discourse Treebank. In *In Proceedings of LREC 2004*, pages 2237–2240.

Guido Minnen, John Carroll, and Darren Pearce. 2001. Applied morphological processing of english. *Journal of Natural Language Engineering*, 7(3):207–223.

Mark Steedman. 2001. *The Syntactic Process*. The MIT Press.

HadoopPerceptron: a Toolkit for Distributed Perceptron Training and Prediction with MapReduce

Andrea Gesmundo
Computer Science Department
University of Geneva
Geneva, Switzerland
andrea.gesmundo@unige.ch

Nadi Tomeh
LIMSI-CNRS and
Université Paris-Sud
Orsay, France
nadi.tomeh@limsi.fr

Abstract

We propose a set of open-source software modules to perform structured Perceptron Training, Prediction and Evaluation within the Hadoop framework. Apache Hadoop is a freely available environment for running distributed applications on a computer cluster. The software is designed within the Map-Reduce paradigm. Thanks to distributed computing, the proposed software reduces substantially execution times while handling huge data-sets. The distributed Perceptron training algorithm preserves convergence properties, thus guaranties same accuracy performances as the serial Perceptron. The presented modules can be executed as stand-alone software or easily extended or integrated in complex systems. The execution of the modules applied to specific NLP tasks can be demonstrated and tested via an interactive web interface that allows the user to inspect the status and structure of the cluster and interact with the MapReduce jobs.

1 Introduction

The Perceptron training algorithm (Rosenblatt, 1958; Freund and Schapire, 1999; Collins, 2002) is widely applied in the Natural Language Processing community for learning complex structured models. The non-probabilistic nature of the perceptron parameters makes it possible to incorporate arbitrary features without the need to calculate a partition function, which is required for its discriminative probabilistic counterparts such as CRFs (Lafferty et al., 2001). Additionally, the Perceptron is robust to approximate inference in large search spaces.

Nevertheless, Perceptron training is proportional to inference which is frequently non-linear in the input sequence size. Therefore, training can be time-consuming for complex model structures. Furthermore, for an increasing number of tasks is fundamental to leverage on huge sources of data as the World Wide Web. Such difficulties render the scalability of the Perceptron a challenge.

In order to improve scalability, Mcdonald et al. (2010) propose a distributed training strategy called *iterative parameter mixing*, and show that it has similar convergence properties to the standard perceptron algorithm; it finds a separating hyperplane if the training set is separable; it produces models with comparable accuracies to those trained serially on all the data; and reduces training times significantly by exploiting computing clusters.

With this paper we present the HadoopPerceptron package. It provides a freely available open-source implementation of the iterative parameter mixing algorithm for training the structured perceptron on a generic sequence labeling tasks. Furthermore, the package provides two additional modules for prediction and evaluation. The three software modules are designed within the MapReduce programming model (Dean and Ghemawat, 2004) and implemented using the Apache Hadoop distributed programming Framework (White, 2009; Lin and Dyer, 2010). The presented HadoopPerceptron package reduces execution time significantly compared to its serial counterpart while maintaining comparable performance.

PerceptronIterParamMix($\mathcal{T} = \{(\mathbf{x}_t, \mathbf{y}_t)\}_{t=1}^{|\mathcal{T}|}$)

Split $\mathcal{T}$ into $\mathcal{S}$ pieces $\mathcal{T} = \{\mathcal{T}_1, \ldots, \mathcal{T}_\mathcal{S}\}$
$\mathbf{w} = \mathbf{0}$
for $n : 1..N$
  $\mathbf{w}^{(i,n)} =$ OneEpochPerceptron($\mathcal{T}_i, \mathbf{w}$)
  $\mathbf{w} = \sum_i \mu_{i,n} \mathbf{w}^{(i,n)}$
return $\mathbf{w}$

OneEpochPerceptron($\mathcal{T}_i, \mathbf{w}^*$)

$\mathbf{w}^{(0)} = \mathbf{w}^*; k = 0$
for $n : 1..T$
Let $\mathbf{y}' = \arg\max_{\mathbf{y}'} \mathbf{w}^{(k)}.\mathbf{f}(\mathbf{x}_t, \mathbf{y}'_t)$
if $\mathbf{y}' \neq \mathbf{y}_t$
  $\mathbf{x}^{(k+1)} = \mathbf{x}^{(k)} + \mathbf{f}(\mathbf{x}_t, \mathbf{y}_t) - \mathbf{f}(\mathbf{x}_t, \mathbf{y}'_t)$
  $k = k + 1$
return $\mathbf{w}^{(k)}$

Figure 1: Distributed perceptron with iterative parameter mixing strategy. Each $\mathbf{w}^{(i,n)}$ is computed in parallel. $\boldsymbol{\mu}_n = \{\mu_{1,n}, \ldots, \mu_{\mathcal{S},n}\}, \forall \mu_{i,n} \in \boldsymbol{\mu}_n : \mu_{i,n} \geq 0$ and $\forall n : \sum_i \mu_{i,n} = 1$.

2 Distributed Structured Perceptron

The structured perceptron (Collins, 2002) is an online learning algorithm that processes training instances one at a time during each training epoch. In sequence labeling tasks, the algorithm predicts a sequence of labels (an element from the structured output space) for each input sequence. Prediction is determined by linear operations on high-dimensional feature representations of candidate input-output pairs and an associated weight vector. During training, the parameters are updated whenever the prediction that employed them is incorrect.

Unlike many batch learning algorithms that can easily be distributed through the gradient calculation, the perceptron online training is more subtle to parallelize. However, Mcdonald et al. (2010) present a simple distributed training through a parameter mixing scheme.

The Iterative Parameter Mixing is given in Figure 2 (Mcdonald et al., 2010). First the training data is divided into disjoint splits of example pairs $(\mathbf{x}_t, \mathbf{y}_t)$ where $\mathbf{x}_t$ is the observation sequence and $\mathbf{y}_t$ is the associated labels. The algorithm proceeds to train a single epoch of the perceptron algorithm for each split in parallel, and mix the local models weights $\mathbf{w}^{(i,n)}$ to produce the global weight vector $\mathbf{w}$. The mixed model is then passed to each split to reset the perceptron local weights, and a new iteration is started. Mcdonald et al. (2010) provide bound analysis for the algorithm and show that it is guaranteed to converge and find a seperation hyperplane if one exists.

3 MapReduce and Hadoop

Many algorithms need to iterate over number of records and 1) perform some calculation on each of them and then 2) aggregate the results. The MapReduce programming model implements a functional abstraction of these two operations called respectively Map and Reduce. The Map function takes a value-key pairs and produces a list of key-value pairs: map$(k, v) \rightarrow (k', v')^*$; while the input the Reduce function is a key with all the associated values produced by all the mappers: reduce$(k', (v')^*) \rightarrow (k'', v'')^*$. The model requires that all values with the same key are reduced together.

Apache Hadoop is an open-source implementation of the MapReduce model on cluster of computers. A cluster is composed by a set of computers (nodes) connected into a network. One node is designated as the Master while other nodes are referred to as Worker Nodes. Hadoop is designed to scale out to large clusters built from commodity hardware and achieves seamless scalability. To allow rapid development, Hadoop hides system-level details from the application developer.The MapReduce runtime automatically schedule worker assignment to mappers and reducers;handles synchronization required by the programming model including gathering, sorting and shuffling of intermediate data across the network; and provides robustness by detecting worker failures and managing restarts. The framework is built on top of he Hadoop Distributed File System (HDFS), which allows to distribute the data across the cluster nodes. Network traffic is minimized by moving the process to the node storing the data. In Hadoop terminology an entire MapReduce program is called a *job* while individual mappers and reducers are called *tasks*.

4 HadoopPerceptron Implementation

In this section we give details on how the training, prediction and evaluation modules are implemented for the Hadoop framework using the

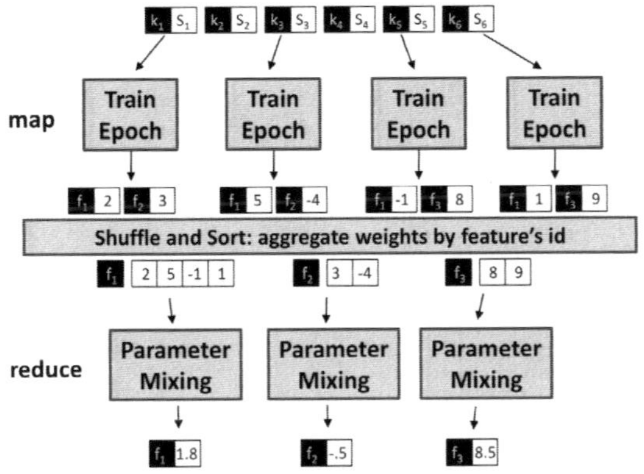

Figure 2: HadoopPerceptron in MapReduce.

MapReduce programming model[1].

Our implementation of the iterative parameter mixing algorithm is sketched in Figure 2. At the beginning of each iteration, the training data is split and distributed to the worker nodes. The set of training examples in a data split is streamed to map workers as pairs (sentence-id, $(\mathbf{x}_t, \mathbf{y}_t)$). Each map worker performs a standard perceptron training epoch and outputs a pair (feature-id, $w_{i,f}$) for each feature. The set of such pairs emitted by a map worker represents its local weight vector. After map workers have finished, the MapReduce framework guarantees that all local weights associated with a given feature are aggregated together as input to a distinct reduce worker. Each reduce worker produces as output the average of the associated feature weight. At the end of each iteration, the reduce workers outputs are aggregated into the global averaged weight vector. The algorithm iterates N times or until convergence is achieved. At the beginning of each iteration the weight vector of each distinct model is initialized with the global averaged weight vector resultant from the previous iteration. Thus, for all the iterations except for the first, the global averaged weight vector resultant from the previous iteration needs to be provided the map workers. In Hadoop it is possible to pass this information via the Distributed Cache System.

In addition to the training module, the HadoopPerceptron package provides separate modules for prediction and evaluation both of them are designed as MapReduce programs. The evaluation module output the accuracy measure computed against provided gold standards. Prediction and evaluation modules are independent from the training modules, the weight vector given as input could have been computed with any other system using any other training algorithm as long as they employ the same features.

The implementation is in Java, and we interface with the Hadoop cluster via the native Java API. It can be easily adapted to a wide range of NLP tasks. Incorporating new features by modifying the extensible feature extractor is straightforward. The package includes the implementation of the basic feature set described in (Suzuki and Isozaki, 2008).

5 The Web User Interface

Hadoop is bundled with several web interfaces that provide concise tracking information for jobs, tasks, data nodes, etc. as shown in Figure 3. These web interfaces can be used to demonstrate the HadoopPerceptron running phases and monitor the distributed execution of the training, prediction and evaluation modules for several sequence labeling tasks including part-of-speech tagging and named entity recognition.

6 Experiments

We investigate HadoopPerceptron training time and prediction accuracy on a part-of-speech (POS) task using the PennTreeBank corpus (Marcus et al., 1994). We use sections 0-18 of the Wall Street Journal for training, and sections 22-24 for testing.

We compare the regular percepton trained serially on all the training data with the distributed perceptron trained with iterative parameter mixing with variable number of splits $\mathcal{S} \in \{10, 20\}$. For each system, we report the prediction accuracy measure on the final test set to determine if any loss is observed as a consequence of distributed training.

For each system, Figure 4 plots accuracy results computed at the end of every training epoch against consumed wall-clock time. We observe that iterative mixing parameter achieves comparable performance to its serial counterpart while converging orders of magnitude faster.

Furthermore, we note that the distributed algorithm achieves a slightly higher final accuracy

[1]The Hadoop Perceptron toolkit is available from https://github.com/agesmundo/HadoopPerceptron .

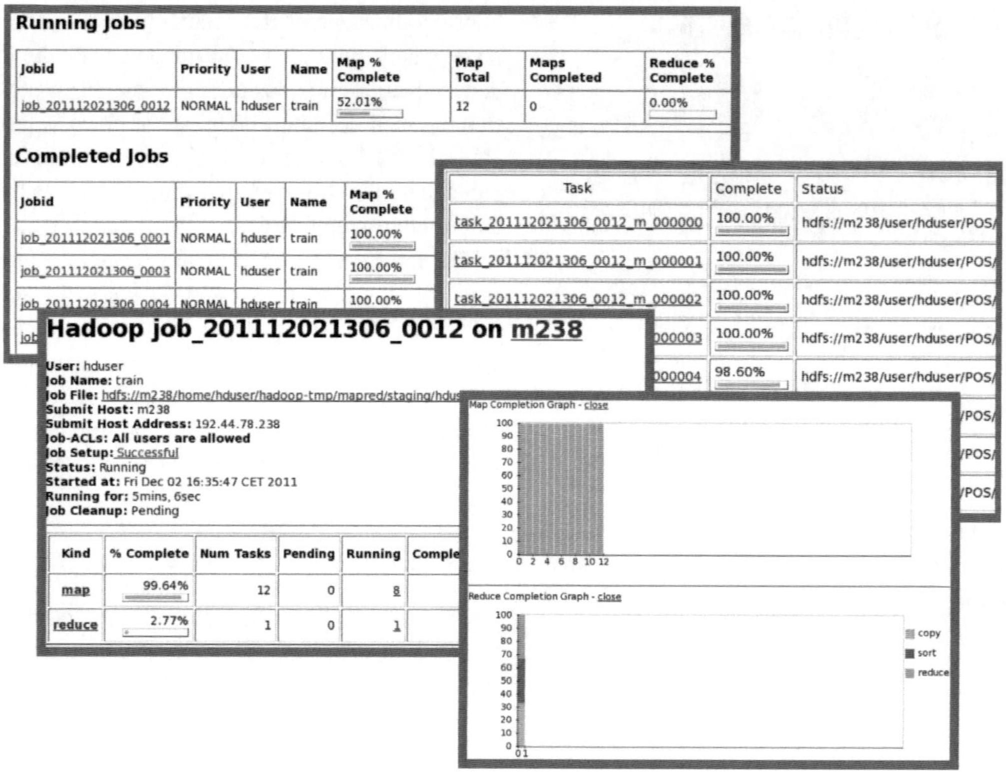

Figure 3: Hadoop interfaces for HadoopPerceptron.

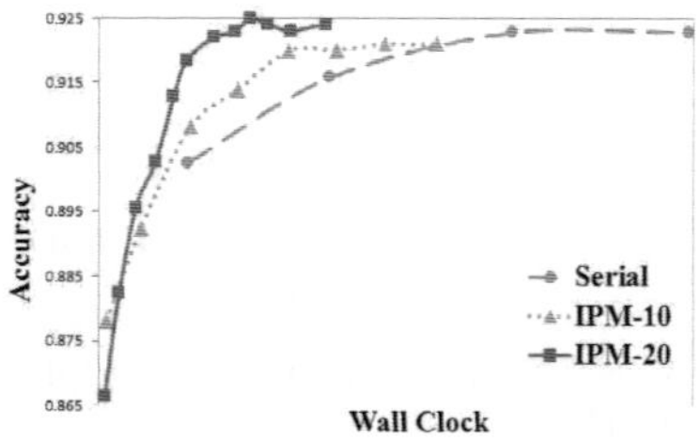

Figure 4: Accuracy vs. training time. Each point corresponds to a training epoch.

than serial training. Mcdonald et al. (2010) suggest that this is due to the bagging effect that the distributed training has, and due to parameter mixing that is similar to the averaged perceptron.

We note also that increasing the number of splits increases the number of epoch required to attain convergence, while reducing the time required per epoch. This implies a trade-off between slower convergence and quicker epochs when selecting a larger number of splits.

7 Conclusion

The HadoopPerceptron package provides the first freely-available open-source implementation of iterative parameter mixing Perceptron Training, Prediction and Evaluation for a distributed Map-Reduce framework. It is a versatile stand alone software or building block, that can be easily extended, modified, adapted, and integrated in broader systems.

HadoopPerceptron is a useful tool for the increasing number of applications that need to perform large-scale structured learning. This is the first freely available implementation of an approach that has already been applied with success in private sectors (e.g. Google Inc.). Making it possible for everybody to fully leverage on huge data sources as the World Wide Web, and develop structured learning solutions that can scale keeping feasible execution times and cluster-network usage to a minimum.

Acknowledgments

This work was funded by Google and The Scottish Informatics and Computer Science Alliance (SICSA). We thank Keith Hall, Chris Dyer and Miles Osborne for help and advice.

References

Michael Collins. 2002. Discriminative training methods for hidden markov models: Theory and experiments with perceptron algorithms. In *EMNLP '02: Proceedings of the 2002 Conference on Empirical Methods in Natural Language Processing*, Philadelphia, PA, USA.

Jeffrey Dean and Sanjay Ghemawat. 2004. Mapreduce: simplified data processing on large clusters. In *Proceedings of the 6th Symposium on Opearting Systems Design and Implementation*, San Francisco, CA, USA.

Yoav Freund and Robert E. Schapire. 1999. Large margin classification using the perceptron algorithm. *Machine Learning*, 37(3):277–296.

John Lafferty, Andrew Mccallum, and Fernando Pereira. 2001. John lafferty and andrew mccallum and fernando pereira. In *Proceedings of the International Conference on Machine Learning*, Williamstown, MA, USA.

Jimmy Lin and Chris Dyer. 2010. *Data-Intensive Text Processing with MapReduce*. Morgan & Claypool Publishers.

Mitchell P. Marcus, Beatrice Santorini, and Mary A. Marcinkiewicz. 1994. Building a large annotated corpus of english: The penn treebank. *Computational Linguistics*, 19(2):313–330.

Ryan Mcdonald, Keith Hall, and Gideon Mann. 2010. Distributed training strategies for the structured perceptron. In *NAACL '10: Proceedings of the 11th Conference of the North American Chapter of the Association for Computational Linguistics*, Los Angeles, CA, USA.

Frank Rosenblatt. 1958. The Perceptron: A probabilistic model for information storage and organization in the brain. *Psychological Review*, 65(6):386–408.

Jun Suzuki and Hideki Isozaki. 2008. Semi-supervised sequential labeling and segmentation using giga-word scale unlabeled data. In *ACL '08: Proceedings of the 46th Conference of the Association for Computational Linguistics*, Columbus, OH, USA.

Tom White. 2009. *Hadoop: The Definitive Guide*. O'Reilly Media Inc.

BRAT: a Web-based Tool for NLP-Assisted Text Annotation

Pontus Stenetorp[1]* Sampo Pyysalo[2,3]* Goran Topić[1]
Tomoko Ohta[1,2,3] Sophia Ananiadou[2,3] and Jun'ichi Tsujii[4]
[1]Department of Computer Science, The University of Tokyo, Tokyo, Japan
[2]School of Computer Science, University of Manchester, Manchester, UK
[3]National Centre for Text Mining, University of Manchester, Manchester, UK
[4]Microsoft Research Asia, Beijing, People's Republic of China
{pontus,smp,goran,okap}@is.s.u-tokyo.ac.jp
sophia.ananiadou@manchester.ac.uk
jtsujii@microsoft.com

Abstract

We introduce the brat rapid annotation tool (BRAT), an intuitive web-based tool for text annotation supported by Natural Language Processing (NLP) technology. BRAT has been developed for rich structured annotation for a variety of NLP tasks and aims to support manual curation efforts and increase annotator productivity using NLP techniques. We discuss several case studies of real-world annotation projects using pre-release versions of BRAT and present an evaluation of annotation assisted by semantic class disambiguation on a multi-category entity mention annotation task, showing a 15% decrease in total annotation time. BRAT is available under an open-source license from: http://brat.nlplab.org

1 Introduction

Manually-curated gold standard annotations are a prerequisite for the evaluation and training of state-of-the-art tools for most Natural Language Processing (NLP) tasks. However, annotation is also one of the most time-consuming and financially costly components of many NLP research efforts, and can place heavy demands on human annotators for maintaining annotation quality and consistency. Yet, modern annotation tools are generally technically oriented and many offer little support to users beyond the minimum required functionality. We believe that intuitive and user-friendly interfaces as well as the judicious application of NLP technology to *support*, not supplant, human judgements can help maintain the quality of annotations, make annotation more accessible to non-technical users such as subject domain experts, and improve annotation productivity, thus reducing both the human and financial cost of annotation. The tool presented in this work, BRAT, represents our attempt to realise these possibilities.

*These authors contributed equally to this work

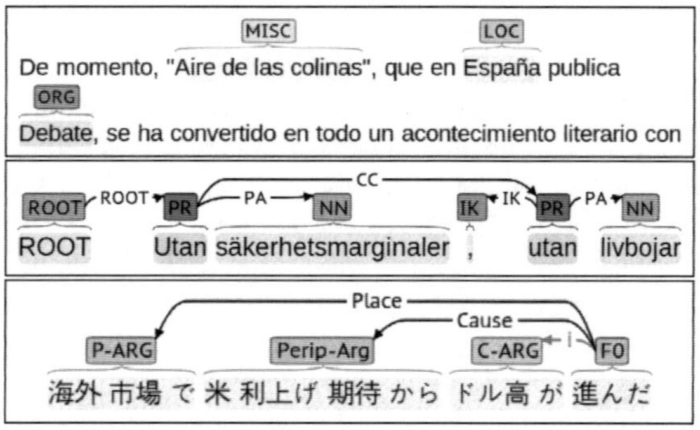

Figure 1: Visualisation examples. Top: named entity recognition, middle: dependency syntax, bottom: verb frames.

2 Features

2.1 High-quality Annotation Visualisation

BRAT is based on our previously released open-source STAV text annotation visualiser (Stenetorp et al., 2011b), which was designed to help users gain an understanding of complex annotations involving a large number of different semantic types, dense, partially overlapping text annotations, and non-projective sets of connections between annotations. Both tools share a vector graphics-based visualisation component, which provide scalable detail and rendering. BRAT integrates PDF and EPS image format export functionality to support use in e.g. figures in publications (Figure 1).

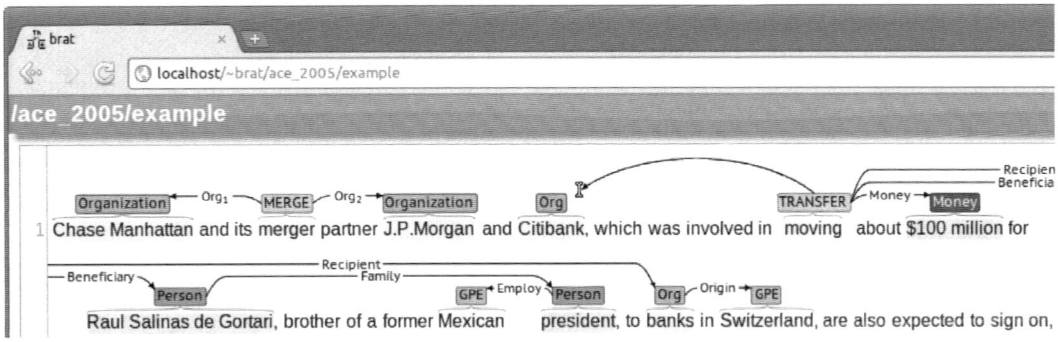

Figure 2: Screenshot of the main BRAT user-interface, showing a connection being made between the annotations for "moving" and "Citibank".

2.2 Intuitive Annotation Interface

We extended the capabilities of STAV by implementing support for annotation editing. This was done by adding functionality for recognising standard user interface gestures familiar from text editors, presentation software, and many other tools.

In BRAT, a span of text is marked for annotation simply by selecting it with the mouse by "dragging" or by double-clicking on a word. Similarly, annotations are linked by clicking with the mouse on one annotation and dragging a connection to the other (Figure 2).

BRAT is browser-based and built entirely using standard web technologies. It thus offers a familiar environment to annotators, and it is possible to start using BRAT simply by pointing a standards-compliant modern browser to an installation. There is thus no need to install or distribute any additional annotation software or to use browser plug-ins. The use of web standards also makes it possible for BRAT to uniquely identify any annotation using Uniform Resource Identifiers (URIs), which enables linking to individual annotations for discussions in e-mail, documents and on web pages, facilitating easy communication regarding annotations.

2.3 Versatile Annotation Support

BRAT is fully configurable and can be set up to support most text annotation tasks. The most basic annotation primitive identifies a text span and assigns it a type (or tag or label), marking for e.g. POS-tagged tokens, chunks or entity mentions (Figure 1 top). These base annotations can be connected by binary relations – either directed or undirected – which can be configured for e.g. simple relation extraction, or verb frame annotation (Figure 1 middle and bottom). n-ary associations of annotations are also supported, allowing the annotation of event structures such as those targeted in the MUC (Sundheim, 1996), ACE (Doddington et al., 2004), and BioNLP (Kim et al., 2011) Information Extraction (IE) tasks (Figure 2). Additional aspects of annotations can be marked using *attributes*, binary or multi-valued flags that can be added to other annotations. Finally, annotators can attach free-form text notes to any annotation.

In addition to information extraction tasks, these annotation primitives allow BRAT to be configured for use in various other tasks, such as chunking (Abney, 1991), Semantic Role Labeling (Gildea and Jurafsky, 2002; Carreras and Màrquez, 2005), and dependency annotation (Nivre, 2003) (See Figure 1 for examples). Further, both the BRAT client and server implement full support for the Unicode standard, which allow the tool to support the annotation of text using e.g. Chinese or Devanāgarī characters. BRAT is distributed with examples from over 20 corpora for a variety of tasks, involving texts in seven different languages and including examples from corpora such as those introduced for the CoNLL shared tasks on language-independent named entity recognition (Tjong Kim Sang and De Meulder, 2003) and multilingual dependency parsing (Buchholz and Marsi, 2006).

BRAT also implements a fully configurable system for checking detailed constraints on annotation semantics, for example specifying that a TRANSFER event must take exactly one of each of GIVER, RECIPIENT and BENEFICIARY arguments, each of which must have one of the types PERSON, ORGANIZATION or GEO-POLITICAL ENTITY, as well as a MONEY argument of type

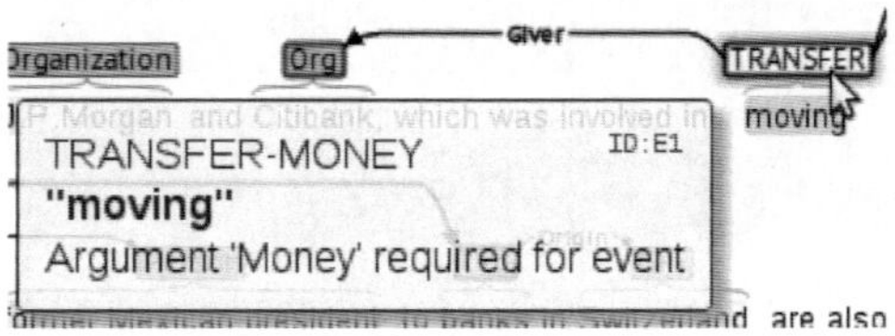

Figure 3: Incomplete TRANSFER event indicated to the annotator

MONEY, and may optionally take a PLACE argument of type LOCATION (LDC, 2005). Constraint checking is fully integrated into the annotation interface and feedback is immediate, with clear visual effects marking incomplete or erroneous annotations (Figure 3).

2.4 NLP Technology Integration

BRAT supports two standard approaches for integrating the results of fully automatic annotation tools into an annotation workflow: bulk annotation imports can be performed by format conversion tools distributed with BRAT for many standard formats (such as in-line and column-formatted BIO), and tools that provide standard web service interfaces can be configured to be invoked from the user interface.

However, human judgements cannot be replaced or based on a completely automatic analysis without some risk of introducing bias and reducing annotation quality. To address this issue, we have been studying ways to augment the annotation process with input from statistical and machine learning methods to support the annotation process while still involving human annotator judgement for each annotation.

As a specific realisation based on this approach, we have integrated a recently introduced machine learning-based semantic class disambiguation system capable of offering multiple outputs with probability estimates that was shown to be able to reduce ambiguity on average by over 75% while retaining the correct class in on average 99% of cases over six corpora (Stenetorp et al., 2011a). Section 4 presents an evaluation of the contribution of this component to annotator productivity.

2.5 Corpus Search Functionality

BRAT implements a comprehensive set of search functions, allowing users to search document col-

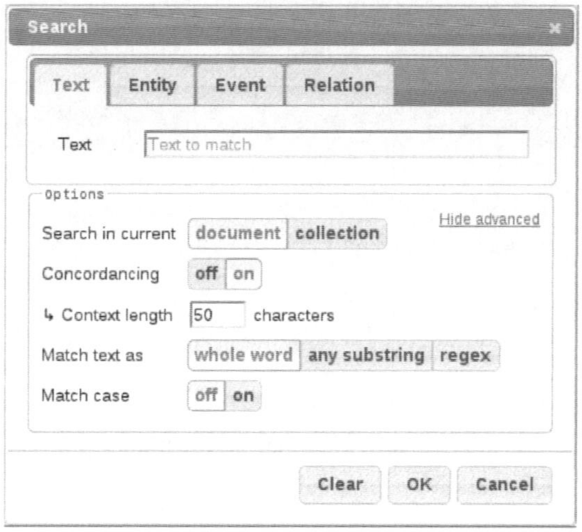

Figure 4: The BRAT search dialog

lections for text span annotations, relations, event structures, or simply text, with a rich set of search options definable using a simple point-and-click interface (Figure 4). Additionally, search results can optionally be displayed using keyword-in-context concordancing and sorted for browsing using any aspect of the matched annotation (e.g. type, text, or context).

3 Implementation

BRAT is implemented using a client-server architecture with communication over HTTP using JavaScript Object Notation (JSON). The server is a RESTful web service (Fielding, 2000) and the tool can easily be extended or adapted to switch out the server or client. The client user interface is implemented using XHTML and Scalable Vector Graphics (SVG), with interactivity implemented using JavaScript with the jQuery library. The client communicates with the server using Asynchronous JavaScript and XML (AJAX), which permits asynchronous messaging.

BRAT uses a stateless server back-end implemented in Python and supports both the Common Gateway Interface (CGI) and FastCGI protocols, the latter allowing response times far below the 100 ms boundary for a "smooth" user experience without noticeable delay (Card et al., 1983). For server side annotation storage BRAT uses an easy-to-process file-based stand-off format that can be converted from or into other formats; there is no need to perform database import or export to interface with the data storage. The BRAT server in-

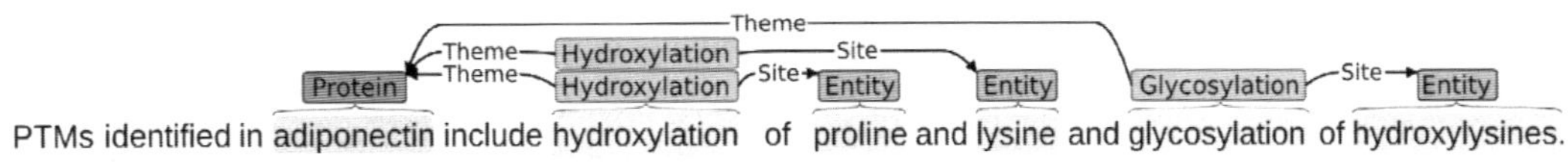

Figure 5: Example annotation from the BioNLP Shared Task 2011 Epigenetics and Post-translational Modifications event extraction task.

stallation requires only a CGI-capable web server and the set-up supports any number of annotators who access the server using their browsers, on any operating system, without separate installation.

Client-server communication is managed so that all user edit operations are immediately sent to the server, which consolidates them with the stored data. There is no separate "save" operation and thus a minimal risk of data loss, and as the authoritative version of all annotations is always maintained by the server, there is no chance of conflicting annotations being made which would need to be merged to produce an authoritative version. The BRAT client-server architecture also makes real-time collaboration possible: multiple annotators can work on a single document simultaneously, seeing each others edits as they appear in a document.

4 Case Studies

4.1 Annotation Projects

BRAT has been used throughout its development during 2011 in the annotation of six different corpora by four research groups in efforts that have in total involved the creation of well-over 50,000 annotations in thousands of documents comprising hundreds of thousands of words.

These projects include structured event annotation for the domain of cancer biology, Japanese verb frame annotation, and gene-mutation-phenotype relation annotation. One prominent effort making use of BRAT is the BioNLP Shared Task 2011,[1] in which the tool was used in the annotation of the EPI and ID main task corpora (Pyysalo et al., 2012). These two information extraction tasks involved the annotation of entities, relations and events in the epigenetics and infectious diseases subdomains of biology. Figure 5 shows an illustration of shared task annotations.

Many other annotation efforts using BRAT are still ongoing. We refer the reader to the BRAT website[2] for further details on current and past annotation projects using BRAT.

Mode	Total	Type Selection
Normal	45:28	13:49
Rapid	39:24 (-6:04)	09:35 (-4:14)

Table 1: Total annotation time, portion spent selecting annotation type, and absolute improvement for rapid mode.

4.2 Automatic Annotation Support

To estimate the contribution of the semantic class disambiguation component to annotation productivity, we performed a small-scale experiment involving an entity and process mention tagging task. The annotation targets were of 54 distinct mention types (19 physical entity and 35 event/process types) marked using the simple typed-span representation. To reduce confounding effects from annotator productivity differences and learning during the task, annotation was performed by a single experienced annotator with a Ph.D. in biology in a closely related area who was previously familiar with the annotation task.

The experiment was performed on publication abstracts from the biomolecular science subdomain of glucose metabolism in cancer. The texts were drawn from a pool of 1,750 initial candidates using stratified sampling to select pairs of 10-document sets with similar overall statistical properties.[3] Four pairs of 10 documents (80 in total) were annotated in the experiment, with 10 in each pair annotated with automatic support and 10 without, in alternating sequence to prevent learning effects from favouring either approach.

The results of this experiment are summarized in Table 1 and Figure 6. In total 1,546 annotations were created in normal mode and 1,541 annota-

[1] http://2011.bionlp-st.org

[2] http://brat.nlplab.org

[3] Document word count and expected annotation count, were estimated from the output of NERsuite, a freely available CRF-based NER tagger: http://nersuite.nlplab.org

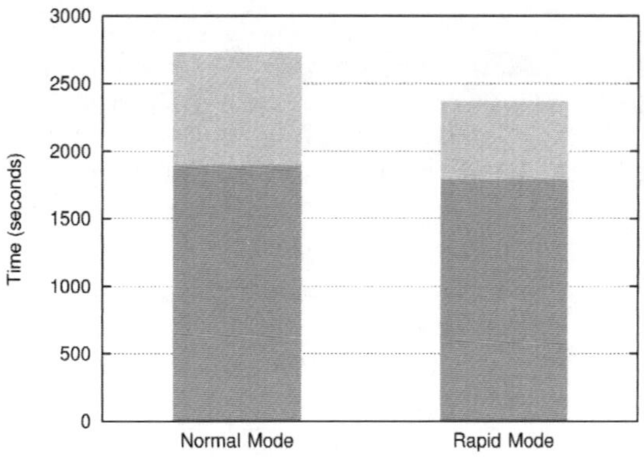

Figure 6: Allocation of annotation time. GREEN signifies time spent on selecting annotation type and BLUE the remaining annotation time.

tions in rapid mode; the sets are thus highly comparable. We observe a 15.4% reduction in total annotation time, and, as expected, this is almost exclusively due to a reduction in the time the annotator spent selecting the type to assign to each span, which is reduced by 30.7%; annotation time is otherwise stable across the annotation modes (Figure 6). The reduction in the time spent in selecting the span is explained by the limiting of the number of candidate types exposed to the annotator, which were decreased from the original 54 to an average of 2.88 by the semantic class disambiguation component (Stenetorp et al., 2011a).

Although further research is needed to establish the benefits of this approach in various annotation tasks, we view the results of this initial experiment as promising regarding the potential of our approach to using machine learning to support annotation efforts.

5 Related Work and Conclusions

We have introduced BRAT, an intuitive and user-friendly web-based annotation tool that aims to enhance annotator productivity by closely integrating NLP technology into the annotation process. BRAT has been and is being used for several ongoing annotation efforts at a number of academic institutions and has so far been used for the creation of well-over 50,000 annotations. We presented an experiment demonstrating that integrated machine learning technology can reduce the time for type selection by over 30% and overall annotation time by 15% for a multi-type entity mention annotation task.

The design and implementation of BRAT was informed by experience from several annotation tasks and research efforts spanning more than a decade. A variety of previously introduced annotation tools and approaches also served to guide our design decisions, including the fast annotation mode of Knowtator (Ogren, 2006), the search capabilities of the XConc tool (Kim et al., 2008), and the design of web-based systems such as MyMiner (Salgado et al., 2010), and GATE Teamware (Cunningham et al., 2011). Using machine learning to accelerate annotation by supporting human judgements is well documented in the literature for tasks such as entity annotation (Tsuruoka et al., 2008) and translation (Martínez-Gómez et al., 2011), efforts which served as inspiration for our own approach.

BRAT, along with conversion tools and extensive documentation, is freely available under the open-source MIT license from its homepage at http://brat.nlplab.org

Acknowledgements

The authors would like to thank early adopters of BRAT who have provided us with extensive feedback and feature suggestions. This work was supported by Grant-in-Aid for Specially Promoted Research (MEXT, Japan), the UK Biotechnology and Biological Sciences Research Council (BBSRC) under project Automated Biological Event Extraction from the Literature for Drug Discovery (reference number: BB/G013160/1), and the Royal Swedish Academy of Sciences.

References

Steven Abney. 1991. Parsing by chunks. *Principle-based parsing*, 44:257–278.

Sabine Buchholz and Erwin Marsi. 2006. CoNLL-X shared task on multilingual dependency parsing. In *Proceedings of the Tenth Conference on Computational Natural Language Learning (CoNLL-X)*, pages 149–164.

Stuart K. Card, Thomas P. Moran, and Allen Newell. 1983. *The psychology of human-computer interaction*. Lawrence Erlbaum Associates, Hillsdale, New Jersey.

Xavier Carreras and Lluís Màrquez. 2005. Introduction to the CoNLL-2005 shared task: Semantic Role Labeling. In *Proceedings of the 9th Conference on Natural Language Learning*, pages 152–164. Association for Computational Linguistics.

Hamish Cunningham, Diana Maynard, Kalina Bontcheva, Valentin Tablan, Niraj Aswani, Ian Roberts, Genevieve Gorrell, Adam Funk, Angus Roberts, Danica Damljanovic, Thomas Heitz, Mark A. Greenwood, Horacio Saggion, Johann Petrak, Yaoyong Li, and Wim Peters. 2011. *Text Processing with GATE (Version 6)*.

George Doddington, Alexis Mitchell, Mark Przybocki, Lance Ramshaw, Stephanie Strassel, and Ralph Weischedel. 2004. The Automatic Content Extraction (ACE) program: Tasks, data, and evaluation. In *Proceedings of the 4th International Conference on Language Resources and Evaluation*, pages 837–840.

Roy Fielding. 2000. REpresentational State Transfer (REST). *Architectural Styles and the Design of Network-based Software Architectures. University of California, Irvine*, page 120.

Daniel Gildea and Daniel Jurafsky. 2002. Automatic labeling of semantic roles. *Computational Linguistics*, 28(3):245–288.

Jin-Dong Kim, Tomoko Ohta, and Jun'ichi Tsujii. 2008. Corpus annotation for mining biomedical events from literature. *BMC Bioinformatics*, 9(1):10.

Jin-Dong Kim, Sampo Pyysalo, Tomoko Ohta, Robert Bossy, Ngan Nguyen, and Jun'ichi Tsujii. 2011. Overview of BioNLP Shared Task 2011. In *Proceedings of BioNLP Shared Task 2011 Workshop*, pages 1–6, Portland, Oregon, USA, June. Association for Computational Linguistics.

LDC. 2005. ACE (Automatic Content Extraction) English Annotation Guidelines for Events. Technical report, Linguistic Data Consortium.

Pascual Martínez-Gómez, Germán Sanchis-Trilles, and Francisco Casacuberta. 2011. Online learning via dynamic reranking for computer assisted translation. In Alexander Gelbukh, editor, *Computational Linguistics and Intelligent Text Processing*, volume 6609 of *Lecture Notes in Computer Science*, pages 93–105. Springer Berlin / Heidelberg.

Joakim Nivre. 2003. An Efficient Algorithm for Projective Dependency Parsing. In *Proceedings of the 8th International Workshop on Parsing Technologies*, pages 149–160.

Philip V. Ogren. 2006. Knowtator: A protégé plug-in for annotated corpus construction. In *Proceedings of the Conference of the North American Chapter of the Association for Computational Linguistics: Human Language Technologies, Companion Volume: Demonstrations*, pages 273–275, New York City, USA, June. Association for Computational Linguistics.

Sampo Pyysalo, Tomoko Ohta, Rafal Rak, Dan Sullivan, Chunhong Mao, Chunxia Wang, Bruno Sobral, Junichi Tsujii, and Sophia Ananiadou. 2012. Overview of the ID, EPI and REL tasks of BioNLP Shared Task 2011. *BMC Bioinformatics*, 13(suppl. 8):S2.

David Salgado, Martin Krallinger, Marc Depaule, Elodie Drula, and Ashish V Tendulkar. 2010. Myminer system description. In *Proceedings of the Third BioCreative Challenge Evaluation Workshop 2010*, pages 157–158.

Pontus Stenetorp, Sampo Pyysalo, Sophia Ananiadou, and Jun'ichi Tsujii. 2011a. Almost total recall: Semantic category disambiguation using large lexical resources and approximate string matching. In *Proceedings of the Fourth International Symposium on Languages in Biology and Medicine*.

Pontus Stenetorp, Goran Topić, Sampo Pyysalo, Tomoko Ohta, Jin-Dong Kim, and Jun'ichi Tsujii. 2011b. BioNLP Shared Task 2011: Supporting Resources. In *Proceedings of BioNLP Shared Task 2011 Workshop*, pages 112–120, Portland, Oregon, USA, June. Association for Computational Linguistics.

Beth M. Sundheim. 1996. Overview of results of the MUC-6 evaluation. In *Proceedings of the Sixth Message Understanding Conference*, pages 423–442. Association for Computational Linguistics.

Erik F. Tjong Kim Sang and Fien De Meulder. 2003. Introduction to the CoNLL-2003 shared task: Language-independent named entity recognition. In *Proceedings of the Seventh Conference on Natural Language Learning at HLT-NAACL 2003*, pages 142–147.

Yoshimasa Tsuruoka, Jun'ichi Tsujii, and Sophia Ananiadou. 2008. Accelerating the annotation of sparse named entities by dynamic sentence selection. *BMC Bioinformatics*, 9(Suppl 11):S8.

Author Index